Spangler and Tverberg, with the rigor of a s
storyteller, and the passion of a disciple, pre
of Jesus as a first-century Jewish teacher that
scholar and the layperson alike. Supported with careful analysis of
ancient sources and recent archaeological discovery, this study is a
profound call to follow the Jesus of Scripture.

RAY VANDER LAAN, AUTHOR AND FOUNDER OF
THAT THE WORLD MAY KNOW MINISTRIES

If we could turn the clock back to the Jewish world of the first century,
what would it be like to follow in the footsteps of Jesus the Jew? This
highly readable work is rooted in rabbinic sources and reflects current
gospel research. Spangler and Tverberg vibrantly introduce the reader
to valuable aspects of the Jewish background, lifestyle, and teachings
of the Rabbi from Galilee. Through their engaging personal style and
reflective Judaic approach toward understanding biblical discipleship,
Spangler and Tverberg have "hit a home run." The authors draw their
readers in to learn at the feet of the Rabbi and leave them begging
for more.

MARVIN R. WILSON, PhD, OCKENGA PROFESSOR
OF BIBLICAL STUDIES, GORDON COLLEGE

For disciples of Yeshua (Jesus) who know little about his Jewishness,
including his rabbinic and Hebraic teaching style, *Sitting at the Feet of
Rabbi Jesus* is the place for them to start. Spangler and Tverberg have
created the perfect introduction for the uninitiated. This book will
have a deep impact on the thinking of ordinary Christians through
the world.

DAVID BIVIN, AUTHOR AND EDITOR, *JERUSALEM PERSPECTIVE*

Last year over a million pilgrims visited the Holy Land. Few, however, would have learned as much about the historical Jesus as you can
by reading this terrific new work by Spangler and Tverberg. Drawing
upon personal experiences as well as the latest Jewish and Christian

scholarship in Israel, the authors skillfully guide you on a wonderful journey into Jesus's first-century Jewish world—exploring his culture, his lifestyle as an itinerant sage, and his well-honed rabbinic teaching methods and subtle but startling messianic claims. This book makes you really eager to sit at the feet of Rabbi Jesus and learn from the One we joyously serve as both Messiah and Lord. I commend it to every follower of Jesus of Nazareth.

DWIGHT A. PRYOR, CENTER FOR JUDAIC-CHRISTIAN STUDIES

SITTING AT THE FEET OF RABBI JESUS

Also by Lois Tverberg

Listening to the Language of the Bible
Walking in the Dust of Rabbi Jesus
Reading the Bible with Rabbi Jesus

Also by Ann Spangler

Finding the Peace God Promises
He's Been Faithful, Carol Cymbala with Ann Spangler
I Am with You: Daily Meditations on Knowing and Experiencing God
Less Than Perfect
Men of the Bible, coauthored with Robert Wolgemuth
The Names of God: 52 Bible Studies for Individuals and Groups
The Names of God Bible (general editor)
The One-Year Devotions for Women
Praying the Names of God
Praying the Names of Jesus
The Rescue, Jim Cymbala with Ann Spangler
She Who Laughs, Lasts!
The Tender Words of God
Women of the Bible, coauthored with Jean Syswerda

SITTING
AT THE
FEET
of
RABBI JESUS

HOW THE JEWISHNESS OF JESUS
CAN TRANSFORM YOUR FAITH

ANN SPANGLER AND LOIS TVERBERG

ZONDERVAN®

ZONDERVAN

Sitting at the Feet of Rabbi Jesus
Copyright © 2009, 2018 by Ann Spangler and Lois Tverberg

Requests for information should be addressed to:
Zondervan, *3900 Sparks Dr. SE, Grand Rapids, Michigan 49546*

Zondervan titles may be purchased in bulk for educational, business, fundraising, or promotional use. For information, please email SpecialMarkets@ Zondervan.com.

ISBN 978-0-310-35041-5 (ebook)

Library of Congress Cataloging-in-Publication Data

Names: Spangler, Ann, author. | Tverberg, Lois, author.
Title: Sitting at the feet of Rabbi Jesus : how the Jewishness of Jesus can
    transform your faith / Ann Spangler and Lois Tverberg.
Description: [Updated edition] | Grand Rapids, MI : Zondervan, [2018] |
    Originally published in 2009. | Includes bibliographical references and
    index.
Identifiers: LCCN 2017056961 | ISBN 9780310330691 (softcover)
Subjects: LCSH: Jesus Christ—Jewishness.
Classification: LCC BT590.J8 S63 2018 | DDC 232.9/06—dc23 LC record
    available at https://lccn.loc.gov/2017056961

Cover design: Gearbox/Chris Gilbert
Art direction: Curt Diepenhorst
Interior design: Denise Froelich

Printed in the United States of America

24 25 26 27 28 LBC 35 34 33 32 31

To Laura and Milt Tverberg,
who dedicated their lives to raising their children
as faithful talmidim of Christ.

—LOIS TVERBERG

•————————•

To the Jewish people,
for preserving a faith upon
which my own is built.

—ANN SPANGLER

Contents

Introduction

Writing this book has been for us a joy and a privilege. How lucky can you get to spend the better part of your day, month after month, steeping yourself in the life of Jesus and the Jewish world in which he lived? Even as we worked, our own lives were often affected. For instance, as Easter approached this year, we found ourselves writing the chapter on Passover. Delving into that feast, already ancient by Jesus's time, made it easier to visualize and understand the profound events of Holy Week. It was not difficult to picture Jesus in agony on that lonely night in Gethsemane, his own disciples too exhausted to stay awake and pray, oblivious to the events unfolding around them after consuming the heavy Passover meal with its multiple glasses of wine. Their beloved rabbi was about to be consumed by forces that would set things in motion for the promises embedded in the feast to be fulfilled. But they had no understanding of its rich depth of meaning until much later.

As we tried to place ourselves in Jesus's Jewish world, layer after layer of history seemed to peel away until we could almost imagine that for a while we, too, had joined the disciples and were sitting at Jesus's feet.

Gabi Barkai, an eminent Jewish archaeologist, has said that "every day in Jerusalem is a day of discovery." Indeed, the last fifty years have seen many exciting archaeological discoveries in the land of the Bible that, far from undermining faith, have bolstered the historical reliability of the Gospels. What's more, a growing number of Christian scholars have begun to explore the Hebraic roots of Christianity because they realize they have much to learn from their Jewish counterparts about the Jewish customs and traditions that have shaped the

Bible. Their research has yielded valuable insights that are not easily available to the general reader.

You might wonder if the authors of this book are Jewish, and the answer is no. We are Christians who are fascinated with our Savior and his life and teachings. If Jesus had been an Eskimo, we'd be studying Inuit (Eskimo) language and culture, learning about igloos, ice fishing, and polar bears. The goal of this book is not so much to help you understand Judaism as to help you hear Christ's life-changing words with greater clarity and force. God promised Abraham that the Gentiles would be blessed through his descendants. When we honor this ancient people by learning about their culture and customs, God blesses us with a deeper understanding of our Scriptures and of Jesus, our Messiah.

No book, however carefully researched and written, is without its flaws and for these we take full responsibility. We are aware, too, that the study of the Hebraic roots of Christianity is a developing field and that future research may well cause us to revise certain details of Jewish life in first-century Israel. Scholars themselves disagree as to the dating of some details, whether they describe Jesus's time or arose afterward. With these issues in mind, we've done our best to explore and weigh the most current research in the field. We have also been careful to place Jesus within his first-century Jewish context rather than that of later ages. We hope the end result will be of help to pastors, students, and laypeople who find their reading of the Bible all the more fascinating and life transforming as they come to appreciate and understand the Jewish context that shaped it.

You may wonder how the current edition differs from the original. Unless otherwise indicated, all of the Scripture passages have been updated from the 1984 edition to the 2011 edition of the NIV. This edition also includes a study guide at the back of the book designed for both individual and small group use. Realizing that many readers are drawn to the richness of the Jewish feasts, Lois has designed a simple Seder to help them celebrate the Feast of Passover either at home or in a church setting.

Ann is grateful for the privilege of beginning her study of the Jewish world of Jesus with someone who has dedicated more than twenty years of her life to carefully investigating the Jewish context in which Jesus lived and ministered. A molecular biologist by training, Lois Tverberg has shifted her interest and expertise to this emerging field of study, dedicating her considerable intellectual gifts and academic training to the kind of careful, balanced, and inspired research that both authors hope is evident in this book. Time after time as Ann questioned her about a particular statement or point of view, Lois's answers surprised and delighted her, revealing not only a wealth of knowledge but something even rarer—a depth of wisdom. Indeed *Sitting at the Feet of Rabbi Jesus* is a book Lois has wanted to write for many years. Ann is thankful that Lois waited until she could come alongside to write it with her.

Lois is especially grateful to her scholarly mentors over the years, David Bivin, Randall Buth, Steve Notley, Dwight Pryor, and of course Ray Vander Laan, who instilled this fascination in her life many years ago. For Bruce and Mary Okkema, good friends through this journey, and for the love and prayers of Laura Tverberg, and David and Lora Tverberg, and the rest of Lois's family, she has never ceased to give thanks. Most of all, Lois thanks the Lord for these months of writing with Ann, whose mentorship, honest critiques, and delightful creativity have given her a new approach to the craft of writing. Seeing how perfectly the circumstances fell together for their meeting, she hardly has enough words of praise for what God has begun through this relationship.

For those who regularly prayed for us as we wrote and researched— for Linda Bieze, Leslie Dennis, Joan Huyser-Honig, Hillari Madison, Dorothy Spangler, Patti Swets, and Stephanie Wiggins—we are amazed and grateful for how faithfully you kept it up. Special thanks go to Josa Bivin for her helpful feedback and to Marylin Bright, Kathleen Coveny, and Shirley Hoogeboom, true *haverot* who grappled with each chapter in its roughest form and whose prayers lifted Lois all the way along.

For associate publisher and executive editor Sandy Vander Zicht, who has enthusiastically supported this project from day one and who has offered many helpful suggestions along the way, we say thank you. For Jana Reiss, we are grateful for your careful and insightful review of the manuscript. Your grasp of the material combined with your understanding of the needs of the general reader is truly amazing. Thanks also go to Bob Hudson, senior editor at large, for his careful eye on the updated edition of the book. We greatly appreciate the feedback of former senior editor at large Verlyn Verbrugge, as well as of Marvin Wilson and Ed Visser on the historical content of the book. Thank you for taking the time to offer such helpful critiques. Thanks as well to Alicia Kasen, senior marketing director, and to her team for the creative ways in which they continue to spread the word about this book.

CHAPTER 1

Joining Mary at the Feet of Jesus

*Let your house be a meeting place for the
rabbis, and cover yourself in the dust of their
feet, and drink in their words thirstily.*

ATTRIBUTED TO YOSE BEN YOEZER (SECOND CENTURY BC)

Bethany's steep dirt roads are hard on your legs, especially when you've spent a hot day walking uphill the entire way from Jericho. But the smell of Martha's lamb stew wafting from a cooking pot in the front courtyard of her house beckons your dusty legs to keep climbing. You try to ignore your aching feet and the sweat-soaked dirt that clumps beneath your toes, thinking instead of the cool drink she will soon offer. The long hike has been worth it, because the conversation along the way has been absolutely profound. Didn't you feel your heart burning within you as you listened to the rabbi?

A person has to have some *chutzpah* and sturdy legs, you think, to push to the front so that he can hear the conversation. But this afternoon you haven't missed a word even on those narrow paths along Wadi Kelt, where only two or three could be in good listening range. Usually Peter, James, and John would angle their way up toward Jesus, but this time you got there first. Finally you had a chance to ask him some of the questions that had been piling up in your head.

But before you have time to make sense of his answers, your thoughts are interrupted by the cackles of chickens that strut across the courtyard and by Martha's joyous laughter greeting you, the sweat

Female Students in the First Century

Women were encouraged to sit in on the advanced discussions at the synagogue if they were able. A few even acquired the high-level education required to contribute to rabbinic debates, and their words are still on record. Some restrictions on women, like separating men and women during worship, actually arose several centuries later.[1]

beading on her forehead from her last-minute flurry of preparation. She and Mary share a small stone house that seems to miraculously expand to embrace all the guests that enter. Mary is there, too, greeting each person. Before you can even sit down, she asks you what Jesus has been talking about on the walk from Jericho.

When family responsibilities allow, Mary sits in on the study sessions at the local synagogue, and she has questions of her own that she's been waiting to ask. She often joins the group for Jesus's after-dinner discussions, and today, even with supper only half-ready, she sits down at Jesus's feet, oblivious of the look on Martha's face, laughing readily with the others over a heated debate that started along the road (Luke 10:38–42).

Wouldn't you love to have joined the boisterous crowd in Martha's house that evening? To have sat with Mary and those incredibly fortunate disciples who were able to travel with Jesus, to listen to him and learn from him for the three years of his public ministry?

What would it have been like to have been counted among Jesus's closest friends? To have him stay at your house whenever he was in town? Besides being an eyewitness, you would have had the great advantage of being a first-century Jew, someone whose life and experience were shaped by the same culture and religious beliefs that helped shape the life and ministry of Jesus. Like Jesus, you would have observed the laws and traditions of Judaism and would have been familiar with the issues of the day. You would have caught the humor and the nuanced remarks that made his words even more captivating, more life-changing.

Much as we might wish to have seen and heard the Lord in person, we are grateful that we can still experience him in Scripture. And yet the Jesus we meet in the Gospels is not always easy to understand. Partially, this is because we perceive his words at the distance of many centuries, from an entirely different culture, and in a different language. Instead of making our hearts burn, sometimes Scripture makes us scratch our heads in confusion.

I (Ann) remember the first time I met one of my roommates in graduate school. Gladisín was from Panama and had only been in the country a week when we first met. I liked her immediately. We seemed to get along well despite the language barrier. But I recall how stumped I was when Gladisín turned to me one day and declared, "I have a pain."

"What is it? What can I do?" I asked. But Gladisín merely stared at me with wide brown eyes and repeated, this time more emphatically: "I have a pain!" The more I tried to discover what was wrong with her, the louder she spoke: "A pain, a paaaiiin!" I wondered if I should call an ambulance or drive her to the hospital myself. But before I had the chance to do anything, it dawned on me. She was merely asking for a pen, a ballpoint pen to fill out some paperwork! I was so relieved I couldn't stop laughing. A simple request had mushroomed into a medical emergency—all because I couldn't understand Gladisín's repeated attempts to say, "Can I have a pen?"

Now consider the challenge of communicating across centuries and religious traditions as well as languages and cultures. No wonder we sometimes find it hard to grasp what Jesus is trying to tell us in the Gospels. But what if we could find a way to fine-tune our hearing, so that we could develop first-century Jewish ears? The words of Jesus that electrified crowds, incensed his enemies, and changed so many lives would have a much greater impact on us.

Is it possible to retune our hearing and thinking so that we can understand Jesus better? We believe it is, because that is exactly what happened to us the moment we began studying Jesus's Jewish culture. Passages that had previously left us cold or puzzled suddenly came to life. Lights turned on, stories took on new meaning, and the mist began to clear.

Tuning into the customs of Jesus's time and to the conversations of the rabbis who lived at that time can deepen your faith as it has ours, transforming the way you read the Bible. With that in mind, we invite you to embark on a journey that will take you back to that house in Bethany to hear Jesus's words again—this time from inside his culture. We hope to teach you how to listen to the Gospels with the ears of a first-century disciple. And once you start tuning in, we are confident you will become even more curious, eager to learn more.

Take the current setting. Why, for instance, were Jesus and his disciples camping out in the home of Mary and Martha? If you had been a first-century Jew, you probably would have heard a saying in circulation for at least a hundred years: "Let your house be a meeting place for the rabbis, and cover yourself in the dust of their feet, and drink in their words thirstily."[2]

The Jews of Jesus's day greatly prized the study of the Scriptures. Many of their most gifted teachers walked from town to town teaching from their Bible, asking no pay in return. People were expected to open their homes, providing food and shelter to these wandering teachers and their disciples. So, as much as we honor Mary for her desire to learn from Jesus, this saying shows us that Martha's hospitality was an important help to Jesus's ministry too.

If we were first-century visitors, we would have recognized the significance of something else in that story. It was customary for rabbis to sit on low pillows or chairs while they were teaching. Their disciples would sit on the ground or on mats around them. That's how the phrase "sit at his feet" became an idiom for learning from a rabbi. In Acts 22:3, Paul described himself as someone who had learned "at the feet of Gamaliel" (NRSV).[3] So when Mary was described as sitting "at the Lord's feet," she was being described as a disciple. Clearly, Jesus welcomed her as such.

But what about the phrase that speaks of "covering yourself in the dust of their feet"? Some scholars think this is yet another reference to the practice of sitting on the floor as a way of honoring a rabbi and submitting to his teaching. Others think that it refers to how disciples traveled from place to place by walking behind their rabbi, following so closely that they became covered with the dust swirling up from his sandals.[4] Both ideas describe the context of the story of Jesus's visit to Mary and Martha's house with his disciples and add color and meaning to God's Word.

Yearning to Dig Deeper

Now that you've begun to get a taste for why we think it's helpful to understand the Jewish background of Jesus, we want to let you know how Lois first became intrigued by the topic. The granddaughter of Lutheran missionaries, she had plenty of Sunday school knowledge. But Lois didn't get serious about her faith until her last year of college. Even then, she was wary of classmates who seemed overly pious. Still, she longed for a way to dig deeper into the Bible—a way that challenged her mind as well as her heart. So she signed up for a course on the New Testament, hoping it would provide some insight. "Instead," she says, "I was discouraged to learn that my professor believed, as did many others, that the New Testament was generally unreliable, composed of documents that had been written very late and were filled with legends from the early church." Her first exposure to the world of biblical criticism deterred her from further academic study of the Bible. Instead she channeled her efforts into obtaining a doctorate in biology.

Many years later, after Lois had become a college professor, her church hosted an adult class on the land and culture of the Bible. The emphasis was on archaeology, history, and the Jewish cultural background of Jesus. "I wondered," she says, "why the presenter didn't share the radical cynicism that my college professor had displayed about the historicity of the Bible." Uncertain what to believe, her instincts as a research scientist drove her to examine the sources behind the course she had recently attended. Her efforts led to a surprising conclusion. In the past few decades, an emerging field of study had unearthed a wealth of information confirming and strengthening the Christian faith. In the years since her college class, many new discoveries had changed the way scholars have understood the New Testament texts, particularly in light of their Jewish setting.[5]

The more Lois read, the more fascinated she became with how much richer Bible study can be when you know about Jesus's first-century context. That's when she started some serious study on her own. Each day seemed to bring some new insight, another aha moment, like the one from the story that follows. It takes place in the home of Martha and Mary, this time toward the end of Jesus's ministry.

You are probably familiar with a dramatic gesture Mary made one day, sitting at the feet of Jesus once again. John 12:3 describes the scene like this: "Then Mary took about a pint of pure nard, an expensive perfume; she poured it on Jesus' feet and wiped his feet with her hair. And the house was filled with the fragrance of the perfume."

Without understanding the cultural background in which this event occurred, it's easy to miss the full significance of Mary's gesture. What exactly was she trying to communicate? Jesus himself clarified one aspect of the story by commenting that Mary was preparing him for the day of his burial (Matt. 26:12). We understand that her act of devotion pointed toward Christ's death at the end of the week. But we miss something else that the disciples would have immediately realized, something so obvious that Jesus didn't even need to mention it. By anointing him with expensive fragrances, Mary may well have been making a statement about who she believed Jesus was, proclaiming him as Messiah. In fact, the Hebrew word for Messiah is *Mashiach*, which literally means "the Anointed One." *Christos*, or "Christ," is the Greek equivalent.

But why "the Anointed One"? The word "Messiah" alludes to the ceremony used to set apart someone chosen by God, like a king or a priest. Instead of being crowned during a coronation, Hebrew kings were anointed with sacred oil perfumed with extremely expensive spices. Only used for consecrating objects in the temple and for anointing priests and

Anointing

Anointing a guest with oil was a common, expected act of hospitality (see Luke 7:46). But Mary's use of a breathtakingly expensive vial of perfumed oil in John 12 made her action hint at the anointing of a king.

kings, the sacred anointing oil would have been more valuable than diamonds. The marvelous scent that it left behind acted like an invisible "crown," conferring an aura of holiness on its recipients. Everything and everyone with that unique fragrance was recognized as belonging to God in a special way.

In the ancient Middle East, the majesty of a king was expressed not only by what he wore—his jewelry and robes—but by his royal "aroma." Even after a king was first anointed, he would perfume his robes with precious oils for special occasions. Listen to a line from King David's wedding song:

> You love righteousness and hated wickedness;
>> therefore God, your God, has set you above your
> companions
>> by anointing you with the oil of joy.
> All your robes are fragrant with myrrh and aloes and cassia.
> (Psalm 45:7–8)

Consider, too, this passage about King Solomon:

> Who is this coming up from the wilderness
>> like a column of smoke,
> perfumed with myrrh and incense
>> made from all the spices of the merchant?
> Look! It is Solomon's carriage,
>> escorted by sixty warriors,
>> the noblest of Israel. (Song of Songs 3:6–7)[6]

During royal processions, the fragrance of expensive oils would inform the crowds that a king was passing by.

Now take a look at another scene from the Old Testament. It describes a newly anointed Solomon being led into Jerusalem from the spring of Gihon, just outside the city, and then parading through the streets on a mule while people stood by and cheered:

> So Zadok the priest . . . went down and had Solomon mount
> King David's mule, and they escorted him to Gihon. Zadok the

priest took the horn of oil from the sacred tent and anointed
Solomon. Then they sounded the trumpet and all the people
shouted, "Long live King Solomon!" And all the people went up
after him, playing pipes and rejoicing greatly, so that the ground
shook with the sound. (1 Kings 1:38–40)

Now consider a striking parallel in the life of Jesus. It happened
the week before his death, right after Mary anointed him with the
expensive perfume.[7] Just as Solomon had done a thousand years earlier,
Jesus rode a donkey on his triumphal entry into Jerusalem. Imagine the
scene as recounted in John 12. The crowd was not greeting an ordinary
rabbi. No, people were shouting out: "Hosannah! Blessed is the king of
Israel!" They were remembering Solomon, the son of David, who long
ago had ridden through their streets on a mule, and now they were
proclaiming that Jesus was the promised "Son of David," whom God
had sent to redeem his people.

The significance of Mary's action doesn't stop there, though. It
seems likely that the smell of the perfume with which Mary anointed
Jesus would have lingered for days. God may have used Mary's act of
devotion to telegraph a subtle but powerful message. Everywhere Jesus
went during the final days of his life, he had the fragrance of royalty.
Jesus smelled like a king.

Imagine, in the garden of Gethsemane, as Judas and the guards
approached Jesus to arrest him, the guards must have sniffed the
air and wondered who stood before them. When Jesus was on trial,
mocked, whipped, and stripped naked, even then the aroma may have
clung to him. What an amazing God we have!

> But thanks be to God, who always leads us in triumphal proces-
> sion in Christ and through us spreads everywhere the fragrance
> of the knowledge of him. For we are to God the aroma of Christ
> [the Anointed One] among those who are being saved and those
> who are perishing. To the one we are the smell of death; to the
> other, the fragrance of life. (2 Corinthians 2:14–16 NIV 1984)

What a fascinating parallel, which shows what Paul meant by the "aroma of Christ." As Jesus's followers, we spread the fragrance of our anointed Messiah everywhere we go.

Why Focus on Jesus's Jewishness?

Ken Bailey is a prominent biblical scholar, known for his unique insights into the gospel, based on his long familiarity with Middle Eastern culture and languages, past and present. When asked whether his discoveries threaten to overturn what Christians think they know about the Bible, Bailey responds, "Suppose I've spent my life going to a beach. I've seen waves splashing against rocks, ships on the water, fishermen casting lines. One day at this beach someone says, 'Ken, I have two snorkels. Let's go.' Suddenly I see coral, seaweed, and fish. These undersea views in no way invalidate the beauty of what's above. In my work, I'm looking for the coral and the fish."[8]

Similarly, instead of undermining our faith, looking at the Jewish background of the Bible deepens our understanding of Jesus and his times, increasing our awe as we look more closely at this extraordinary rabbi and his astonishing claims. In *The Jesus I Never Knew*, Philip Yancey wisely comments, "I can no more understand Jesus apart from his Jewishness than I can understand Gandhi apart from his Indianness. I need to go way back, and picture Jesus as a first-century Jew with a phylactery on his wrist and Palestinian dust on his sandals."[9]

As Christians we can never forget that the Bible—from Genesis through Revelation—is essentially a Jewish document. Once we begin to read it from a Jewish perspective, our experience of it will be transformed, as though we have just swapped an old black-and-white TV with its scratchy image for the latest flat screen, high-definition set. Suddenly the Bible takes on new depth and color as we read the familiar stories once again, but this time from the perspective of its original audience.

A couple of cautions. It's not hard to become fascinated with Judaism for its own sake simply because of the antiquity of its traditions and because many of its practices are wise and biblical. But keep in mind that more than two thousand years have passed since Jesus was born. Over the centuries a lot has changed. Some Jewish practices and traditions hearken back to his time, but many others do not. Bearing these cautions in mind, let's dive in and begin looking for the "coral and the fish," the wonders that lie just beneath the surface.

A Glimpse of Life in the First Century

As we begin to explore, looking beneath the surface of things, let's take a quick look at Israel in the first century. Already the picture of Jewish life painted by the Old Testament is hundreds of years out of date. During the Old Testament, for instance, there is no mention of rabbis, synagogues, Pharisees, Sadducees, or Zealots.

Sadducees

The Sadducees came primarily from the ruling priestly and aristocratic classes. Unlike the Pharisees, they did not believe in the resurrection of the dead, and they considered only the written Torah (i.e., the first five books of the Hebrew Bible) as binding. Despised as collaborators with Rome, they controlled the temple worship. Their influence ceased with the destruction of the temple in AD 70.

Most of the people living in the land of Judea and Galilee are the descendants of pious Jews who returned to Israel after their exile in Babylon. Since then, life for the chosen people has been anything but idyllic. Their Roman occupiers are universally hated for their brutality and pagan ways, to say nothing of the oppressively high taxes they levy. Little wonder that everyone is longing for a Messiah to come and deliver them by throwing out their harsh oppressors.

Though anticipation is high, opinions vary about just how or when the Messiah will finally arrive. Sadducees, Zealots, Essenes, and Pharisees—each has a different take on what has happened and why, and on how the future will unfold. Political tension and spiritual fervor are both on the rise. It is into this time of intense spiritual searching that another rabbi comes striding onto the scene. He hails from Nazareth. Can anything good come out of Nazareth?

CHAPTER 2

Why a Jewish Rabbi?

*Pore over it again and again, for everything
is contained in it; look into it, grow old and
gray over it, and do not depart from it, for
there is no better pursuit for you than this.*

ON STUDYING THE SCRIPTURES (FIRST CENTURY AD)[1]

Predictably, the midsummer flight to Tel Aviv was packed. Though our plane was still sitting on the tarmac in New York, I (Ann) realized that my adventure had already begun. From the moment I stepped onto the jetway, it seemed as though I had been transported into another world. I had chosen El Al because of its reputation for security, little knowing that this Israeli airline was also famous for catering to religious Jews, serving only kosher foods and refusing to fly on the Sabbath regardless of how much money it might lose by doing so.

As I took my seat, I scanned the plane to see how many "ordinary-looking Americans" like myself were aboard. I found few. Instead I noticed several men wearing *yarmulkes* on their heads. And despite the heat, some of them had prayer shawls wrapped around their shoulders.

I tried not to stare as a bearded man three rows ahead stood up and began carefully winding a long strip of leather around his arm. He was observing a daily custom common among Orthodox Jews—binding small boxes, called *tefillin*, to both head and arm. These boxes, I knew, contained parchment scrolls inscribed with the ancient command recorded in Deuteronomy 6:6–8:

These commandments that I give you today are to be on your hearts. Impress them on your children. Talk about them when you sit at home and when you walk along the road, when you lie down and when you get up. Tie them as symbols on your hands and bind them on your foreheads.

As the young man wound the dark strand of leather around his arm, I could hear him speaking in Hebrew. Later I learned that he was echoing the words of Hosea 2:19–20:

> "I will betroth you to me forever;
>> I will betroth you in righteousness and justice,
>> in love and compassion.
> I will betroth you in faithfulness,
>> and you will acknowledge the LORD."

I had seen the *tefillin*, or phylacteries, before, but had not realized that their wearers consider them an outward sign of the love that exists between God and his people. By binding his arm in this way, the man was joining millions of Jews across the centuries and throughout the world in expressing the deeply held conviction that he was both "bound up" with God and with his law, and "wrapped up" with God and with his protection. In fact, he had carefully wrapped the leather straps around his hand in a configuration that formed the Hebrew letter *shin* (שׁ) which stands for *Shaddai*, one of the Hebrew names of God.

In the seat next to me was a teenage girl, piously bent over her prayer book. When she wasn't sleeping through the long flight, she was reading and praying, rocking rhythmically back and forth as she read and meditated on the Hebrew words. Later, I asked a white-haired rabbi I met in Israel about this practice, called *davening*. The rocking motion during prayer, I discovered, is a way of expressing that one's whole self, body and soul, is caught up with God. The old rabbi explained that the movement of the body mimics the flickering flame of a candle, calling to mind the saying that "the candlestick of God is the soul of a man."

As I settled in for the long flight, I realized that I had much to learn about the customs and beliefs that had shaped Judaism throughout the centuries, particularly ones that were current in the time of

Jesus. But I was certain that my own faith would be enriched as I traveled to Israel, a land that some have called "the fifth gospel" because so many places in it bear witness to Jesus Christ. On this, my second trip to Israel, I was hungry to learn more about the Jewishness of Jesus and how it had shaped his teaching and his message. One of many questions I pondered was why God, in the person of his Son, had chosen to enter the world and become a Jewish rabbi more than two thousand years ago.

Why a Rabbi?

A visit to Israel makes it easier to picture many of the scenes in the Gospels. On my most recent trip, I met a graduate student named Brian. Both of us were enrolled in a class on Second Temple Judaism. Headed to a prestigious seminary on America's East Coast, Brian is unquestionably bright. But he's something else as well. With shoulder-length brown hair, a long beard, and medium build, this fair-skinned Californian is a dead ringer for Jesus, at least the one in all the Sunday school paintings. One day our class took a dip in the Sea of Galilee. As water ran down Brian's matted hair and beard, I could almost see a dove hovering over him as he stood waist-deep in the lake.

One day, as we were walking up the southern steps of the Temple Mount in Jerusalem, steps that Jesus would have climbed on his way up to the temple, a group of twenty-something Israeli students suddenly began poking each other and pointing at Brian. Then they held out their hands, shouting: "Jesus, Jesus!" The students' good-natured bantering made it clear they were in on the joke—Brian exactly fit the stereotype of a Hollywood Jesus—a stereotype, of course, that completely ignores Jesus's Semitic heritage.

Rabbi

Rabbi literally means "my master." In Jesus's day, it was a term of respect for teachers of the Scripture. It wasn't until after AD 70 that "rabbi" became a formal title.

Though most of us have grown beyond such historically inaccurate images of Jesus, at least when it comes to movies, we often fail to realize the significance of his Jewish heritage in other respects. Just how Jewish was Jesus, and how pious were the people around him? Were they as devout as the Jews on my El Al flight or were most of them far more casual about their faith? And why, for that matter, should we place so much emphasis on understanding Jesus as a rabbi? Isn't it enough to know him as Redeemer and Messiah?

To answer these questions, we must begin by realizing that Jesus entered history at what could be described as the best and the worst of times. It was the best of times in Israel because people were hungry to know how to live for God. They knew from their own tragic history how painful life could become when their nation strayed from the path that God had laid out for them in Scripture.

Despite this spiritual hunger, it was also the worst of times in Israel because life under the Romans was unbearably brutal. Not only did Rome demand oppressively high taxes, they harshly suppressed every whiff of opposition.

In Sepphoris, for instance, a town just three miles from Nazareth, the Romans quelled a rebellion by burning the city to the ground and then selling its survivors into slavery. This happened in 4 BC, around the time of Jesus's birth. Imagine what it would have been like growing up so close to such a disaster. It would be like being born in Manhattan on September 11, 2001. Though you hadn't witnessed the destruction of the World Trade Center towers, you would grow up hearing the story until it became seared into your mind.

Because of their continuing oppression by the Romans, the Jewish people cried out to God daily, begging for a Messiah to deliver them. It was into this hotbed of social ferment and religious longing that the greatest of all rabbis appeared on the scene. No wonder he attracted a crowd wherever he went.

Torah Study

How might Jesus's Jewish upbringing have shaped his life and ministry? For one thing, Jesus probably began learning to read and memorize the Torah and much of the Hebrew Scriptures by the time he was just five or six years old. This was a typical pattern for Jewish boys. After age ten, he would have begun to learn the Oral Torah, the rabbinic traditions handed down for interpreting the Written Torah. Though girls were not required to have formal training in the Torah, they would frequently have heard the Scriptures recited and would have been expected to know many prayers by heart, both at home and in the synagogue.

By the age of thirteen most boys would have concluded their formal study and then begun to learn a trade. The most talented among them would have been encouraged to continue studying throughout their teenage years at the *bet midrash* ("house of interpretation") at the synagogue until they married at the age of eighteen or twenty. Only the most brilliant would go on to become disciples of a great rabbi.[2]

Though pious Jews had an avid interest in all of Scripture, they focused primarily on the Torah, the first five books of the law that God gave Moses. For them the Torah was not an onerous rulebook or a vast catalog of laws as we might think, but a gift from God that taught them how to live.

> **Torah and Oral Torah**
>
> *Torah* is Hebrew for "teaching" or "instruction." It refers to the first five books of the Bible, also called the Pentateuch. Christian Bibles often translate *torah* as "law," while Jewish translations usually render it "teaching." It sometimes is used to refer to the Scriptures as a whole.
>
> The "Oral Torah" consists of the explanations and interpretations of the laws given to Moses in the Pentateuch (the "Written Torah"). These were passed down in oral form by rabbinic teachers in Jesus's day. Other rabbis added to the teachings, which were recorded in the Mishnah around AD 200.

During the first century, knowledge of the Scriptures was widespread. Even ordinary people devoutly studied the Torah, meeting together in their local synagogue, an institution that developed during the Babylonian exile when it was no longer possible to offer sacrifices in the Jerusalem temple. For both men and women, the synagogue had become the center of Jewish life.

Each Sabbath a member of the congregation would read from the

Scriptures and expound on the day's passages. Gifted rabbis, like Jesus, who happened to be in town would also be asked to speak. In the early first century, many people were involved in living and teaching their faith, not just an educated few. Jewish historian Shmuel Safrai writes:

> Torah study was a remarkable feature in Jewish life at the time of the Second Temple and during the period following it. It was not restricted to the formal setting of schools and synagogue, nor to sages only, but became an integral part of ordinary Jewish life. The Torah was studied at all possible times, even if only a little at a time . . . The sound of Torah learning issuing from houses at night was a common phenomenon. When people assembled for a joyous occasion such as a circumcision or a wedding, a group might withdraw to engage in study of the Law.[3]

When Lois first heard about this Jewish fascination for study, she found it utterly incomprehensible. Just imagine standing up in the middle of a party and saying to your friends, "Hey, everybody, let's go talk about a bunch of old documents!"

Over time, though, she realized that there really are few thrills greater than digging deep into the Scriptures and discovering fresh insight from the Word of God. For many people this passion often ignites after a study trip to Israel. When Lois's group arrived home after her first trip, they all bubbled over with new "ahas" whenever they opened their Bibles. "Each of us," she recalls, "had tasted the historical reality of Jesus, and it made all the difference. After that, whenever we read the Gospels, we could see him walking across the Galilee region, preaching to the crowds, healing the sick, and debating with other rabbis."

"When my friends and I returned with a group from our last trip, dirt from the steps

Bet Midrash

The *bet midrash* is a center for study and teaching of the Torah and its rabbinic interpretation. In the first century, it was usually located within a synagogue, serving as a "high school" where boys between the ages of thirteen and seventeen studied religious texts. Adults would have continued to study there in their free time.

of the recently excavated Pool of Siloam in Jerusalem still clung to our sandals. Our eyes had been opened in the very place where Jesus had opened the eyes of a blind man (John 9). Suddenly, my friends and I were as eager to tear into the latest issue of *Biblical Archaeology Review* as we were to launch into the Sunday paper or go to the latest movie. I've since realized that a plane ticket to Israel isn't necessary— wonderful insights are as close as your own Bible."

Would it surprise you to learn that the rabbis thought that study, and not prayer, was the highest form of worship? They pointed out that when we pray, we speak to God, but that when we study the Scriptures, God speaks to us. Of course they weren't advocating a coldly intellectual approach to Scripture, but the kind of study that is motivated by a deep reverence for God's Word. The Talmud says that a person who studies without reverence "is like a man with a treasure chest who owns the inner keys but not the outer keys."[4] Such a person might think he understands, but the true meaning of Scripture remains hidden, locked away.

The Life of a Rabbi

In the centuries prior to Jesus's time, certain men distinguished themselves by their earnest desire to study and teach the Torah. In Jesus's day, a person would honor one of these learned men by addressing him as "my master," which in Hebrew is *rabbi*. Some decades after Jesus's time, this became a formal title, and these teachers became known as "rabbis."[5] For the most part these teachers did not hail from wealthy or priestly classes, but from the ranks of ordinary folk. They could be blacksmiths, tailors, farmers, tanners, shoemakers, woodcutters, and of course, carpenters.[6] Many of them worked seasonally, traveling and teaching in the months when they were free.

Rabbis interpreted the Torah, explained the Scriptures, and told parables. Some traveled from village to village, teaching in synagogues. Though they relied on the hospitality of others, rabbis were never paid. They often took disciples who would study under their direction for

Synagogue

Synagogues probably developed during the Babylonian exile in the sixth century BC when the Jews were unable to worship at the Jerusalem temple. As the local community center, the synagogue served as the place where people gathered, prayed, and studied the Scriptures. In the first century, all kinds of meetings were held in the synagogue—school during the week, and prayer and study of the Torah on the Sabbath.

years, traveling with them everywhere they went. Study sessions were often conducted outdoors in vineyards, marketplaces, beside a road, or in an open field.[7] Disciples would then go out on their own, holding classes in homes or in the synagogue.

Knowing more about the life of a rabbi sheds considerable light on the life of Jesus. Remember Dan Brown's enormously popular but historically flawed book, *The Da Vinci Code*? It advances the notion that Jesus was married. Brown bases this assertion on the idea that Jewish society would not have allowed him to remain single. Listen to what he says through the lips of his main character, Robert Langdon, "According to Jewish custom, celibacy was condemned, and the obligation for a Jewish father was to find a suitable wife for his son. If Jesus were not married, at least one of the Bible's gospels would have mentioned it and offered some explanation for his unnatural state of bachelorhood."[8]

Brown is right in one respect. Most Jewish men married at a fairly young age, often between the ages of eighteen and twenty.[9] But he seems ignorant of the fact that rabbinic scholars spent many years in study and travel, causing some to postpone marriage until much later in life. As David Bivin points out, "A bachelor rabbi functioning within Jewish society of the first century was not as abnormal as it might first appear. Rabbis often spent many years far from home, first as students and then as itinerant teachers. It was not uncommon for such men to marry in their late thirties or forties."[10]

This fits perfectly with Jesus's statement that others had renounced marriage "for the sake of the kingdom of heaven" (Matthew 19:12), and Paul's affirmation of singleness as well. Singleness was not an impossibility, but a sign of a rabbi's great commitment to God.

Jesus among the Rabbis

As far as we know, Jesus belonged to none of the main religious groups active in the first century—Sadducees, Zealots, Essenes, or Pharisees. Still, his teaching comes closest to that of the Pharisees (the group who reestablished Judaism after the temple was destroyed in AD 70), and the rabbinic Judaism that survives today is their legacy. This may seem surprising, since Jesus called the Pharisees "hypocrites" and a "brood of vipers" on at least one occasion. Sometimes the Gospels seem to imply that everything Jesus said directly contradicted the teaching of the Pharisees. But it's important to realize that debate was a central aspect of study—the rabbis believed that a mark of an excellent student was his ability to argue well. One rabbi lamented the death of his stiffest opponent, because he had no one to spar with, no one who would force him to refine his thinking![11] Though some of Jesus's listeners tried to trap him with clever questions, others debated him simply because this was how study and teaching was done.[12]

In *The Gospel According to Moses*, the Christian writer Athol Dickson tells the fascinating story of his involvement with a Torah study group at the local synagogue. One day, when the presiding rabbi was having trouble generating group discussion, he fired off question after question, finally tossing out a provocative comment to stir things up. But still the group was silent. Exasperated, the rabbi exclaimed, "Come on people! Somebody disagree with me! How can we learn anything if no one will disagree?"[13]

Luke's gospel tells us that Jesus had been teaching in synagogues even before his ministry formally began (Luke 4:15). Why is this important? Because it tells us two things about Jesus's Jewish reality. First, Jesus must have been quite learned by the standards of his time. If not, he would never have been invited to teach. Even his toughest critics never questioned his scholarship. Second, Jesus must have been observant of the Torah. If he hadn't been, he would have been barred from even attending the synagogue, let alone speaking in it.[14] So it seems clear that Jesus was an integral part of the Jewish world of his day, making sophisticated contributions to the high level of conversation that was going on among the rabbis of his time.

Other than reading through the Gospels, how can we get a feel for the Jewish thinking of Jesus's day? Surprisingly, some of what was under discussion in the first century is still being discussed and studied by Jews today. The Jewish people considered the Oral Torah (the teachings of the rabbis of Jesus's time) authoritative, as though it had been given by God to Moses on Mount Sinai when the Written Torah was given. This oral tradition was finally written down around AD 200 in a book called the Mishnah. Composed primarily of legal rulings, the Mishnah preserves the discussions of Jewish thinkers from between 200 BC and AD 200. Over the next few centuries, the Mishnah was compiled together with an expansive commentary into the Talmud and completed around AD 500. For the past two thousand years, the discussions contained in the Mishnah and Talmud have formed the main body of study for Orthodox Jews, even up to the present day.

Talmud

The *Talmud* is a large volume of commentary on the Mishnah. The commentary is printed section by section following each verse of the Mishnah. There are two Talmuds: the *Jerusalem* (or Palestinian) *Talmud*, completed about AD 400; and the *Babylonian Talmud*, completed about AD 500. The Babylonian Talmud is considered authoritative by Jews today.

In fact, Jesus lived in the midst of a golden age of study that provided the germinating seed of Jewish thought today. Two of its founding thinkers, Hillel and Shammai, were teaching immediately prior to Jesus's time, between 30 BC and AD 10. Many of the debates between the disciples of Hillel and Shammai are preserved in the Mishnah, and more than once Jesus was asked to comment on their rulings. When Jesus was queried on his opinion on divorce, for instance, he was being asked which side he took between their two camps.[15] Sometimes Jesus agreed with other rabbis and sometimes he went beyond their thinking, building on their ideas and bringing them to a new level.[16]

The Rabbis Told Parables

It's not hard to see how perfectly the vocation of a rabbinic teacher suited Jesus. Like other rabbis, Jesus walked the land, taught in parables, engaged in debates, interpreted Scriptures, and raised up disciples. His teachings, too, fit well within rabbinic styles.

Take the parables. You may be surprised to learn that Jesus was not the only rabbi who told parables. Most rabbis used traditional motifs, themes that shed light on the parables Jesus told. For instance, parables often included a character who represented God—a king, a shepherd, or a farmer with a vineyard. The rabbis drew these images of God directly from Scripture.[17] Consider what one rabbi said:

> When a sheep strays from the pasture, who seeks whom? Does the sheep seek the shepherd, or the shepherd seek the sheep? Obviously, the shepherd seeks the sheep. In the same way, the Holy One, blessed be He, looks for the lost.[18]

Doesn't this rabbi's words remind you just a little of Jesus's parable about the shepherd leaving the ninety-nine sheep to rescue the one lost sheep (Matthew 18:12–13)? Like Jesus, this rabbi was saying that God is the one who pursues us when we stray. Both Jesus and the rabbi were basing their parables on Scriptures. Once we identify the traditional forms of rabbinic parables, we can better understand what Jesus was saying.

Consider the following rabbinic parable:

> There are four types among those who sit in the presence of the rabbis: the sponge, the funnel, the strainer, and the sieve. "The sponge," which soaks up everything. "The funnel," which takes in at this end and lets out at the other. "The strainer," which lets out the wine and retains the dregs. "The sieve," which removes the chaff and retains the fine flour.[19]

This is what's called a "four types" parable, where four kinds of people are compared in their way of living. It reminds us of Jesus's parable in

Luke 8:4–11 about the seed that fell in four places: the rock, the path, the thorns, and the good soil. Each parable focuses on how various people respond to God's Word.

In the above parable, the rabbi is saying that the best disciple is not—contrary to our preconceptions—the "sponge," who retains absolutely everything, but the "sieve," who sifts through the teaching to retain what is best. What great advice for Christians! It reminds us that we are not called to be parrots, unquestioningly repeating whatever we learn from a favorite teacher. Instead, we are to exercise wisdom and discernment, continually asking questions, weighing answers, seeking understanding, and grounding our beliefs within the context of God's Word and the wisdom of Christian tradition.

A Rabbi as Redeemer

By comparing Jesus to other rabbis of his time, we do not mean to imply that he is just another rabbi. Nor are we merely singling him out as a rabbi among rabbis, much as you might distinguish an Olympic gold medalist from other athletes. Jesus was an extraordinary rabbi, but he was so much more than that.

Remember that the Jewish people longed for a Messiah, a deliverer, who would be like Moses. Many of Jesus's contemporaries were looking for a new Moses to deliver them from their Roman oppressors. But did you know that Moses is revered not only as Israel's great deliverer but as Israel's great teacher? In fact he is often called *Moshe Rabbenu*, "Moses Our Rabbi," by the Jewish people, who honor him for bringing them the Torah after his encounter with God on Mount Sinai.

Like Moses, Jesus brought God's word to earth. More than that, he was God's Word incarnate. With this in mind, it is hardly surprising that he spent his life as a Jewish rabbi. In both life and death he is our Great Teacher, redeeming us so that we can learn from him how to live.

Imagine for a moment that you possess the sheet music of the most beautiful piano concerto ever written, but you have never heard the whole piece perfectly performed. Then one day, you meet the composer's son, who is himself a great pianist. This man knows his father's music by heart. As he sits down to play with the orchestra, the music is so achingly beautiful that you begin to weep. At last, you are hearing the most magnificent concerto in the world being played exactly as the composer intended. This is a rough analogy of what Jesus has done for us, not merely *telling* us but *showing* us what human beings, created in God's image, were meant to become.

In addition to pointing toward a deliverer like Moses, the Scriptures also promised a king whose reign would be as glorious as that of King David, Israel's greatest monarch. But what does being a king have to do with being a rabbi?

Let's look for a moment at Jewish thinking about what a messianic king might look like. Orthodox rabbi Meir Zlotowitz points out that the Scriptures predict the messianic king will be a great teacher of the Torah. "The messianic king," he writes, "plays a unique role. He, as first citizen of the nation, is the living embodiment of Torah." He goes on to say that as the "holder of immense and almost unbridled power, he submits to the laws in the Scriptures which he carries with him at all times, and he does not rest until his people know the rigors of Torah study." Rather than being above the law, the king is to be the best possible role model for living out the Torah.[20] This modern rabbi is basing his thoughts on Deuteronomy 17, which talks about the qualities God desires in a king:

> Be sure to appoint over you a king the LORD your God chooses . . .
> When he takes the throne of his kingdom, he is to write for himself on a scroll a copy of this law . . . It is to be with him, and he is to read it all the days of his life so that he may learn to revere the LORD his God and follow carefully all the words of this law and these decrees. (Deuteronomy 17:15–19)

The king was to study and obey the law, to love the law so much that he would write it on a scroll to be carried with him wherever he went. Gradually this idea of the law-abiding, law-cherishing king was extended to the Messiah. The great King of kings would be consumed with the study of the Scriptures and would "carry it" to the people as a great teacher. He would not seek his own glory, but would intentionally point people toward obedience of God's Word.

In our materialistic, entertainment-oriented culture, people look at business titans, sports heroes, and movie stars as people to be emulated. Our society honors those who possess beauty and wealth. But in Jesus's time and throughout the ages, the Jewish people believed that becoming a great scholar of the Scriptures represented life's supreme achievement. In such a culture, it made sense that the Messiah should be the greatest of teachers. No wonder Jesus became a Jewish rabbi!

The Goal of a Rabbi

Along with instructing the crowds, a rabbi's greatest goal was to raise up disciples who would carry on his teaching. This was not merely an academic exercise, a matter of downloading volumes of data into someone else's head. As important as knowledge of Scripture was, there was one thing more important—a rabbi's moral character. It was said that "if the teacher is like an angel of the Lord, they will seek Torah from him, but if not, they will not seek Torah from him."[21]

The mission of a rabbi was to become a living example of what it means to apply God's Word to one's life. A disciple apprenticed himself to a rabbi because the rabbi had saturated his life with Scripture and had become a true follower of God. The disciple sought to study the text, not only of Scripture but of the rabbi's life, for it was there that he would learn how to live out the Torah. Even more than acquiring his master's knowledge, he wanted to acquire his master's character, his internal grasp of God's law.

This approach to learning makes perfect sense. Imagine handing an instruction sheet to a five-year-old who wants to learn to ride a bike. It would be far better to begin by showing her how to ride and then putting training wheels on her bike. Then, once she's ready for the wheels to come off, she will need someone to run alongside her as she makes that first thrilling attempt. That's what the rabbi-disciple relationship was all about. From ancient times, God had told his people: "Be holy because I, the LORD your God, am holy" (Leviticus 19:2). What better way to teach people to be like him than to walk the earth as a rabbi?

So often we focus on Jesus's mission on the cross to save us from our sins. As marvelous as that is, it's critical for us to grasp the importance of his mission on earth as a rabbi. His goal was to raise up disciples who would become like him. As followers of Jesus, we are still called to live out the adventure of discipleship, becoming like Jesus through the power of his Spirit at work within us.

To do that, we need to tune into what he was saying by developing the ears of a first-century Jew. As we do, we'll discover that there are many times in the Gospels when knowing what Jesus *doesn't say* becomes just as important as knowing what he *does say*. Let's explore the deeper meaning that lies behind his words.

AT THE FEET OF THE RABBI

1. Jesus quoted from the book of Deuteronomy more than any other book of the Torah. Consider reading through this Old Testament book to see if you can identify some of the passages he quoted. Or try scanning the cross references to Deuteronomy in the Gospels. You may want a good study Bible for this.

2. Disciples were expected to know the words of their rabbi by heart. Choose a favorite quote from Rabbi Jesus and commit it to memory. See if you can make this a regular habit.

3. Which type of disciple are you—a funnel, a sponge, a strainer, or a sieve?

CHAPTER 3

Stringing Pearls

*When they were "stringing pearls," the words
in the Pentateuch with those in the Prophets,
and the Prophets with the Writings, the fire
flashed around them and the words rejoiced as
on the day they were delivered from Sinai.*

SONG OF SONGS RABBAH 1:10 (THIRD TO SIXTH CENTURY AD)

One afternoon late in 1946, dust particles danced in a ray of sunshine filtering into a remote cliff cave in the Judean desert. Bedouin shepherd boys peeked into the cave and made an astonishing discovery. Pottery jars full of scrolls that had been carefully hidden for twenty centuries were suddenly illuminated. These boys had stumbled on the most important biblical archaeology find of the twentieth century—the Dead Sea Scrolls. In 1948, news of the discovery of ancient biblical manuscripts and Jewish writings from around the first century dumbfounded the scholarly world.

But forty-five years later, many of the manuscripts were still inaccessible to all but a tiny team of researchers, much to the outrage of scholars everywhere. A young graduate student by the name of Marty Abegg had been introduced to the ancient documents by one of his professors, Emanuel Tov. In the course of doing other research, Abegg stumbled on a way to reconstruct the text of the other scrolls, and in 1991, he published a section for all the world to see. "The effect was like a thunderbolt. The cat was out of the bag," he said. Soon the rest of the scrolls were forthcoming. Abegg had forced the hand of Tov, who had by then become chief editor of the Dead Sea Scrolls team.

Tension was thick in the air when Tov and Abegg encountered each other at a scholarly meeting later that year. The balding Jewish scholar paused, uttering just three words to his former student:

"*Banim gidalti veromumti.*"

"I have reared children and brought them up."[1]

What on earth was he saying? Abegg vaguely recalled the phrase, recognizing it as a passage from the book of Isaiah. But it wasn't until later in his hotel room, when he cracked open his Bible and read Isaiah 1:2, that he felt the brunt of Tov's rebuke: "I reared children and brought them up, *but they have rebelled against me!*"

Abegg winced, knowing that Tov was using a classic rabbinic technique, quoting part of a verse and leaving the rest unsaid. As an observant Jew, Emanuel Tov had been living in a world that was deeply knowledgeable of the Scriptures, and he had expressed his sense of betrayal in a powerful but subtle way. He knew Abegg would get the point as soon as he discovered the full context of the message.

Now listen to the words of another brilliant Jewish scholar two thousand years earlier. He had been preaching and healing people within the temple grounds. The crowds were cheering for him. Even children were shouting, "Hosanna to the Son of David!" Indignant, the priests and teachers of the law stormed over to Jesus to confront him: "Do you hear what these children are saying?" they asked.

Jesus replied, "Have you never read, 'From the lips of children and infants you have ordained praise'?" (Matthew 21:16 NIV 1984). Instantly, the rest of Psalm 8:2 would have reverberated in their minds:

> From the lips of children and infants
> > you have ordained praise
> > *because of your enemies,*
> > to silence the foe and the avenger. (italics added)[2]

The psalmist is saying that God's glory is so great that even children instinctively worship him, to the shame of those who hate him. In the same way, the children who acclaimed Jesus were responding to his ministry the way his interrogators should have, but refused to do.

Just like Emanuel Tov, Jesus was using a quote from Scripture to invoke a longer passage that his opponents knew well. God's Word delivered the rebuke they deserved.

"Hinting" to the Scriptures

Both Jesus and Emanuel Tov were using a rabbinic technique well known throughout the centuries. To increase the impact of a statement, rabbis would quote part of a Scripture and then let their audience fill in the rest. It was common for them to pepper their teachings with brief quotations and distinctive phrases from the Bible. As contemporary American rabbi David Wolpe explains, "Rabbinic documents are so densely allusive not because the rabbis were straining to display erudition, but because the rabbis were educated Jews and as such lived those texts. The stories and the laws of the Bible were common coinage. They were the yardstick against which life was ceaselessly measured."[3]

As Wolpe suggests, the rabbis weren't trying to show off, they were simply communicating within the framework of the Scriptures that they knew so well. Jesus did the same. If you doubt it, just open a study Bible and check the cross references in the Gospels. Jesus did not reserve this technique for trained religious elites. He used it everywhere he went, whether preaching to the crowds or fielding questions from ordinary people.

Sometimes his references were obvious and sometimes subtle— only a word or two. In fact, there are times when knowing what Jesus *doesn't* say becomes as important as knowing what he *does* say. In other words, the passages from which Jesus quoted provide background for understanding his meaning more fully. If we miss his reference, we may miss his point.

Here's a well-known example. In Matthew 18:21 Peter asks, "Lord, how many times shall I forgive my brother or sister who sins against me? Up to seven times?"

Jesus responded, "I tell you, not seven times, but *seventy-seven times*" (v. 22, italics added). What did Jesus mean? Most of us immediately check the footnote in our Bible, which says "*Or, seventy times seven*." We like the fact that 490 is so much larger than 77. So that's what Jesus was saying! Believe it or not, we are still missing the punch line.

The key to understanding Jesus's meaning is embedded in the passage to which he alluded. The phrase "seventy-seven times" is found in only one place in the entire Bible—Genesis 4:24, in the ancient song of Lamech. But who was this obscure biblical character? Lamech was a descendant of Cain who had inherited his forefather's murderous instinct, but who, in his shocking lust for revenge, outdid even Cain:

> I have killed a man for wounding me,
>   a young man for injuring me.
> If Cain is avenged seven times,
>   then Lamech seventy-seven times. (vv. 23–24)

Anybody who crossed Lamech would have been paid back big time—not just seven times, but seventy-seven times! In Scripture, seven is a significant number. It symbolizes completeness. But Lamech lusted for a vengeance that went far beyond completeness.[4]

Once you catch Jesus's reference, you understand the contrast he is making. He is saying that his followers should be as eager to forgive as Lamech was to take vengeance. Just as Lamech was vowing a punishment that far exceeded the crime, we should let our forgiveness far exceed the wrong done to us. We should be Lamech's polar opposite, making it our goal to forgive as extravagantly and completely as possible. Amazing what you can learn from a single word or phrase.

Here's another example: "The kingdom of heaven is like yeast that a woman took and mixed into a large amount of flour until it worked all through the dough" (Matthew 13:33 NIV 1984). What the NIV translates

Midrash, Midrashim

Midrash (plural, *midrashim*) is a rabbinic explanation or commentary on the biblical text. In later centuries, *midrash* often included imaginative legends about biblical characters. *Midrash* can also refer to a compilation of commentaries on the Scriptures. These commentaries were handed down orally and later compiled in written form, becoming a sourcebook for the preaching of later rabbis.

as "a large amount of flour" was literally "three *seahs*." Everyone in Jesus's time would have recognized this as a reference to the story of when God and two angels visited Abraham. As Abraham was hurrying off to catch his fattest calf, he caught up with Sarah and told her, "Quick . . . get three seahs of the finest flour and knead it and bake some bread" (Genesis 18:6). Three *seahs* is about fifty pounds of flour, enough to feed a hundred people![5] The huge quantity of bread that Sarah baked for just three strangers must have awed ancient listeners, and the details of the event would have stuck in their memory.

Usually women saved enough leavened dough from one day in order to act as a starter for the next day's loaf. The fact that Sarah's leavening was sufficient for such a huge baking project must have seemed like a tiny miracle. When Jesus referred to this passage, his audience (especially the women) would have smiled as they visualized Sarah's leaven causing such an enormous batch of dough to rise.

Knowing that this story was in Jesus's mind also yields a clue about why he uses leaven as an image of the kingdom of God. Often leaven is a negative image, as when Jesus uses it to refer to hypocrisy in Luke 12:1. Why would he speak of it here in a positive way? Perhaps Jesus "hints" to Abraham and Sarah's feast because here leaven is used for the best of all purposes—in preparing an extravagant meal to be shared with three heavenly visitors.[6]

Though this practice of alluding to passages from Scripture may sound strange, it's not so different from the way we often communicate. For instance, what would come to mind if you saw an op-ed column entitled, "Iraq May Become Another Vietnam"? Instead of imagining thousands of Vietnamese immigrants flooding into Iraq, you would probably recognize the reference to the United States's long and losing conflict in Vietnam. Similarly, if a news story were to describe a piece of evidence as a "bloody glove," you would probably think of O. J. Simpson's over-publicized murder trial. A single distinctive word or phrase can evoke a visceral reaction whenever it is embedded within a larger recognizable context. When you know the Bible well, even a short reference to an important passage can pack a punch.

Discovering Jesus's Library

You might wonder what Bible Jesus knew. The Scriptures he read (and Jews still consider this their Bible today) are the same books as those in the Protestant Old Testament.[7] However, Jews in Jesus's day (and today as well) divided their Bible into three sections, referring to them as "the Law of Moses, the Prophets and the Psalms" (Luke 24:44). Nowadays, Jews refer to their Scriptures as the *Tanakh*. The word is an acronym derived from the first letters of these three sections of Scripture:

T: *Torah* (Teaching/Law)—the five books of Moses
N: *Neviim* (Prophets)—the historical and prophetic books
  (Joshua, Judges, Isaiah, etc.)
K: *Ketuvim* (Writings)—Psalms, Proverbs, Job, Ecclesiastes, etc.

Jesus's words brim with allusions to the Torah, the Prophets, and the Writings. His three favorite books came from each section: Deuteronomy (Torah), Isaiah (Prophets), and Psalms (Writings). Interestingly, these books are also best represented among the Dead Sea Scrolls.[8] It seems that Jesus favored the same texts as other Jews of his day.

Jesus also used the same methods for quoting and interpreting the Scriptures that other rabbinic teachers did. One set of guidelines was called the "Seven Rules of Hillel," and scholars have found examples of Jesus using a number of them.[9] One rule, for example, is called *geze-rah shavah*, a "comparison of equals." This rule said that you could use one passage to expand on another if they share the same word. In other words, Scripture interprets Scripture. The rabbis would look for places where the same word or phrase comes up in different places. Then they would meditate on how these passages might expand upon each other.

Look at how Jesus responded when asked to identify the greatest commandment in the law:

> "Love the Lord your God with all your heart and with all your soul and with all your mind." This is the first and greatest commandment. And the second is like it: "Love your neighbor as yourself." (Matthew 22:37–39)

The first command, "Love the Lord your God . . ." is from Deuteronomy 6:5, a famous part of the *Shema*, the prayer uttered by Jews morning and evening. The second command, "Love your neighbor as yourself," comes from Leviticus 19:18. Both passages contain the Hebrew word *ve-ahavta* (veh ah-HAHV-tah), literally translated "and you shall love." According to the rule of *gezerah shavah*, these passages can be linked because they share the same word.[10]

Did Jesus's first-century audience catch these references? Probably they did. Most observant Jews would have been thoroughly familiar with their Scriptures. Even those without much formal schooling would have heard and prayed large amounts of the biblical text every week at the synagogue. So it seems likely that most of his listeners would have recognized and understood the context of the passages to which Jesus alluded. Rather than rejecting the religious people of his day, Jesus used their love for the Scriptures to teach them about himself.

Lois remembers how surprised she was to learn how vital the Old Testament was for understanding Jesus. She relates, "My Bible had a well-worn crack in the binding at the first page of the New Testament, bypassing three quarters of the text that Jesus had faithfully learned by heart as he grew up. His library was right at my fingertips, but to my embarrassment, those were the pages I had hardly read. Now when I read the Gospels, I always glance at the cross-references, checking for the passage Jesus was quoting from in the Bible that *he* read, our Old Testament."

Books of the Tanakh

These are the books of the *Tanakh* as they are arranged within the three sections that Jesus knew and Jews still use today:

Torah (Law, Teaching)

Genesis	Numbers
Exodus	Deuteronomy
Leviticus	

Neviim (Prophets)

Joshua	Obadiah
Judges	Jonah
Samuel	Micah
Kings	Nahum
Isaiah	Habakkuk
Jeremiah	Zephaniah
Ezekiel	Haggai
Hosea	Zechariah
Joel	Malachi
Amos	

Ketuvim (Writings)

Psalms	Ecclesiastes
Proverbs	Esther
Job	Daniel
Song of	Ezra
Solomon	Nehemiah
Ruth	Chronicles
Lamentations	

Often these quotations are obscured by the English translation. Keep in mind that Jesus was quoting from the part of the Bible written in Hebrew (or sometimes Aramaic). The Gospels, on the other hand, are in Greek. Don't worry if you can't read either Hebrew or Greek, because you can learn a lot simply by reading the footnotes in a good study Bible. If you do your own digging, however, it's important to use discernment. A phrase might at first sound like it refers to a certain passage in the Old Testament, but it may actually be a concept found widely in Scripture, or an expression commonly used in Jesus's day.

While Jesus frequently cited passages from the Hebrew Scriptures, he was not doing so in order to look for hidden meanings. Some have made the mistake of assigning methods of interpretation to Jesus that only came into use hundreds of years after his time, when rabbis developed interpretative styles that went beyond the plain sense of the biblical text. For instance, in later centuries, some assigned meanings to a passage by adding up the numeric equivalents of the words, insofar as Hebrew letters also functioned as numbers. But practices like these did not begin until well after the time of Christ.[11] While we need to look deeply into the Scriptures Jesus knew, we needn't look *beyond* them for things that aren't there.

Stringing Pearls

Having said that, it is difficult to overestimate the love that the rabbis had for their Bible. On a good day, they would link text after text after text. A story is told about Ben Azzai, a rabbi from the early second century. One day while Ben Azzai was teaching, it is said that "the fire flashed around him"—he was setting his audience ablaze with his preaching. When someone asked him what his secret was, he replied:

> I was linking up the words of the Torah with one another, and then the words of the Prophets, and the Prophets with the Writings, and the words rejoiced as on the day they were delivered from Sinai. And were they not originally delivered from Sinai in fire?[12]

Ben Azzai was said to be "stringing pearls"—bringing together passages from different places in order to explore their great truths. When he did this, it was as if the words themselves became so excited to be together that they burst into flames!

Jesus did the same thing. Listen to the Beatitudes in Matthew 5:3–12. These passages are thick with references to Isaiah and the Psalms.

> Blessed are the poor in spirit . . .
> Blessed are those who mourn . . .
> Blessed are the meek . . .

Each of these passages would have reminded the crowd of passages in the Bible in which God had promised to rescue his faithful followers. Jesus was pulling together various Scriptures to make one major point: God is faithful. He cares for us and will bless us if we seek him even when life is painful.

Believe it or not, God himself seems to enjoy "stringing pearls." Do you remember the scene in which Jesus is being baptized by his cousin John? Listen to how the Father spoke from heaven at Jesus's baptism (Mark 1:11): "You are my Son, whom I love; with you I am well pleased."[13] At face value this seems like a simple, though wonderful, affirmation. But it's so much more than that. Did you catch all the references? If not, here they are:

- "You are my Son" is from Psalm 2:7: "He said to me, '*You are my son*; today I have become your father.'"
- "whom I love" is from Genesis 22:2: "Take your son, *your only son, whom you love*—Isaac—and go to the region of Moriah. Sacrifice him there as a burnt offering on a mountain I will show you."
- "with you I am well pleased" is from Isaiah 42:1: "Here is my servant, whom I uphold, my chosen *one in whom I delight*; I will put my Spirit on him, and he will bring justice to the nations."

What was God saying by making use of these quotations? To answer this question, you need to know two things: the context from which each passage is drawn and the way in which the people of that time understood the passage. Both Psalm 2 and Isaiah 42 were understood as powerful messianic prophecies. In Psalm 2, God makes a royal proclamation announcing his Son, the King of kings who would rule over the whole earth.

But in Isaiah 42, God speaks about his "servant" (also understood to be the Messiah). Paradoxically, God's Messiah is both a king *and* a servant. This passage from Isaiah also proclaims that God's Spirit is upon his servant. How fitting since the Father utters these words as the Spirit descends on Jesus in the Jordan River.

The reference "whom I love" is likely drawn from Genesis 22, one of the most poignant scenes in the Old Testament. Abraham is about to sacrifice Isaac out of obedience to God. Genesis heightens the drama by emphasizing how precious Isaac is to Abraham, foreshadowing the Father's own feelings for his only Son. When Jesus is baptized in the Jordan, the Father is saying, "Here is *my* precious son, *my* Isaac," hinting at the sacrifice he will soon ask of Jesus.

In just three brief quotes from the Scriptures, God speaks of Jesus as a king, a servant, and his Son, who will become a sacrifice. When God speaks, he packs a lot into his words! And be sure to notice where these three passages come from: the Torah (Genesis 22), the Prophets (Isaiah 42), and the Psalms (Psalm 2). Just like Ben Azzai, God links together the words from the three parts of Scripture. By quoting all three, he is proclaiming that the entire Scriptures point to Jesus as their fulfillment.[14]

Jesus's Words about Himself

One of the most fascinating ways Jesus used the Scriptures was to point toward his own identity as the one who would fulfill them. Some of his most powerful claims to be the Messiah were delivered in this subtle way.[15] Let's look deeper into the biblical texts that Jesus quoted.

One of the most popular images of Jesus is as the "good shepherd." Who hasn't seen painting after painting depicting Jesus with a lamb slung tenderly across his shoulders? This image comes from Jesus himself, who said: "I am the good shepherd; I know my sheep and my sheep know me—just as the Father knows me and I know the Father—and I lay down my life for the sheep" (John 10:14–15). His words conjure another favorite image, that of the shepherd in Psalm 23:1–3:

> The LORD is my shepherd,
> I lack nothing . . .
> he leads me beside quiet waters,
> he refreshes my soul.

Any rabbi worth his salt would have known that the mere mention of the word "shepherd" would have caused the rest of that passage to float through the minds of his listeners. Even now we find great comfort in this psalm.

Yeshua

Jesus's name in Hebrew is *Yeshua*, a shortened form of *Yehoshua*, which in English is "Joshua." Both mean "Yahweh's salvation," or "Yahweh is salvation." In a dream, Joseph had a vision of an angel who told him: "You are to give him the name Jesus, because he will save his people from their sins" (Matthew 1:21).

But Jesus was doing more than evoking a comforting image of himself. He was also evoking an image of power, because shepherd imagery is often used to describe kings. In Isaiah, for instance, King Cyrus of Persia is called a "shepherd" (44:28), and Psalm 78:71–72 says King David "shepherded" his people. Most interestingly, in Ezekiel 34, God expresses his anger at the leaders of his people by describing them as "bad shepherds." He then promises to save his flock and to send a good shepherd to lead them. Could this be what Jesus was thinking of in John 10?

Listen to what Herod's counselors told him after his encounter with the wise men who had come looking for the newborn king of Israel. They quoted Micah 5:2 when they said:

> "But you, Bethlehem, in the land of Judah,
> are by no means least among the rulers of Judah;
> for out of you will come a ruler
> who will shepherd my people Israel." (Matthew 2:6)

When Jesus called himself a "shepherd" in John 10, he was hinting at his identity as the messianic king, the future ruler of God's kingdom.

Such a reference would have astonished his listeners. But they would have been stunned by another allusion. Listen to what Jesus says in Matthew 25:31–32:

> "When the Son of Man comes in his glory, and all the angels with him, he will sit on his glorious throne. All the nations will be gathered before him, and he will separate the people one from another as a shepherd separates the sheep from the goats."

Now listen to Ezekiel 34:17:

> "As for you, my flock, this is what the Sovereign LORD says: I will judge between one sheep and another, and between rams and goats."

What is so stunning about Jesus's words is that by using the metaphor of a shepherd sorting his sheep, he is linking himself to God, who is often called the "Shepherd of Israel."[16] No doubt many of his listeners were shocked. Others would have been scandalized. We need first-century ears to hear Jesus's claims to oneness with God the Father.

The Son of Man

One of the most enigmatic phrases that ever came from Jesus's lips is his unique name for himself, the "Son of Man." Over eighty times in the Gospels, Jesus uses this phrase in the third-person to refer to himself. What does he mean?

Many Christians have assumed that Jesus is showing great humility by using this phrase. Though divine, Jesus relates to our human condition. Indeed, "son of man" in Hebrew (*ben adam*) and Aramaic (*bar enash*) can both be used in an idiomatic way to refer to a human being in general. When associated with Jesus, the phrase could also have pointed to the fact that he is the true fulfillment of what a human being was supposed to be.

Jesus sometimes uses "Son of Man" in an ordinary way. But more often he uses it in a very special sense, making bold claims about his messianic mission. To catch what he is saying, we need to understand how the Jewish people of Jesus's time interpreted a key messianic prophecy from the book of Daniel about an enigmatic figure called the "Son of Man." One night Daniel had a vivid dream in which he saw a great, heavenly court in session. Suddenly, he saw "one like a son of man, coming with the clouds of heaven." Immediately this exalted figure approached the Ancient of Days and was "given authority, glory and sovereign power." Daniel goes on to say that "all nations and peoples of every language worshipped him. His dominion is an ever-lasting dominion that will not pass away, and his kingdom is one that will never be destroyed" (Daniel 7:13–14).

In the first century, this passage was universally understood as a reference to the coming Messiah. The book of Daniel predicted the rise of great kingdoms, which would eventually fall to the authority of one supreme king, a king who would rule forever. The pinnacle of Daniel's prophecy was this scene in which a humanlike figure enters God's throne room, is crowned, and then sits down on the throne to reign.

According to the Jewish scholar David Flusser, this passage from Daniel was considered the most potent messianic prophecy in all of Scripture.[17] While other messianic passages could be interpreted as pointing to a human king descended from David's line (2 Samuel 7:12–13), this one predicted the Messiah would be divine. Why? Because it spoke of "one *like* a son of man." This person seemed merely human, but he was actually far more.

Jesus also speaks about himself as the Son of Man who will come in glory on the clouds (Mark 13:26; 14:62; Luke 21:27), a clear reference to this passage from Daniel. His audience would know exactly what he is saying.[18]

Why is it important to consider the claims Jesus is making about himself? Over the last century skeptics have made the case that Jesus was only a humble rabbi from Nazareth, nothing more. They say that it was not Jesus but the Gentile church that exalted him as the Christ. The Jesus Seminar, a collaborative scholarly group that aimed to deconstruct the "real" historical Jesus from the Christ of faith, has argued that the Jesus of the Gospels is only an imagined creation, embellished by later New Testament writers who wanted to bolster their hero's claims to divinity.[19]

Ironically, instead of achieving greater historical accuracy, the members of the Jesus Seminar may have propagated a misunderstanding about what the historical Jesus claimed. By failing to understand the very Jewish way in which Jesus communicated to his first-century audience, skeptics miss the shocking assertions he made about himself.

Actually, even early on in church history, Gentile believers failed to realize the implications of Jesus's use of the phrase "Son of Man." The church fathers rarely used the phrase because they couldn't understand why Jesus seemed to be speaking about himself as a lowly human being. Jesus's Jewish claim to be the fulfillment of Daniel's prophecy went sailing right past them.[20] In other words, Jesus, not the early church, was the source of this exceedingly powerful self-declaration.

Once we begin to hear Jesus's words as though we are his contemporaries, steeped in an understanding of the Scriptures and the cultural context in which they were spoken, the power of his claims become both obvious and striking. We realize that by calling himself the "good shepherd," Jesus is not just invoking a lovely and comforting image but is identifying with God himself. Likewise, the enigmatic phrase "Son of Man" becomes a multifaceted summary of Christ's entire redemptive mission, speaking of his humanity, his coming glory, and his role as Judge and Savior of all the earth. No wonder so many of his listeners responded with either awe or anger at his words!

AT THE FEET OF THE RABBI

1. Are you as unfamiliar with Jesus's Bible as Lois was when she first learned about its importance in understanding the Gospels? If so, consider following a simple reading plan that will take you through the Old Testament in a year or two, or sign up for an Old Testament overview class at a local church so that you can begin to dig deeper into Jesus's Scriptures.

2. Consider developing a greater familiarity with Bible stories from the Old Testament. A book the whole family might enjoy reading aloud is *The Jesus Storybook Bible* by Sally Lloyd Jones.[21] Unlike other children's Bibles, this one is written on the premise that every story—from Noah to Moses to King David—"whispers his name," offering fascinating insights for adults as well as children.

3. For a wonderfully rich study, read the Beatitudes in Matthew 5:3–12. Then read the passages that would have entered the minds of people in Jesus's audience as they heard his words. Think about the surrounding context too, which only makes his words more meaningful:

   - Blessed are the poor in spirit . . . (Isaiah 57:15; 66:1–2)
   - Blessed are those who mourn . . . (Isaiah 61:1–2; 66:2–3, 10, 13)
   - Blessed are the meek . . . (Psalm 37:11)
   - Blessed are those who hunger and thirst for righteousness . . . (Isaiah 25:6; 55:1–2)
   - Blessed are the pure in heart . . . (Psalm 24:4)
   - Blessed are you when people insult you . . . (Isaiah 51:7–8; 66:5)

CHAPTER 4

Following the Rabbi

Disciples of the wise increase peace in the world, for
it is said, "And all your children shall be taught of the
Lord, and great shall be the peace of your children."

BABYLONIAN TALMUD, *BERAKHOT* 64A.

One of Ann's favorite movies is *Young Frankenstein*. Its warped sense of humor invariably induces out-of-control laughter whenever she sees it. One of the scenes, played by bug-eyed Marty Feldman, is borrowed from an old vaudeville routine. After meeting the young Dr. Frankenstein at the train station in Transylvania, Feldman, playing a hunchback named Igor, hobbles down the steps, instructing his new master: "Walk this way." Interpreting him literally, Gene Wilder, in the role of young Frankenstein, hunches over obligingly, lurching down the steps after him.

Ridiculous as this scene is, it points to an important difference between our Western idea of instruction and the kind of instruction given by Jewish rabbis to their disciples. To follow a rabbi meant something other than sitting in a classroom and absorbing his lectures. Rather, it involved a literal kind of following, in which disciples often traveled with, lived with, and imitated their rabbis, learning not only from what they said but from what they did—from their reactions to everyday life as well as from the manner in which they lived. The task of the disciple was to become as much like the rabbi as possible.

This approach to teaching is much more like a traditional apprenticeship than a modern classroom. Around the world, and for thousands of years, apprenticeship traditions have been largely unchanged. Westerners are hardly aware of this very different, but surprisingly effective, way of teaching.

Consider the experience of Ange Sabin Peter, an accomplished potter who recently served a six-month apprenticeship under Masaaki Shibata, a well-known Japanese potter.[1] Before journeying to Japan, Ange imagined herself studying with the aged craftsman, an artist she had long admired. She envisioned herself shaping beautiful pottery on his wheel, his decades of skill sharpening her own expertise. Aware that his apprentices usually served for four years, but impatient about taking too much time away from her work, she hoped a short tutorial would suffice.

At the start of her apprenticeship, Ange knew little or nothing of an ancient Japanese tradition that Masaaki Shibata would have been well aware of—the tradition of becoming an *uchi deshi*, an apprentice to a skilled craftsman. To learn a craft, a teenage boy would be "adopted" into his master's household, living as a member of the family during his apprenticeship and participating in every aspect of the life of the home and the shop. He would have much more to learn than just how to throw and glaze pottery and would begin by performing menial tasks, including housework. The boy had to learn to do *everything* in just the right way. Only after years of apprenticeship would the *uchi deshi* be trusted to throw the pots that the master craftsman would embellish with his designs and sign with his famous name.[2]

"You cannot separate life from work," Shibata told Ange, his new apprentice, one day. "The way you do the most insignificant activity in your daily life will reflect in your work." Then he sent her to the rice fields to dig for clay instead of inviting her to sit down at his wheel. Her pride chafed at not being asked to demonstrate her own skill. In fact, Shibata did not allow her to throw even one piece of pottery during her six-month stay in Japan.

One day over lunch, Shibata's wife confided, "When you came to us, you were like a fully grown tree with big branches. We have to cut those branches for something new to be able to grow," but all Ange felt was the cutting. Still, as she toiled at her humble chores, she snatched every chance to watch the master potter at work.

Returning home, she felt deflated and defeated, afraid that her six months in Japan had been a complete waste. But when she sat down at her wheel, she began to sense a subtle difference. Something had changed. Then, as the kiln door opened on her new work, she marveled at the result. Without knowing it, she had been absorbing a new way of doing things. Her eyes had gained an aesthetic sense for distinguishing excellent work from merely acceptable work. Thanks to her time with Masaaki Shibata, Ange Peter's approach to her craft had been transformed. Delightedly she caressed each new vessel, admiring how the influence of her Japanese master had blended beautifully with her own personality to transform each of her new creations.

A Different Way to Learn

Like Jesus's disciples, Ange Sabine Peter had tasted a different kind of learning. She had entered an ancient way, a time-honored method of training common throughout the world for many centuries.

This was precisely the way Jewish boys and girls learned in Jesus's day. They didn't take math classes. Instead, they watched how their fathers measured and calculated as they were building, and they noticed how their mothers counted their money at the market. The girls didn't take home economics classes but learned to pluck and cook a chicken by helping their mothers and sisters. Children didn't crack open their history textbooks either. Instead, they learned the epic stories of their ancestors as their family gathered around the glow of the evening fire. Though most Jewish people were educated in the Scriptures and though Jewish boys learned to read in school, the usual method of learning was through hands-on experience, imitating someone who possessed the skills they wanted to acquire.

Likewise, after finishing school at the age of thirteen, a boy learned his life's work by joining his father and brothers in the family trade. Sometimes a father would apprentice his son to another craftsman and the boy would move into his master's home for a number of years.[3] Working all day at his mentor's side, he would also perform menial chores, gradually gaining know-how as he observed the craftsman's expert hands. Learning wasn't so much about retaining data as it was about gaining essential wisdom for living, absorbing it from those around him. This was also the ancient method whereby rabbis trained their *talmidim*, or disciples.

Why should we spend time talking about ancient discipling methods? Because we, too, are followers of a rabbi. Like Jesus's first *talmidim*, we are to become his faithful disciples. And like them we are called by our Master to "go and make disciples of all nations" (Matthew 28:19). Remember what happened when Jesus's first followers carried out his great command? Within a few centuries the early church exploded with growth, as believers spread across the Roman empire to transform the face of ancient history. Beginning with an army of only twelve, God took on the world.

Go and make disciples. How did the disciples understand these mountaintop words of Jesus? For three years they had been following him closely and in the process their own "big branches" were being cut off so that something new and better could grow within them. What exactly had they learned? What does their Jewish culture reveal about our own call to become transformed disciples of Jesus Christ?

The call to discipleship is one that has echoed down the centuries, not just within the Christian church. It has characterized Judaism as well. Even today rabbis are commissioned during their ordination ceremonies to "raise up disciples," a quotation known

Talmidim

Talmid (tahl-MEED; plural, *talmidim*, tahl-mee-DEEM). A disciple or student, one who dedicated himself to learning a rabbi's understanding of Scripture and his way of living it out. In Greek, a disciple is a *mathetes* (plural, *mathetai*). In both languages the words mean "student" or "learner." A female disciple would be a *talmidah* in Hebrew, or *mathetria* in Greek. But were there any female disciples? Surprisingly, in Acts 9:36 Dorcas (Tabitha) is called a *mathetria*, a (female) disciple.

from Jesus's time.[4] Perhaps we can recapture some of the original passion and effectiveness of Jesus's first followers by exploring how discipleship worked in the ancient Jewish world.

How to Raise a Disciple

Where did the rabbis develop their ideas of discipleship? They found their model in Scripture, especially in the relationship of two men—the prophets Elijah and Elisha.[5]

Elijah, of course, was one of Israel's greatest prophets, known for the amazing miracles he performed, like raising the dead and calling down fire from heaven to defeat false prophets. But despite the powerful way God used him, or maybe even because of it, Elijah had his low moments, times in which his adversaries threatened to overwhelm him. It was after one of these that God spoke to him, instructing him to anoint Elisha as his successor, and Elijah obeyed:

> So Elijah went from there and found Elisha son of Shaphat. He was plowing with twelve yoke of oxen, and he himself was driving the twelfth pair. Elijah went up to him and threw his cloak around him. Elisha then left his oxen and ran after Elijah. "Let me kiss my father and mother goodbye," he said, "and then I will come with you."
>
> "Go back," Elijah replied. "What have I done to you?"
>
> So Elisha left him and went back. He took his yoke of oxen and slaughtered them. He burned the plowing equipment to cook the meat and gave it to the people, and they ate. Then he set out to follow Elijah and became his servant. (1 Kings 19:19–21)

When Elijah called Elisha, the younger man gave up everything, abandoning his prosperous farm to become Elijah's personal servant, humbly attending to his needs, and accompanying him everywhere he went. Like any disciple, Elisha's goal was not just to study from Elijah, but to become *like* Elijah in order to carry on his ministry as a prophet to Israel.

Several aspects of Elisha's life exemplified discipleship in Jesus's time. First of all, Elisha went to live with Elijah, spending year after year with him. That made sense in light of the fact that the goal wasn't just academic learning but personal transformation. As the Jewish historian Shmuel Safrai explains it, a disciple "did not grasp the full significance of his teacher's learning in all its nuances except through prolonged intimacy with his teacher, through close association with his rich and profound mind."[6] To that end, the disciple would accompany the rabbi on all of his daily rounds: going to court, helping the poor, burying the dead, redeeming slaves, and so on. The disciple sought to be a humble and caring companion, doing personal acts of service and helping the teacher in all things.

The Gospels make it clear that this is the kind of relationship Jesus had with his own disciples. His *talmidim* followed him everywhere. And as they did, their hearts were challenged and changed.

Imagine, for instance, how it would have felt to follow Jesus through the door of Matthew's house, eating with tax collectors, sinners who were considered the stooges of Rome. Such people were reviled in Jewish society not only because they raked in money for a foreign power, but also because they inflated the high Roman taxes in order to pay themselves a handsome salary. For the disciples to eat with such despicable men would have been scandalous. Sharing a meal was considered a sign of wholehearted friendship and peace—so how could righteous men sit at table with the worst of sinners?

Jesus was constantly surprising his disciples both by his words and by his actions. He was challenging their way of looking at God and at others, welcoming sinners into his kingdom and associating with people that other rabbis would have scorned.

But the changes that he worked in his disciples' lives did not come instantly or even easily. Our culture is fascinated with instant fixes and extreme makeovers. Just like Ange Peter, we chafe at the years it takes to train as an apprentice. But discipleship has always been about a process.

As Christians we can become addicted to stories of miraculous change, believing that if God is listening to our prayers, every sinful urge we feel will be healed immediately. Contrast this with the record of the Gospels. Think how often the disciples messed up. They made mistakes to the very end—even on the last night they spent with Jesus prior to his death. After eating the Passover meal, his closest disciples fell asleep while men armed with clubs and swords made their way up the Mount of Olives to arrest Jesus. At the precise moment their rabbi most needed them, they failed him.

While the Gospels record many instances of Jesus instantly healing people's illnesses, we know of not even one instance in which he simply waved his hand to immediately fix an ugly habit for one of his disciples. Instead, he simply kept teaching and correcting them, giving them time to grow.

God seems to work like this much of the time in our own lives. He lets our weaknesses and difficulties drive us to himself, keeping us close. Miracles happen, but the inner transformation we so desperately desire can only be achieved over time. God seems to prefer it this way, perhaps because he knows we can only become like him by maintaining a constant close connection.

Utter Commitment

It must have been a remarkable experience for Elisha to realize that Elijah had invited him to become his successor. But still Elisha hesitated. He wanted to follow the great prophet, but he also wanted to kiss his parents goodbye. But as soon as Elijah challenged his commitment, Elisha promptly sacrificed twelve pairs of oxen, burned his plow, and left everything to follow him. He said goodbye to wealth, home, and family, even to his ability to make a living. Clearly, Elisha hadn't just acquired a new hobby or signed up for an evening Sunday school class he could skip whenever life became too busy.

Jesus referred to this story when responding to a potential disciple who wanted to follow him—but not right away. First, the man wanted to return home and bid his family goodbye (Luke 9:61). Jesus's words to this would-be disciple are telling: "No one who puts his hand to the plow and looks back is fit for service in the kingdom of God" (v. 62). This is one of the places where Jesus alluded to the Scriptures to make a point. He was reminding the man of the "plow of Elisha," a metaphor for making a sacrifice showing his commitment.

Jesus often spoke of leaving everything, saying that he himself had nowhere to lay his head (Luke 9:57–58). By this he meant that his calling was to serve God through the wandering life of a rabbi, walking from village to village to draw people into God's kingdom. It was a difficult existence. Long days spent hiking up and down the hot, dusty hills of Galilee, preaching to whomever would listen, and depending on the hospitality of others for his most basic needs. Here's how other rabbis described this kind of life: "This is the path of Torah: a morsel with salt shall you eat, and you shall drink water by measure, and sleep upon the ground, and live a life of painfulness, and in Torah shall you labor. If thou do this, happy shall you be and it shall be well with you."[7]

The disciples would have shared the difficult life of their rabbi. But they would also have experienced great joy in the midst of it. After all, they were the *talmidim* of an extraordinary rabbi, learning from him about the deep things of God.

Modern Christians have sometimes been confused about what discipleship is, equating it with discipline. Of course discipline is vital to the spiritual life. Jesus himself said, "Whoever wants to be my disciple must deny themselves and take up their cross and follow me" (Mark 8:34). But the overall goal of discipleship is not simply to grow in self-discipline, but to be transformed into the likeness of Christ.

Imagine for a moment if someone were to define parenting *only* as discipline. Of course children need discipline. But we would have great cause for worry if discipline was the only thing a parent focused on.

Sometimes we hear the word "disciple" and conclude that it's too hard to become one. But think about the alternative. To refuse to become Jesus's disciples is to consign ourselves to perpetual childhood and condemn ourselves to a wasted, frustrating life. The more we enter into relationship with Rabbi Jesus, the more joy we will experience.

To become more like Christ will deepen our relationships and allow us to live more authentically. It may not always be easy but it will certainly be good, and, as we follow him, we will find ourselves living with greater passion and purpose, experiencing a life of greater fulfillment.

The Rabbi-Disciple Bond

Over time the relationship between Elijah and Elisha grew deep, like that of a father and son. On Elijah's last day on earth, Elisha followed him everywhere, clinging to him as though he could keep him tethered to earth one more day. When the heavenly chariots finally whisked Elijah away, Elisha tore his garment in a sign of mourning, crying out in anguish, "My father! My father!" (2 Kings 2:12). The loss of his beloved mentor overwhelmed him.

Like these two Old Testament prophets, a rabbi and his disciple were expected to form a close, personal bond—hardly surprising given the amount of time they spent together and the important life issues they were constantly discussing. This closeness between rabbi and disciple was considered essential to the learning process. It has been said, just as one candle lights another only if it is brought close, so a rabbi only teaches well when he is close to his *talmidim*.

During the time of Jesus, one's rabbi was considered to be as dear as one's own father, and it was traditional for disciples to show the same reverence for their rabbi as their father, or even more. It was said, "Your father brought you into this world, but your rabbi brings you into the life of the world to come!"[8]

We find statements like, "If a man's father and his rabbi are both taken captive, a disciple should ransom his rabbi first," and, "If his father and his master are carrying heavy burdens, he removes that of his master, and afterward removes that of his father."[9] The point of such sayings was to highlight the utter devotion a disciple should display to his rabbi. Rabbis were also deeply committed to their disciples, as evidenced by such sayings as this: "If a disciple is sent into exile, his rabbi should go with him."[10] A famous sage by the name of Rabbi

Akiva once cared for a sick disciple, coming to his home and even performing housework until he returned to health.

No wonder Peter told Jesus, "We have left everything to follow you!" (Mark 10:28), and later, "Even if I have to die with you, I will never disown you" (Mark 14:31). He was reflecting the deep devotion that disciples felt for their rabbis at that time. Peter's devotion stands in direct contrast to Judas's disloyalty, highlighting how unthinkable it would have been for a disciple to betray his rabbi with a kiss! By understanding the traditional bond between rabbi and disciple, we can also sense the depth of Peter's anguish after denying Jesus three times, and then his overwhelming gratitude on the shores of the Sea of Galilee when the risen Christ made him breakfast and reinstated him (John 21:17).

Serving the Rabbi

Like Elisha, disciples were supposed to become servants of their rabbi, attending to his personal needs. Elisha was described as the one who "used to pour water on the hands of Elijah," meaning that he served as his personal attendant (2 Kings 3:11). How appropriate since Elisha was, in a sense, Elijah's "apprentice."

The Gospels make it clear that Jesus's disciples also served him. They went into town to buy food (John 4:8), and they arranged for the Passover celebration according to his directions (Luke 22:8). Disciples were expected to take turns preparing the common meal and serving the needs of the group. It was said, "All acts a slave performs for his master, a disciple performs for his rabbi, except untying the sandal."[11] To untie someone's sandal was considered demeaning, the task of a slave. With that as background, we can understand the impact of John the Baptist's comment that he felt unworthy even to untie Jesus's sandal (John 1:27).

Disciples were supposed to be their rabbi's servants because, as Safrai points out, "some laws could not just be studied theoretically or merely discussed, but could only be learned by serving the teacher."[12]

By learning obedience to his rabbi's directions, a disciple learned reverence for doing God's will. And by putting himself in the position of a servant, he opened himself to correction so that his conduct could be honed and refined. Furthermore, the rabbis believed that humility was an indispensable condition for learning: "Just as water flows away from a high point and gathers at a low point, so the word of God only endures with the learner who is humble in his knowledge."[13]

Like many others before him, Jesus compared the relationship between rabbi and disciple to that of master and servant, saying, "The student is not above the teacher, nor a servant above his master" (Matthew 10:24). As we have seen, the title "rabbi" literally means "my master." It was the very same term a slave would have used to address his owner. Despite Jesus's own humility, his expectations for his followers were clear, illustrated by sayings like, "Why do you call me, 'Lord, Lord,' and do not do what I say?" (Luke 6:46).

Let's return once more to the scene in the upper room. How distraught Jesus must have been to find that after three years of instructing his twelve disciples, they missed the point entirely. Instead of acting like humble servants, they were jockeying for position, arguing who was greatest (Luke 22:24–30). What would it take to get the message through their thick heads and even thicker hearts? Jesus then knelt down and did the unthinkable. Wrapping a towel around his waist, exactly as a slave would have done, he began to wash their feet. Then he said:

> "You call me 'Teacher' and 'Lord,' and rightly so, for that is what I am. Now that I, your Lord and Teacher, have washed your feet, you also should wash one another's feet. I have set you an example that you should do as I have done for you." (John 13:13–15)

Discipling by Example

So we see that on the night before his death, Jesus bent down and wiped away the grime on the feet of his disciples. This startling and intimate act of kindness embodied another rabbinic method: a rabbi was to model how to live by using examples from his own life.

Paul did the same, telling the Corinthians: "In Christ Jesus I became your father through the gospel. Therefore I urge you to imitate me. For this reason I have sent you Timothy, my son whom I love, who is faithful in the Lord. He will remind you of my way of life in Christ Jesus, which agrees with what I teach everywhere in every church" (1 Corinthians 4:15–17). Paul was urging the Corinthian believers to imitate him just as he was imitating Christ (see 1 Corinthians 11:1).

Like other rabbis, Paul saw himself as a "father," sending the Corinthians his beloved disciple Timothy, whom he called his "son." He wanted the Corinthians to learn about his own way of life through the example of Timothy. Paul was using this "whole person" method of discipling in order to transform their lives.

But didn't Christ warn his disciples, saying, "You are not to be called 'Rabbi,' for you have only one Master and you are all brothers. And do not call anyone on earth 'father,' for you have one Father, and he is in heaven. Nor are you to be called 'teacher,' for you have one Teacher, the Christ." (Matthew 23:8–10 NIV 1984)? Jesus knew too well the human propensity for self-exaltation.

In a recent op-ed column for the *New York Times*, David Brooks made an insightful comment about one of the most powerful positions in the world—that of the presidency of the United States:

> The presidency is a bacterium. It finds the open wounds in the people who hold it. It infects them, and the resulting scandals infect the presidency and the country. The person with the fewest wounds usually does best in the White House, and is best for the country.[14]

Brooks's remark offers a new twist on the old saying that "power corrupts and absolute power corrupts absolutely." Jesus is the only one to whom all power can safely be given. And in that sense he is our only true rabbi.

Even though Christ called his followers to go out and make

disciples, he was not endorsing a model of self-important leadership. An authoritarian style of leadership has little to do with Christ and everything to do with human ego. Some Christians, out of ignorance or passivity, have given away personal responsibility for their lives. Tragically, some leaders have encouraged them to do so.

Still, just because there have been abuses shouldn't make us disrespectful or suspicious of the legitimate authority God has given to leaders in the church. Despite human imperfection, we are still called to disciple others. That was true of Paul even though he called himself the "worst" of sinners (1 Timothy 1:15). And it will sometimes be true of us as well. Parents, for instance, must be disciple-makers of their children. Knowing that Christ is our true Master will help us to humbly disciple others.

Jesus's words that "you are not to be called 'Rabbi'" should make us wary of wanting to pridefully hold ourselves up as "rabbi," acquiring disciples to become just like ourselves. Yet, discipling often seems to happen whether we want it to or not. Any parent, for instance, can tell you that children are amazing mimics. Ann remembers when her daughter Katie was about a year old. "She was only nine months when I adopted her from China," she explains, "so it took her a while to catch up in the language department. One day when Katie was spouting a steady stream of baby gibberish, my mother commented that she sounded just like me. My mother wasn't trying to insult my command of the English language. She was only noting that my daughter had already managed to master my inflections."

This tendency toward imitation doesn't end when you grow up. Back when Lois was teaching college biology classes, she would tell her students how to do a lab procedure and then show them exactly how to do it. Before long, she noted something interesting. If she took a shortcut or ignored a step when demonstrating the procedure, her students would do the same. Invariably, they imitated her *actions* rather than her *words*.

Over the years Lois became keenly aware of her influence, realizing, for instance, that she couldn't ask research students to work long hours on a project if she intended to leave early every night. She knew, too, how important it was to keep good lab records and express enthusiasm for their research. If she was sloppy or lackadaisical, her students would likely become the same. As Jesus said, "It is enough for students to be like their teachers, and servants like their masters" (Matthew 10:25).

"Speaking of our tendency to imitate," Lois says, "I find that my own mind seems remarkably malleable, impressed by whatever I read or see modeled around me. A steady diet of cynical political commentary always makes me more negative. Being with friends who gossip can make me more careless about how I speak. None of us is so mature that we cannot be influenced. The question is: Who or what do we want to shape our lives? Even the culture around us will try to 'disciple' us if we have not placed ourselves under the transforming influence of Jesus Christ."

Remember the analogy we made at the beginning of this chapter citing the scene in *Young Frankenstein*, where Igor urges Dr. Frankenstein to "walk this way"? Months after developing the analogy between this scene in the movie and the way that rabbis train their disciples, Ann heard a sermon in which a pastor told the story of a friend who had recently returned from a visit to Israel. One day while this man was in Jerusalem, he noticed a bent-over rabbi, shuffling through the streets. Behind the rabbi walked several men, presumably his disciples. Remarkably, each man was also walking bent over.[15] What a picture of the rabbinic model of learning through imitation!

An Eastern View of Discipleship

"I used to think," Lois says, "that Jesus's command to make disciples simply meant teaching people certain beliefs about God, helping them to accept Christ as Lord, and then educating them in doctrinal truth later on. Though all these are important, this way of defining discipleship showed that I, like many Westerners, approached the gospel primarily as information." Unfortunately, such an approach tends to produce efforts at evangelism that are thinly disguised power grabs. We try hard to foist our belief system onto others, debating with people until they declare our way the best.

An Eastern view of discipleship seems far more in keeping with the gospel. The Eastern view encompasses the understanding that Jesus died for our sins and that belonging to him involves repenting and receiving him as Lord. But it also recognizes that Jesus lived transparently in front of his disciples in order to teach them how to live. They, in turn, were to live transparently before others, humbly teaching them the way of Christ. This approach involves not just *information* but *transformation*. God's goal isn't simply to fill the world with people who believe the right things. It is to fill the world with people who shine with the brilliance of Christ.

Shepherding in Israel is a wonderful metaphor for this kind of discipleship. In many countries, sheep spend their lives in fenced-in pastures where they spend their time grazing and milling about. Many Christians seem to think that the Great Commission is a matter of getting sheep "into the pen"—inviting people to accept Christ, the high point of their spiritual lives. In Israel, however, where grass has difficulty growing in the arid soil, sheep must know their shepherd, following him obediently from pasture to pasture. There, shepherding is a much more active task.

Judith Fain is a doctoral candidate at the University of Durham. As part of her studies, she spends several months each year in Israel. One day while walking on a road near Bethlehem, Judith watched as three shepherds converged with their separate flocks of sheep. The three men hailed each other and then stopped to talk. While they were conversing, their sheep intermingled, melting into one big flock. Wondering how the three shepherds would ever be able to identify their own sheep, Judith waited until the men were ready to say their goodbyes. She watched, fascinated, as each of the shepherds called out to his sheep. At the sound of their shepherd's voice, like magic, the sheep separated again into three flocks. Apparently some things in Israel haven't changed for thousands of years.

Just like these sheep, what distinguishes us is not so much the "pen" we inhabit but the shepherd we follow. Some sheep come running as soon as their shepherd calls, but some struggle to obey his lead, going astray whenever temptation strikes. It takes a lot more energy to follow a wandering shepherd than to be cooped up in a pen.

But we are called to be disciples of a Rabbi who is always on the move, one who wants us to go with him, making disciples to the ends of the earth. We need to learn how to recognize his voice, to go where he wants us to go, and to serve and imitate him so that we can share his good news with the world.

AT THE FEET OF THE RABBI

1. Discipleship involves gradual change over a period of years. Ask a friend who knows you well to comment on changes he or she has observed in you as you have matured as Christ's disciple.

2. Disciples were expected to serve their rabbi with humility and to learn through that service. Ask yourself how you have been actively serving Christ in your day-to-day life. What has he been teaching you through your service?

3. What of your parents' traits, even those you dislike, are evident in your own life? Ask God to show you how to improve the example you are to your own children.

4. Someone once said that we should always be discipling at least one person, and being discipled by another. Who are you being discipled by? And who are you discipling?

CHAPTER 5

Get Yourself Some Haverim

*Much have I learned from my teachers, even more
from my haverim, but from my disciples, most of all.*

BABYLONIAN TALMUD, *TAANIT 7A*

If you crack open the door of an Orthodox Jewish *yeshiva* (seminary) study hall, you might expect to be greeted by utter silence. After all, the students need to learn massive amounts of information. But if you anticipate a scene in which all heads are bowed, with each student poring silently and intently over the ancient texts, you will be mistaken.

Instead what will greet you is the din of multiple conversations. Pairs of students will be standing at podiums facing each other, animatedly discussing the fine points of each text. Bespectacled students will have one hand poised over an open volume while the other hand gestures wildly, the debate waxing and waning. If one student doesn't understand a passage, the other tries to explain it. Together they think of possible interpretations of the text. This gathering of students is called a *havruta*, and each student is studying with a *haver* (pronounced hah-VAIR; literally a "friend") to master the text.

> **Yeshiva**
>
> A *yeshiva* is a modern Orthodox Jewish school for religious learning. Some *yeshivas* teach younger students, while others are designed to prepare adults to become ordained as rabbis.

At first glance, this seems like such a strange study technique. But through the ages Jewish thinkers have considered it vital to study the Scriptures in the presence of other people. A famous line of rabbinic advice from before Jesus's time was this: "Acquire for yourself a rabbi, and get yourself a *haver*."[1] In ordinary usage, the word *haver* can simply mean a companion or a close friend. But here it actually means someone who is willing to partner with you in grappling with Scripture and with the rabbinic texts.

As critical as it was to study with a rabbi, it was considered essential to have one or two people who could learn right along with you. Fellow students could ask each other questions that they might be too embarrassed to ask their teachers. Also, partners could learn from each other.

Was Jesus aware of this approach to studying Scripture? Consider the words of the early rabbis, who said: "When two sit together and exchange words of Torah, then the Divine Presence dwells among them."[2] Now, listen to the words of Jesus: "Where two or three gather in my name, there am I with them" (Matthew 18:20). You can hardly miss the similarity. Like other Jewish teachers of his time, Jesus affirmed his followers' need for community. What's more, since Jesus is himself the Word of God, it makes sense that he would promise to be present as we come together to study the Scriptures.

Our Westernized minds may struggle with this idea. We tend to believe that the only way to deeply encounter God is through solitary prayer and study. But Jesus implies that his presence will be felt *most often* in the presence of a small group of *haverim*.

Haver, Haverah

A *haver* (plural, *haverim*) is a male student who partners with another student to enhance learning. Together, *haverim* study and discuss the religious texts. A female study partner is a *haverah* (plural, *haverot*).

Throughout the centuries, Jews have greatly emphasized family and relationships. Jesus himself was very much a part of this Eastern cultural setting, and his words reflect this emphasis on community. Let's look at what we can learn from Jesus's culture about the importance of community and of having *haverim*.

Community, Past and Present

On Lois's first trip to Israel, she visited a class of Orthodox Jewish boys between the ages of thirteen and sixteen. As the boys took her group on an informal tour of their synagogue, they brought out a pair of antique Torah scrolls, proudly placing them on the *bimah* (lectern). As they carefully unrolled the handwritten Hebrew text inscribed on yellowed parchment, someone asked the boys what Scripture passage they had been studying that week. Since the scrolls contain no indications of chapter or verse, they had to rely on their own intimate familiarity with the text to find the passage. Scanning column after column of ornate calligraphy, the boys rolled the enormous scrolls back and forth in their search. Naturally, they easily located the passage.

As interesting as this exercise was, even more fascinating was one student's description of the week's Scripture text. Here's what he said: "We're reading the story of how God brought us out of Egypt and saved us from the Egyptians." Note that he said "us," not "them," as though he and his classmates had just crossed the Red Sea along with Moses and the Israelites.

Because Jewish people understand that Scripture tells the story of their people, they commonly use the pronoun "us" when discussing various stories in the Bible. These students were reading the Bible as their own family history, considering themselves as much a part of it as their ancestors were thousands of years ago.

In his autobiography, the Jewish leader Nahum Goldmann describes how a traditional Jew feels a sense of connectedness even to long-distant Bible characters or historical figures. "When, as a child, he learned about Moses, he saw him not as a mythical figure, but as an important though perhaps somewhat distant uncle," Goldmann explains. "When, as a student at the rabbinical academy, the *yeshiva*, he analyzed Rabbi Akiba or Rabbi Judah, he was not an antiquarian studying history so much as a man engaged in a living discussion with an older, wiser relative."[3]

Perhaps this is why Jews have such a love for studying the ancient texts—they view them as cherished family memoirs. When they read about their ancestors' weaknesses and sins, they can empathize, because they are reading about their own flesh and blood.

"What a contrast," Lois says, "to the way I used to read about the

Branches of Judaism

Orthodox Jews believe that Scripture is inspired, that God has called Jews to live according to the Torah, and that he will someday send a Messiah. Orthodox Jews adhere strictly to dietary laws and other Jewish traditions, but otherwise adopt modern practices. This particular form of Judaism has existed from the first century until today.

Ultra-Orthodox (Hasidic) Jews belong to a branch of Judaism that began in Europe in the late 1700s. Stricter than the Orthodox, this small minority emphasizes mysticism and joyful obedience. They can be recognized by their distinctive dress. Like the Orthodox, they believe in a coming Messiah.

Conservative Jews generally accept traditional Jewish beliefs and practices, but believe that such practices can be adapted to modern culture. Their views of the inspiration and authority of Scripture fall midway between that of the Orthodox Jews (high) and the Reform Jews (low).

Reform Jews believe the Bible was written by human beings and that it contains wise teaching that can be adapted to the culture of the times. They generally do not believe in a Messiah. The movement began in Europe in the 1800s.

Israelites wandering in the desert. I couldn't help wondering why on earth God had chosen such a whiny people. It never occurred to me to think of them as *my* people. Had I learned to read Scripture the way those Jewish students had, I would have pictured myself trudging through the desert right along with them, eating manna day after day and then complaining just as they had. Since Christians emphasize the reality of universal human sinfulness much more than Judaism does, I should have been among the first to identify with their failings."[4]

Noted Christian author Eugene Peterson emphasizes our vital need for connection with our spiritual ancestors. Pointing out that we would dismiss as frivolous a poll that merely interviewed one person for his views on a television special that he had watched for only ten minutes, Peterson remarks, "That is exactly the kind of evidence that too many Christians accept as the final truth about many much more important matters—matters such as answered prayer, God's judgment, Christ's forgiveness, and eternal salvation. The only person they consult is themselves, and the only experience they evaluate is the most recent ten minutes." We need to learn from the centuries of experience provided by our brothers and sisters in the church and in the Bible. Peterson continues:

> A Christian who has David in his bones, Jeremiah in his blood-stream, Paul in his fingertips and Christ in his heart will know how much and how little value to put on his own momentary feelings and the experience of the week. To remain willfully ignorant of Abraham wandering in the desert, the Hebrews enslaved in Egypt, David battling the Philistines, Jesus arguing with the Pharisees and Paul writing to the Corinthians is like saying, "I refuse to remember that when I kicked that black dog last week he bit my leg." If I don't remember it, in the next fit of anger I will kick him again and get bitten again.[5]

Both Peterson and the Jewish boys Lois met in Israel know the wisdom of connecting to our spiritual forefathers and foremothers, of having David in our bones and Jeremiah in our bloodstream. This sense of unbroken connection with the past is especially prominent at Passover, when everyone is instructed to imagine that they themselves have been redeemed from Egypt. Listen to what Exodus 12:26–27 says:

> When your children ask you, "What does this ceremony mean to you?" then tell them, "It is the Passover sacrifice to the LORD, who passed over the houses of the Israelites in Egypt and spared our homes when he struck down the Egyptians."

The way the rabbis read this text, God wasn't just telling the first Israelites to share their story with their children. He was speaking to future readers too, exhorting us to realize that God has spared our homes as well.

At Passover, Jewish families gather to celebrate a big meal and then retell the story of the redemption of their "family." Wouldn't it be great if Christian families were to make a point of sharing their own stories at least once a year, telling each other how God has acted on their behalf?

Without intending to, my family has created a tradition of telling such stories. I come from a long line of Lutheran Tverbergs. For more than sixty years, our Tverberg clan has been having the kind of family reunions that Garrison Keillor might envy. We are so Lutheran, in fact, that at every reunion we hold our own services on Sunday morning, complete with a choir. Though we Lutherans may be loyal churchgoers, we're normally tight-lipped about our religious feelings.

Surprisingly, in spite of our stony-faced Norwegian sense of privacy, it is at these family worship times when people in my family have stood up and told stories about what God has been doing in their lives. At one service, my cousin filled in the details of a terrifying ordeal that had happened just months before. We knew that two youths had broken into his home in the middle of the night, stabbing him and leaving him seriously wounded. But that morning we heard the rest of the story.

Pesach

Pesach is the Hebrew word for "Passover," held in March or April, the first of the seven biblical feasts. It recalls the events of the exodus from Egypt. This ancient feast is still observed by Jews today once a year with a special ceremonial meal, or *Seder*, usually eaten at home.

At the moment he was being attacked, a woman from his church had awoken from a sound sleep with an overwhelming urge to pray for him. Amazingly, my cousin's wife was able to wrest the knife away from the youth, causing it to miss vital organs by a hairsbreadth. Though my cousin suffered great trauma, his life was spared, in part because an experienced surgeon who was supposed to have been out of town that day had an unforeseen change of plans. Several other remarkable details showed God's powerful presence in that dark hour.

Personal accounts like these have had far greater impact on my faith than the best sermon I've ever heard. How could they not? Faith has become not just about assenting to a list of abstract truths, but about my own family having a real-life encounter with Jesus Christ.

Similarly, when God told his people to recount their redemption at Passover each year, he knew how important it would be for them to remember their family story. He wanted coming generations to understand exactly what he had done for them.

What if we could find a way to identify with our own Christian history in the way that Jewish people identify with their sacred history? Perhaps it is time to reacquaint ourselves with the great stories of men and women of faith throughout the ages, people like Perpetua, one of the early Christian martyrs, or Monica and her famous son, Augustine, or Francis of Assisi, or William and Catherine Booth, or Dietrich Bonhoeffer. The stories of God's faithfulness are as varied as the lives of those in our Christian family who have lived them. Today his grace is as generous as it was when Jesus was alive and throughout all the centuries that have passed.

Reconsidering Solitude

Close your eyes and picture the first painting of Jesus that pops into your head. Most likely it depicts Jesus in a solitary scene, praying in Gethsemane, or holding a lamb, or nailed to the cross. From earliest Christian times, Jesus has often been portrayed as a solitary, lonely man.

Of course Jesus did have times of solitude. The Gospels tell us that he sometimes went off on his own to pray. He even spent forty days alone in the desert fasting and praying. Because of this, many have tried to imitate Christ by seeking solitude. Early monks, viewing Jesus's desert fasting as the essence of spirituality and discipleship, often confined themselves to their cells to pray for hours and days on end. And others have emphasized the need for solitude as well. Listen to one author's top four recommendations for developing spiritual disciplines:

1. Solitude
2. Silence
3. Fasting
4. Scripture memorization

Even though these disciplines can be helpful, the author leaves something essential off the list. What about community? If the goal of discipleship is to become Christlike, it's important that we spend time with others, learning how to love and be loved and letting our rough edges be sanded away. We need to learn to tolerate each other's flaws and to admit our own so that Christ's Spirit can refine and reshape us.

Even the extroverts among us don't often engage in the kind of community that is necessary for discipleship. And what about those of us who by personality find ourselves attracted to solitary discipleship? For some of us, being alone is an escape from embracing people who annoy or challenge us. But Jesus's words about being present when two or more are gathered in his name should make us think twice about becoming spiritual Lone Rangers.

As Western individualists, we forget what Jesus's reality was like. Just think—most of his ministry was spent living side by side with his faithful *talmidim*, traveling with them on foot from town to town, camping out everywhere they went. Many an evening would have been spent sharing a meal with strangers who had generously invited them into their homes, as was the custom with visiting rabbis. Even when Jesus made a point of getting away from the clamorous crowds, he usually did so in the company of his disciples. Remarkably, Jesus never sent his students out alone, but always in pairs. He knew their critical need for *haverim*.

If anything, we see Jesus relishing the company of others. The disciples were surprised, for instance, at the delight he took in little children. On one occasion, when they wanted to shoo away the hungry crowd, Jesus multiplied a few loaves of bread and a couple of fish so that everyone could eat dinner together. In fact, his public ministry was initiated in the midst of a party, when he turned water into wine at a wedding feast. Following Jesus means sharing our lives in community, where the richness of life will unfold.

Yet solitude is still to be prized in the craziness of our modern world. Times alone with God and away from daily pressures can help us discern the still, small voice of God. But for most of us solitude should not be the norm. Instead, we should look for opportunities to connect with others in meaningful ways, especially since modern culture seems to be spiraling in on itself, with each person becoming ever more isolated.

As writers we both know what it's like to spend much of the day sitting alone in front of our computers. Many others spend eight hours a day at the office sitting in tomb-like cubicles. What happens when people return home and zone out online? YouTube videos, video games, and Facebook are poor substitutes for the laughter and love of family and friends.

Pastor Robert Stone points out that Americans are some of the loneliest people on the planet, saying that in most societies, people don't experience loneliness as acutely as Americans do. "In other cultures people are rarely alone, physically or emotionally. Relatives, neighbors, and even strangers are a normal part of everyone's life," Stone observes. "Not so in America!"[6]

Our individualism and our wealth have allowed us to minimize our contact with others—to our detriment. This problem of friend-lessness exists even in our churches. In *The Friendless American Male*, Larry Richards is reported as saying that "in church we sit together and sing together and greet one another cheerily as we leave at the end of a service. We do all of these things, sometimes for years, without form-ing any real personal Christian relationships. Our words often seem superficial. The church, therefore, becomes a place where Christians live alone together."[7] Attending church may enable us to hear a great sermon and sing rousing songs, but we are missing out if we are not also befriending and relating to each other in deeper ways.

On Becoming *Haverim*

"Looking back over my life," Lois says, "I can see the wisdom of having *haverim*. When I'm part of an excellent Bible study group, all sorts of insights surface that I would not find on my own. And when I hear stories of how God is working in other people's lives, it makes my read-ing of Scripture all the more powerful. Some of the best relationships I have developed are with my *haverim*. How easy it is to become close to others when you are spending time together discussing God's Word and praying for each other."

But there's more to being a *haver* than just being a Christian friend. A *haver* is a fellow disciple who earnestly desires to grapple with others over issues of faith—someone who wants to delve into God's Word, to be challenged and refined. A *haver* is like a spiritual "jogging partner"— someone for whom you'll crawl out of bed on a rainy morning, putting on your running shoes instead of hitting the snooze button. Once you're up and running together, your pace is a little faster, you keep going a little longer. You are pushed intellectually and spiritually. If we really want to mature in faith and as disciples, we need to develop relationships that force us to grow, by getting ourselves some *haverim*.

Being a *haver* is not a casual commitment. It requires stretching. We will need to carve out time for preparation and study, wrestling with the Scripture text beforehand so that we have something to share. For most of us this will be a challenge, but we should heed the advice of the rabbi who said, "Do not say, 'I will study when I have more time.' You may not have more time!"[8]

Also, it's impossible to be a good *haver* if you hold on to an extreme sense of privacy about spiritual matters. Plenty of study groups never move beyond superficial, impersonal conversation. *Haverim* need to learn to trust one another, openly expressing their thoughts and feelings, confident that what is shared within the group will not go beyond the group. They must also learn the art of respectful disagreement, challenging each other when necessary. Remember, debate was a normal part of the life of disciples, an essential way to learn.

Becoming each other's *haverim* is an effective way to fulfill Jesus's command to raise up disciples. Rather than viewing ourselves as the "rabbi" and others as our "disciples," becoming *haverim* allows us to take on the role of "co-disciples." We can help others grow by learning right alongside them.

"I wasn't the most mature Christian when I was in college," Lois observes. In fact, the obvious piety of some of the other students put her off—the Bibles they carried to every class, their group prayers in the cafeteria, how they seemed to cling to each other. *Are these people even real?* she wondered. *Are they capable of befriending another Christian not of their great spiritual depth?* She decided to test them by acting a little extra worldly, saying things that pushed the edge. "I played the part so well," she says, "that, to my embarrassment, they concluded I wasn't even a Christian."

"It wasn't until a few months later, when I joined a Bible study with them, that they actually began to become my good friends. Once they realized that I was already a Christian, they relaxed, opening up about their own struggles. That's when I discovered how Christlike they could be. Brian, who was in many of my classes, mentioned that he was giving up study time to counsel another student through emotional problems. Instantly, my competitive instincts rebelled. I couldn't imagine putting my success on the line in order to help someone else.

"Another friend, Steph, amazed me with her easy, natural way of befriending foreign students, people who often felt like outsiders on campus. With my own rural Iowa background, I had no clue how she did it. Slowly, her ability to love people from other cultures rubbed off on me, and I've since developed many precious relationships with people of other nationalities."

The Christ that Lois saw in her college friends challenged her to change the way she lived. Ironically, their initial anxiety about her spiritual status was what had prevented them from effectively sharing the gospel with her. These young Christians thought their job was to get her into the "sheep pen" by giving her a perfect sermon or by helping her pray a certain prayer. But the issue wasn't that she was "lost." Lois simply needed to become a better disciple. "Once they allowed themselves to become honest and authentic," she says, "to become my *haverim*, their lives became powerful witnesses to my immaturity."

Many of us see disciple-making as something that only happens at the "fence." We view our primary job as getting people into the fold. But a lot of sheep are like Lois, inside the fence but just milling about munching on grass. They need to be brought closer to Christ by becoming his true disciples.

What about people who aren't at all interested in Jesus or those who are downright angry or hostile toward the church? How are we supposed to relate to them? Perhaps the solution is *to live transparently around everyone* regardless of their faith or lack of it. We can share openly and sensitively about our own struggles and what Christ is doing in our lives without worrying so much about where people are, relative to the "fence." Then every bit of our lives will become a source of witness, no matter who our friends are. Sometimes we will open the gate and let someone in. But just as often we may find ourselves helping other believers become more effective disciples. In the process, we will discover that we are being discipled as well. The key is to stay close to Jesus, living transparently as we seek to follow our Rabbi.

———•———

One way to strengthen our discipleship and stay close to Jesus is through deepening our prayer life. Imagine what it must have been like for the disciples to spend night after night under the stars, waking at dawn to see that their Master was already up, praying to his Father in heaven. Of course they were curious about Jesus's spiritual life, and so they begged him: "Lord, teach us to pray" (Luke 11:1). What can we learn from the way Jewish people prayed in the first century? What can we learn about prayer from the greatest of all rabbis?

AT THE FEET OF THE RABBI

1. If you don't yet have a study partner, a *haver*, ask God to send you one. Perhaps your spouse can be your *haver* or *haverah*. Whether you are single or married, look for another person in your neighborhood, your church, your workplace, or among your circle of friends who shares your interest in Scripture. Make sure your *haver* is someone capable of challenging you to go deeper rather than someone who will simply agree with everything you say. Remember, debate is a helpful method for learning.
2. Consider holding a *havruta*, a study session, in your home or in your church. Invite one or more people to study a particular text with you. If several people show up, arrange them in pairs and have them discuss the text aloud. Before beginning, offer a little background on this method of study. See what insights emerge as this lively session unfolds.
3. The next time you read the Bible, try to relate to the Israelites as though they are part of your own family—your aunts, uncles, siblings, or parents. How does your emotional reaction change when you consider the people in the stories as "us" instead of "them"?
4. Encourage older relatives to tell stories about how God has worked in their lives, especially during hard times. Think about ways to record the faith stories of your family members, preserving them for future generations.
5. One church we know of dedicates an entire service each spring to celebrating the great things God has done throughout the previous year. Each person with a story to tell stands up and shares it, and the whole church has a party afterward. Consider holding a similar celebration in your own church.

CHAPTER 6

Rabbi, Teach Us to Pray

Prayer is an invitation to God to intervene in
our lives, to let His will prevail in our affairs; it
is the opening of a window to Him in our will,
an effort to make Him the Lord of our soul.

RABBI ABRAHAM JOSHUA HESCHEL[1]

Remember Ann's El Al flight from New York? As soon as she arrived in Tel Aviv, she headed by taxi into Jerusalem, one of the world's most religious cities. Everywhere she went she saw men striding by in black fedoras, dark suits, and plain white shirts. Other men wore long beards with side curls hanging from beneath barrel-shaped fur hats. And there were women dressed in long-sleeved blouses and floor-length skirts. If possible, the city seemed even more religious than she had remembered it. Though none of the people Ann saw that day were making a fashion statement, all were saying something loud and clear about their religious beliefs and the community to which they belonged.

"I couldn't help but be impressed by their outward show of devotion," Ann remarks, "especially during the hottest part of summer! I even wondered what would happen if Jesus came striding onto the scene. Would he blend into this crowd better than I did with my wrinkle-free traveling pants, short-sleeved blouse, camera bag slung casually over my shoulder, and small gold cross on a chain around my neck? I wondered, too, whether the customs and habits of today's observant Jews would bear any resemblance to those held by Jesus and his contemporaries.

"I knew it would be foolish to project later religious traditions on Jesus by assuming that the Judaism of today is identical to that practiced by ancient Jews. But might there be some similarities? Did Jesus and his disciples wear *tefillin* (phylacteries), *yarmulkes*, or prayer shawls? Did they recite any of the prayers uttered by Jews today? Should I imagine Jesus and his disciples *davening*, swaying rhythmically back and forth as they prayed, like the young girl who sat next to me on the plane from New York?

"As I was to discover, both history and the gospel accounts reveal a surprising relationship between certain of the distinctive customs of Orthodox Jews today and those shared by the Jewish people of Jesus's time."

For instance, the custom of binding *tefillin*, small black boxes on the head and arm, was already hundreds of years old when Jesus was born. In one of the caves of Qumran near the Dead Sea, archaeologists in 1969 found intact *tefillin* from the first-century era that still had parchment scrolls inside.[2] The boxes were quite small, less than the size of a postage stamp.

Tefillin

Tefillin or phylacteries are leather boxes containing Scripture that are worn on the forehead and left arm to fulfill the command in Deuteronomy 6:8, "Tie them as symbols on your hands and bind them on your foreheads." In Jesus's time, *tefillin* were worn all day long. Today they are worn only during prayer.

Davening

Davening is a Yiddish word that means "praying." It is often used to describe the practice of swaying while reciting prayers. This custom arose among Jews in the Middle Ages.

Jesus probably wore *tefillin* most of the time, not just during prayer, as is the custom today. Ancient manuscripts describe how Jewish men wore them during the daylight hours, removing them only when eating, working, or entering an unclean place. If this was his practice, then Jesus was probably wearing small *tefillin* when he criticized those who were wearing large *tefillin* in order to advertise their super piety (Matthew 23:5).[3]

Jesus, however, would not have worn a *yarmulke* (or *kippah*), a man's head covering. That became customary several centuries later, beginning among the Jews in Babylon.[4] In 1 Corinthians 11, Paul tells us that men's heads were uncovered, whereas women's heads were covered.

Though Jesus would have worn the ceremonial tassels (*tzitziyot*, plural of *tzitzit*), he would not have worn a prayer shawl, which developed only later. The point of the prayer shawl is to carry the tassels, and it is worn only for prayer and religious occasions. In Jesus's case, the tassels would have been attached to the outer woolen garment he wore every day. We see them in Matthew 9:20, when a woman grasped the tassels on his robe and was healed. Jesus's practice of wearing *tzitziyot* all the time, rather than just at prayer, continues among Orthodox and Hasidic Jews of today. During the time of Jesus, women were not required to wear tassels, but some wore them on their outer cloaks anyway, because some husbands borrowed their wives' cloaks occasionally.[5]

Also, the long side curls (*peyot*) that some Jewish men wear in order to observe Leviticus 19:27 ("Do not cut the hair at the sides of your head") are a fairly recent tradition observed by some groups in the past few hundred years, mostly from Poland and Russia. Interestingly, one tradition links the side curls to a command in Leviticus 19:9–10:

> When you reap the harvest of your land, do not reap to the very
> edges of your field or gather the gleanings of your harvest. Do not
> go over your vineyard a second time or pick up the grapes that
> have fallen. Leave them for the poor and the foreigner.

Some think that by leaving the corners of their heads uncut, these Jewish men are reminding themselves and others of the importance of leaving the corners of their fields uncut—in other words, of providing for the poor.[6]

Similarly, the wool coats and fur hats of Hasidic Jews arose out of seventeenth-century Polish fashion. And *davening* began in Europe in the Middle Ages. Not everything Jewish is a picture of Jesus.

Yet some of the customs that seem the strangest, like wearing *tefillin* and tassels, were very much a part of Jesus's everyday experience. Come to think of it, Jesus may also have been more at home on my El

Al flight from New York than I was. He would have been most famil-iar with the prayers the passengers were reciting, especially since they were in Hebrew, the language of prayer since Jesus's day.[7]

He could certainly have joined in as they said the *Shema* (pro-nounced "shmah"), three Scripture passages spoken as a declaration of utter devotion. Jesus would have recited this each morning and evening, as Jews have done for thousands of years. The name *Shema* comes from the first word of the first line, "Hear [*Shema*], O Israel, the Lord is our God, the Lord alone. You shall love the Lord your God with all of your heart and with all of your soul and with all of your might."[8] (The complete text of the *Shema* appears in Appendix A). When a teacher of the law asked Jesus which was the greatest command-ment, Jesus responded by quoting from the *Shema* (Mark 12:28–30). This prayer expressed the essence of his own deep commitment to the Father. For many Jews the words of the *Shema* are the very last words on their lips before they die, confirming their devotion to God.

What other prayers might the passengers on my flight to Israel have been praying? Most likely they were reciting a series of bene-dictions thought to date back to the time of Nehemiah, hundreds of years before Jesus was born. The *Amidah*, also known as the *Eighteen Benedictions* (there are nineteen now), forms the heart of Jewish wor-ship. Sometimes people refer to it simply as *Tefillah*, meaning "Prayer," because it is so central to worship.[9]

Twice a day, from his boyhood, Jesus would have heard his father Joseph praying this traditional prayer,[10] though not in the exact same words as it is prayed today. The *Amidah* wasn't organized into a formal liturgy until about fifty years after Jesus's time, by the grandson of Paul's rabbi, Gamaliel.[11] Since then, for almost two thousand years, it has remained largely unchanged. Along with prayers of praise and thanks-giving, the *Amidah* includes petitions for God to send the Messiah and to grant wisdom, forgiveness, healing, and deliverance. Like all Jewish prayer, it is filled with references to the Scriptures, especially to Psalms. (See Appendix A for the text.)

The beautiful *Amidah* liturgy begins with the words: "Blessed are You, O Lord, our God and God of our fathers, God of Abraham, God of Isaac, and God of Jacob." Commenting on how repetitious this opening prayer is, Rabbi Wayne Dosick observes:

> The prayer book writers understood that each of these "founding fathers" of Judaism had to create a separate, individual, personal, relationship with God—each in his own time. Isaac's world was not the world of his father; Jacob's world was not the world of his father or his grandfather. Each man had to discover God for himself, for each man has his own needs and expectations of God.[12]

In addition to the *Amidah*, ordinary people would have prayed many other prayers in the early first century. Jewish life, in fact, was saturated with prayer. After the destruction of the temple in AD 70, the Jewish people came to think of their prayers as a substitute for the sacrifices that could no longer be offered. Thrice daily—morning, afternoon, and evening—the timing of prayer is patterned after the timing of the temple sacrifices.

Jews pray before eating, before enjoying any pleasure in life, and even in the midst of misfortune. An observant Jew recites at least a hundred blessings a day. The priority placed on prayer is evident by virtue of the fact that the first book (or tractate) of the Mishnah, entitled "*Berakhot*" (meaning "blessings"), is devoted entirely to the subject of how and when to pray.

Jesus, too, placed a priority on prayer. Evidence sprinkled throughout the Gospels shows that he observed the rich customs of Jewish prayer. He often arose early or went off alone to pray. He taught about prayer, wove parables about prayer, and even gave his disciples crib notes with words that they could pray to the Father. What can we learn from Jewish prayer customs that can help us to pray more like he did?

Jewish Insights on the Lord's Prayer

Realizing how Jesus would have practiced the customs of his own religious culture can yield many insights into his teachings on prayer.

Think for a moment about the Lord's Prayer. As beloved as it is, many of us scratch our heads over phrases like "hallowed be your name" or "your kingdom come." These lines are at the same time familiar but strange. We struggle to understand them not because of any thickheadedness on our part but because Jesus's words are so Jewish. His teaching on prayer relies on classic themes that still resonate with Jews today.

It has been suggested that the Lord's Prayer is a summary of the *Amidah* because it encompasses several of its themes.[13] Other rabbis of Jesus's time taught summary versions of the *Amidah* in order to illustrate what prayer should be like at its essence. Furthermore, the early church prayed the Lord's Prayer three times each day, just as the *Amidah* was prayed.[14] Whether or not Jesus had the *Amidah* in mind when he taught the Lord's Prayer, the fact that it shares similar themes shows that Jesus's prayers exemplified the wisdom of Jewish prayer.

Even the first two words of the Lord's Prayer—"Our Father"—can teach us a lot. The Lord's Prayer reflects Jewish tradition by using the phrase "our Father" rather than "my Father." Unlike our tendency to focus on our own individual needs, Jewish prayers tend to involve community prayer for the needs of the whole people. Even today, some prayers cannot be offered unless a *minyan* (ten adult male Jews[15]) are present to represent the people as a whole.

Notice, however, that while Jesus taught his disciples to address God as "our Father," he himself spoke to God as "my Father," in the singular. In Jewish prayer, God was sometimes called "our Father," but "my Father" was daring, almost unheard of. Many would have marked this as evidence that he was the Messiah because several prophecies describe the Messiah as someone who would be in an especially close

> **Amidah**
>
> The *Amidah* is the central prayer of the Jewish liturgy, prayed three times a day since the first century AD. It is also called the *Shmoneh Esreh*, meaning "eighteen," because originally it was composed of eighteen benedictions; a nineteenth petition was added about a hundred years after Jesus lived.

relationship with God.[16] Every time Jesus referred to God as "my" Father, his listeners would have heard it as a bold claim.

Remarkably, Jesus spoke of God as "my Father" when he was only twelve years old. Remember his response to his parents when they discovered him conversing with scholars at the temple: "Didn't you know I had to be in my Father's house?" (Luke 2:49). It seems that the boy Jesus was well aware of his identity and mission.

What about the phrase "give us today our daily bread"? Why does Jesus tell us to pray for bread? Why not tell us to pray for roast beef or bananas? In Hebrew, the word for bread, lechem, can also mean food in general. When Jesus held up bread, broke it, and thanked his Father in heaven, he was giving thanks for the entire meal, just as a Jewish father would have done. Lechem represents not only all the food but God's sustenance as a whole. When we pray this way, we are asking God to provide for all our needs. Grasping this can broaden our understanding of what Jesus was saying when he said, "I am the bread of life" (John 6:35). Jesus himself is the deepest sustenance of all.

Even today, bread has special significance in Jewish thinking. Some people believe that bread should never be discarded because doing so shows ingratitude for God's gracious provision. Josa Bivin, an American who has lived in Israel for many years, writes:

> Instead of dumping their bread along with the rest of their garbage into the garbage carts parked along the streets, they [Israelis] save the bread in plastic sacks and hang it from the metal projections on the sides of the carts (used to hoist the carts into the garbage trucks). That way, the bread is potentially available to the poor.[17]

This sensitivity to the poor and gratitude for God's provision is admirable. Lois remembers chatting one day with a Ugandan pastor who had become a good friend while he was studying at a nearby seminary. "I asked my friend what he would remember most about America when he returned home, and his answer shocked me," she says. "'All my life,' he replied, 'I will never forget having this one year when I did not need to worry about food.' I could hardly believe that a friend of mine had lived for most of his life worrying about not getting enough to eat!" Jesus's prayer for "daily bread" makes complete sense in light of the basic anxiety shared by most people throughout human history.

What about the line "deliver us from evil" (ESV)? What kind of evil is Jesus talking about? We can find clues both in the Scriptures and in Jewish prayer. Several places in the Old Testament speak of God "delivering [someone] from evil."[18] But the Hebrew word for evil, *ra*, is broad, meaning danger or misfortune as well as sin. The rabbis realized that the word *ra* can encompass many things, so one prayer from around AD 200 asks specifically: "Deliver me . . . from a bad person, a bad companion, a bad injury, an evil inclination, and from Satan, the destroyer." Four times the Hebrew word *ra* is used, first as a way of asking for physical protection, but then to ask for protection from being tempted to do evil by others, as well as by one's own desires, and even by Satan. This prayer asks God's help both physically and spiritually to avoid those things that will ultimately destroy our lives.

> **Minyan**
> A *minyan* is a gathering of at least ten adult male Jews required for certain public prayers. In the first century, women could also be included in this number.

Perhaps this ancient rabbinic prayer can help us better understand our own Rabbi's teaching. It parallels Jesus's words "lead us not into temptation," which is a Jewish way of saying, "Don't let us succumb to our own evil inclinations. Help us avoid temptation and sin." We certainly won't go wrong if we hear Jesus's words as a plea for God to protect us from the evil that is both within and without.[19]

How *Not* to Pray

We will return to the Lord's Prayer in chapter 13, when we look more closely at the phrase "your kingdom come," but let's take a moment now to consider another aspect of Jewish prayer—how *not* to pray.

You may wonder whether Jews only prayed fixed prayers at fixed times. Though they had many set prayers, Jewish people also prayed spontaneously. One first-century rabbi even warned against making one's prayers "fixed," meaning praying empty, rote repetitions.[20] He seemed to be making the same point Jesus did when he spoke about praying in "vain repetitions" (KJV) by babbling on and on (Matt. 6:7). Other rabbis offered wisdom on how we should pray in our spontaneous, reflective moments. Interestingly, they, like Jesus, discussed what it meant to pray "in vain." One said:

> If one's wife was pregnant and he said, "May it be thy will that she give birth to a male"—lo, this is a vain prayer. If he was coming along the road and heard a noise of crying in the city and said, "May it be thy will that those who are crying are not members of my household"—lo, this is a vain prayer.[21]

Why are these vain or empty prayers? Because there is no point in asking God to change the sex of an unborn baby, something God had already determined at the time of conception. To pray that God would change the gender of a child would be to pray that God would alter history, magically changing reality to suit us. The second idea is that if we should hear cries of distress, we should refrain from praying that they are not coming from members of our own family. Once again, we would be asking God to change history. Even worse, we would be wishing evil on others—asking God to send trouble on someone else for the sake of the people we love.

These ideas aren't just legalisms about what counts as a "vain prayer." By considering how *not* to pray, we are reminded that we have been given the awesome privilege of speaking to a God who is truly listening. We should always remember to approach him with reverence and love.

A Sense of God's Presence

To many people in the modern world, God seems remote and unconcerned, living light years away in another dimension called "heaven." Does God, the Creator of the entire universe, honestly care about our infinitesimally small problems? Most of us would say yes because we know that's the way we should answer the question. But we ache for a deeper, more immediate sense of God's nearness. We want rock-solid assurance of his faithful care.

Why is it sometimes so difficult to believe God cares about us? Many of us have been shaped not so much by a biblical worldview as by a secular one. Our Western world has been heavily influenced by Enlightenment philosophers who pictured God as a "divine watch-maker"—a being who set the universe in motion and then sat back to watch it tick. But the Bible says the opposite. It pictures God not far away but intimately close, speaking to people like Abraham, Jacob, Joseph, and Moses. He actively intervened on behalf of his people, leading them out of Egypt and into the Promised Land. Years later God came to earth in the person of Jesus Christ. And now his Spirit is alive in those who believe. Scripture reveals a God neither distant nor uncaring but one intensely interested in the world he has made. But Western philosophy has made us doubt the biblical picture.

To remind people of God's active presence in the world, some synagogues have inscribed the words *Da Lifne Mi Atah Omed*, meaning, "*Know Before Whom You Stand,*" above the ornate Torah scroll cabinet at the front of the synagogue. These words inspire a sense of awe, perhaps even a little terror, because they are saying: *Don't forget that you are standing in the presence of God himself.*

The idea that we are continually in the presence of God is greatly emphasized in some branches of Judaism. The reason many Jewish men wear *yarmulkes* is to remind themselves to be humbly in awe of God's presence all around them.[22] The writer Annie Dillard has a memorable way of highlighting Christians' relative nakedness before God, emphasizing how cavalierly we treat the privilege of standing in God's presence Sunday after Sunday:

> Why do people in church seem like cheerful, brainless tourists
> on a packaged tour of the Absolute? . . . Does anyone have the
> foggiest idea what sort of power we blithely invoke? Or, as I sus-
> pect, does no one believe a word of it? The churches are children

playing on the floor with their chemistry sets, mixing up a batch
of TNT to kill a Sunday morning. It is madness to wear ladies'
straw hats and velvet hats to church. We should all be wearing
crash helmets.[23]

In a sense, that's what Jewish head coverings are—little "crash
helmets" reminding them of the God who is infinitely powerful, but
yet so near.

Is it possible to cultivate a sense of God's presence, particularly
during prayer? There is a Hebrew word that deals with the question:
kavanah, which means "intention" or "direction." The word conveys the idea of being profoundly aware of the One to whom you are speaking as you direct your heart toward heaven. "A prayer without *kavanah* is like a body without a soul," say the rabbis. It's a lifeless, dead corpse. Because so many Jewish prayers are repeated, the rabbis emphasized the need for *kavanah*, so that each time a person prays, the words are fresh and full of passion, with a sense of reverence for the awesome God who is their focus.

Yarmulke

A *yarmulke*, also called a *kippah*, is a fabric skullcap worn traditionally by Jewish men. Some men wear one at all times, while others wear it only for religious occasions.

Ann remembers standing at the Western Wall in Jerusalem in
midsummer during the hottest part of the day. Called the "Wailing
Wall," it is part of the ancient retaining wall of the Temple Mount
and Judaism's most sacred site. Though the heat was excruciating, she
thinks of that day as the highlight of her time in Israel. "It is hard
to describe the awe I felt," she explains, "not because of the ancient
stones, but because of the sense I had of being in the presence of the
Father. If I could choose only two words to describe the experience,
they would be these: *immense* and *love*. I had been to the Western
Wall on a previous trip and felt nothing out of the ordinary. But now,
here in this place, all the devotion and the reverence I had witnessed
since I boarded my flight in New York seemed to coalesce. I sensed the
greatness of God as never before."

The Jewish theologian and writer Abraham Heschel says that *kavanah* is "attentiveness to God, an act of appreciation of being able to stand in the presence of God . . . It is one's being drawn to the preciousness of something he is faced with. To sense the preciousness of being able to pray, to be perceptive of the supreme significance of worshipping God is the beginning of higher *kavanah*."[24]

Kavanah goes beyond prayer too. The rabbis say that we should have *kavanah* in four activities:

- prayer
- studying the Scriptures
- performing acts of loving-kindness
- doing our life's work[25]

Ideally, each should be done with a profound awareness of the fact that God is present, desiring to speak and work through us at every moment. Imagine how meaningful each day would be if we undertook all our endeavors this way.

Living with *kavanah* utterly changes our experience of life. A few years ago some friends of Lois got fed up with the routine of sending out Christmas cards; it felt hollow to write one more braggy letter about their kids, mass-producing it for dozens of names in their address book. That year her friends decided to write their cards prayerfully. They still put together a letter of family news, but instead of just signing their names, they wrote a heartfelt note, telling each person how much they valued their relationship with them. Then, as they addressed the envelopes, they prayed for the recipients, reflecting on their memories together. That year, their Christmas cards took a lot longer to write, but this family felt joy rather than stress because their cards were filled with *kavanah*, a sense of the presence of God.

———•———

Jewish life, from morning until evening, is saturated in prayer. Remember how Paul exhorted the Thessalonians to pray continually

(1 Thessalonians 5:17)? At first blush, this sounds like an impossible command. How could anyone pray all the time? Let's turn our attention now to an ancient Jewish prayer custom, one that sheds light on what Paul was saying. It has the potential to enrich and deepen our own experience of prayer.

AT THE FEET OF THE RABBI

1. This week try to find a way to increase your *kavanah*, your attentiveness to God's presence, when you are at work. Whether digging a ditch, baking a soufflé, writing a sermon, or chairing a meeting, pray for the grace to realize that no matter where you are, you are in the presence of the Lord. To remind yourself, consider printing the word *kavanah* on an index card. Place it where it will catch your attention throughout the day.

2. Pray the following blessings from the *Amidah* over the next few days. If one of them particularly strikes you, try memorizing it:

   Lead us back, our Father, to your Torah; bring us near, our King, to your service, and cause us to return in perfect repentance before you. Blessed are you, O Lord, who accepts repentance.

   • • •

   Heal us and we shall be healed, help us and we shall be helped, for you are our joy. Grant full healing for all our wounds, for you, O God and King, are a true and merciful physician. Blessed are you, O Lord, who heals the sick of his people Israel.

· · ·

Bless for us, O Lord our God, this year and all of its yield for good, and shower down a blessing upon the face of the earth. Fill us with your bounty and bless our year, that it be as the good years. Blessed are you, O Lord, who blesses the years.

· · ·

We acknowledge to you, O Lord, that you are our God as you were the God of our fathers, forever and ever. Rock of our life, Shield of our salvation, you are unchanging from age to age. We thank you and declare your praise, for our lives that are in your hands and for our souls that are entrusted to you. Your miracles are with us every day, and your benefits are with us at all times, evening and morning and midday. You are good, for your mercies are endless; you are merciful, for your kindnesses are never complete; from everlasting we have hoped in you. And for all these things may your name be blessed and exalted, always and forevermore. Let every living thing give thanks to you and praise your name in truth, O God, our salvation and our help. Blessed are you, O Lord, your name is good, and to you it is right to give thanks.

CHAPTER 7

For Everything a Blessing

The grateful soul of the wise man is the true altar of God.

PHILO OF ALEXANDRIA (FIRST CENTURY AD)[1]

If you have ever seen the movie *Fiddler on the Roof*, you will probably remember the delightful give-and-take that Tevye, the Jewish milkman, has with God.[2] He is always pausing midscene to discuss something with the Lord right out loud. Back and forth he goes, arguing with God, arguing with himself, pleading, cajoling, even waving his fist, bantering with God as though he's an old friend who can be buttonholed for advice or a favor anytime. God might be invisible, but his presence is palpable. Tevye has a profound sense of God's continual nearness and an easy comfort in his prayer life that many of us might envy.

What if there were a way to feel a little more like Tevye? What was it about his culture that cultivated a sense of God's immediacy? Believe it or not, Tevye understood an ancient practice that dates from Jesus's time, one that can greatly enrich our lives today.

At one point in the movie, someone questions the rabbi of the Russian village in which Tevye lives, asking him, "Is there a blessing for the sewing machine?"

"There's a blessing for everything!" the rabbi replies. He was talking about the rich Jewish tradition of the blessing. This little habit of prayer can be truly transformational, instilling a sense of God's continual presence in those who practice it. Let's take a closer look.

A few hundred years before Jesus's time, Jews began to pay close attention to the words Moses spoke on the edge of the Promised Land:

"When you have eaten and are satisfied, you shall bless the LORD your God for the good land which He has given you" (Deuteronomy 8:10 NASB). He then went on to warn the people that when their silver and gold multiplied, they would be tempted to forget the Lord's great gift, thinking that their own efforts had produced their prosperity (8:14).

In order to heed this warning, the Jewish people developed a tradition of offering specific, short prayers throughout the day, from the instant they awoke until the moment they fell asleep. This has been the practice of many Jews from Jesus's time until today, to remind themselves of God all day long by saying short prayers of blessing.

Each tiny prayer is called a *berakhah* or *brakha* (bra-KHAH), which means "blessing." In English, the word "blessing" often has the sense of bestowing favor on someone. But the Bible often speaks of people "blessing the Lord," as when David said, "Bless the LORD, O my soul, and all that is within me . . ." (Psalm 103:1 NASB). To bless God is to "praise" him (see NIV), to acknowledge him as the source of all blessing. A *berakhah* is actually a prayer of thanksgiving. One way Jews often explain it is to note that the word for "bless," *barakh*, can also mean "to kneel." It is as if you are momentarily "kneeling down" mentally, and humbly praising God for his goodness.[3]

In Jesus's day each prayer was just one short line that started with "Blessed is he." But within a couple hundred years, the rabbis declared that one should always call upon the name of the Lord in prayer, and that one should always pray to God as "King of the universe."[4] So, the traditional first line for each blessing, in use for the past seventeen hundred years, is this: "Blessed are you, O Lord our God, King of the universe," or, in Hebrew, "Barukh atah, Adonai Elohenu, Melek ha-olam . . ."

Saturating Life in Prayer

Clearly, Jewish life is saturated with prayer. But how would this approach to prayer have played out in the first century? In Jesus's time, you would probably have woken up to a rooster's crow. After thanking

God for returning your soul to you for yet another day, you may have said: "Blessed is he who has given the rooster understanding to distinguish between day and night."[5] (Have you ever thanked God for giving people the intelligence to create clock radios?)

As you opened your eyes you would have prayed: "Blessed is he who opens the eyes of the blind," and then you would have said another dozen or so short prayers praising God for every body part still functioning. Believe it or not, there's even a blessing (dating from around AD 400) that is said after using the bathroom![6] How often do we appreciate the miracle of how our bodies function?

Nowadays the ancient blessings said upon awakening are prayed during the morning prayer service. The very first words on the lips of Jews are these: "I am grateful before You, living and eternal King, for returning my soul to me with compassion. You are faithful beyond measure." What a beautiful way to begin the day.

Just walking outside presents many opportunities for blessing the Lord. When you see the first flowers budding on the fruit trees each spring, you can say, "Blessed is he who did not omit anything from the world, and created within it good creations and good trees for people to enjoy!" After a long, cold winter, who isn't happy to see these gorgeous little signs of new life?

You bless God when you see the ocean for the first time in a long while or a king in his royal procession. You bless him if you see an exceptionally beautiful person or a gifted rabbi. You utter a word of praise if you are reunited with a long-lost friend. When you peel a fresh orange and whiff its bracing, zingy scent, you praise God, saying, "Blessed is he who has given a pleasant smell to fruits."

Even in times of grief, when someone dies or upon hearing tragic news, Jewish people bless God, saying: "Blessed is he who is the true judge." Such a prayer is designed to remind them that, no matter how grievous their ills, God is still good and that he will ultimately bring justice, righting the wrongs of this world.

Why do this? Because the *Shema* says that we are supposed to love God with *all* of our hearts. To the rabbis, that meant we shouldn't merely love God with the part of our heart that is happy, but with the angry, sad, mourning part of our heart as well.

Philip Yancey, in his excellent book on prayer, tells the story of a rabbi by the name of Reb Dovid Din, who was trying to help a man undergoing a crisis of faith. He listened for hours to the man's complaints until finally questioning him. "Why are you so angry with God?" he asked.

Stunned by the rabbi's question, because he had not even mentioned God during the course of his long outburst, the man replied, "All my life I have been so afraid to express my anger to God that I always directed my anger at people who are connected with God. But until this moment I did not understand this."

After that the rabbi led the man to the Wailing Wall, as Yancey says, "away from the place where people pray, to the site of the ruins of the Temple. When they reached that place, Reb Dovid told him that it was time to express all the anger he felt toward God. Then, for more than an hour, the man struck the wall of the *Kotel* with his hands and screamed his heart out. After that he began to cry and could not stop crying, and little by little his cries became sobs that turned into prayers. And that is how Reb Dovid Din taught him how to pray."[7]

Blessings in the Gospels

Is there evidence from the Gospels that such blessings were commonly prayed? Before multiplying the fish and loaves to feed five thousand hungry people, Matthew's gospel tells us that Jesus "blessed and broke and gave the loaves to the disciples" (Matthew 14:19 NKJV).[8] Matthew didn't record Jesus's exact words, probably because everyone would already have known them. Jesus would have been praying like a Jewish father, breaking the bread at the beginning of a meal and then saying: "Blessed is he who brings forth bread from the earth."[9] Even today, Jewish people pray this same prayer, though slightly altered: "Blessed are you, Lord our God, King of the universe, who brings forth bread from the earth."

Some Bible translations unwittingly confuse the text by adding the words "the food." That makes it appear as though Jesus blessed the *food*, instead of blessing the Lord who gave it.[10] The Christian tradition of asking God to bless our food arises from this misunderstanding. The reason we pray before eating is not to make the food holy, but to express our gratitude to God for providing it.

The Gospels contain other traces of these blessing prayers as well. After Jesus healed the paralytic, people praised God, who had given such authority to humans. (Matthew 9:8). They may have shouted, "Blessed is he who has performed a miracle in this place!" That was the traditional blessing prayed when encountering a site where God had performed a miracle in the past.

David Flusser, a Jewish scholar, says that Matthew 9:8 may contain a blessing that was not preserved in other rabbinic writings: "Blessed is he who has given of his power (or authority) to men."[11] He points out how similar this line is to other traditional blessings. When you saw a king, you praised God for giving some of his *glory* to humans, and when you met a brilliant rabbi, you praised him for giving some of his *wisdom* to humans. Here, God was sharing some of his *power* to heal and forgive sin. In the rabbis' thinking, every kind of human excellence (power, glory, and wisdom) ultimately comes from God, who graciously shares a tiny portion of his own nature with human beings. Of course in Jesus's case, God was sharing much more of his nature than ever before.

Understanding these blessing customs can also help us make sense of Luke 17:12–19. Jesus had just healed ten lepers, but only one of them, a Samaritan, came back and blessed the Lord in a loud voice. The prayer that he might have said was this: "Blessed is he who does good to the undeserving and has rendered every kindness to me!"[12] This is the blessing people prayed whenever God healed them from a terrible illness or delivered them from great danger. Jesus wondered why the other nine hadn't acted as the Samaritan had. It might seem as though he was annoyed at not being thanked. But Jesus was really asking why the nine former lepers hadn't returned to pray the traditional blessing, thanking God publicly for the great thing he had just done for them.

The apostle Paul alludes to this "blessing" tradition as well. You might think the rabbinic idea that we should "bless the Lord a hundred times a day" is excessive, but listen to what Paul says about being thankful at all times. Consider how often he says this in his letters:

- Always [be] giving thanks to God the Father for everything (Ephesians 5:20).
- Whatever you do . . . do it all in the name of the Lord Jesus, giving thanks to God the Father (Colossians 3:17).
- Pray continually, give thanks in all circumstances (1 Thessalonians 5:17–18).

Rather than urging us to praise God with vague superlatives, perhaps Paul was thinking of this habit of prayer so ingrained in his culture.

Prayers That Change Your Attitude

This tradition of blessing God is one that takes a "glass half full" approach to life. What a great way to avoid negativity and ingratitude, opening our eyes to God's provision! What might the world be like if more of us were to adopt this wonderful Jewish prayer custom?

Consider the simple blessing one says nowadays upon getting dressed in the morning or when wearing something new: "Blessed are you, O Lord our God, King of the universe, who clothes the naked." Thanking God for something as basic as clothing strips us of our many pretensions, exposing the shallowness of using clothes as a status symbol. It even calls to mind the words of Job, who so clearly articulated the human condition when he said: "Naked I came from my mother's womb, and naked I will depart" (Job 1:21). Counter to our materialistic culture, this blessing reminds us of the primary purpose of clothing—to protect and cover our bodies, to provide warmth and modesty. As we thank God for his provision, we may even become more sensitive to the needs of people throughout the world who have little to wear and even less to eat.

Or, what if all the sun lovers among us were to exclaim every time it rained: "Blessed are You, O Lord our God, King of the universe, who is good, and gives good things!" Many of us live in places blessed by frequent rainfall—too frequent, we are tempted to think. But what if we lived in Israel, where no rain falls between May and October? Rain, for us, would be a source of joy. Indeed, the rabbis said, "Rain gives joy to the whole world, including birds and animals."[13] One rabbi quipped that the best time to pray is when it is raining—it shows that God is in a good mood, ready to hand out blessings.

Consider how Jesus and his contemporaries would have responded to a rainstorm. When they heard the first thunderclap, they would have exclaimed, "Blessed is he whose strength and power fill the world." When they saw the lightning, they would have said, "Blessed is he who has made creation." And afterward, if a rainbow appeared, they would have prayed, "Blessed is he who remembers the covenant, is faithful to his covenant, and keeps his promise." Of course our own food supply is dependent on rain as well, though we often forget it. Next time there is a thunderstorm brewing in your neck of the woods, step outside before the rain begins and feel the awesome strength of the wind, watch the majestic clouds rolling in, and then bless God for his amazing power.

Ann and I live near Lake Michigan, in cities that are blessed with an abundance of clouds in winter. Trouble is, neither of us love day after day of gray, overcast skies. It's second nature for Michiganders to complain about the weather, especially in winter. When I began learning about how the Jewish people bless God for the rain, I started to realize how much I complain about the lack of sunshine, as though an overcast day were a sign of God's neglect. Determined to change this minor bad habit, I was surprised by how much my outlook on life improved when I stopped finding something to grumble about every time I stepped outside.

"For many years," Ann says, "I have paraphrased an old proverb whenever I go shopping. Here's what I say to myself as I walk from store to store: 'A fool and her money are soon parted.' Now it occurs to me that after every trip, assuming I have heeded the warning, I should bless God, saying, 'Blessed are you, O Lord our God, King of the universe, who once again has kept the fool and her money together!'"

One rich blessing prayer is called the *Shehehiyanu*. It is prayed on special occasions, whenever you celebrate some happy event for which you have waited a long time. "It's particularly special to me," says Lois, "because of how I saw it lived out once. It happened at a Jewish wedding. I remember how fascinated I was by the *huppah* ("canopy") and the *ketubah* ("marriage contract") and how the bride and groom shared the *kiddush* wine together. It all seemed so joyous. But as a friend of the groom's parents, I knew that the most joyous thing about that evening was what it meant to their son. Watching their bright son struggle through years of loneliness and depression, they wondered if he'd ever marry. But all that changed when he met a wonderful girl who loved him for who he was and whose own love for life was contagious.

"After the wine goblet was ceremoniously smashed, the crowd let up a cheer, and the party began. A close friend approached the groom's mother, hugging her and then quietly recited with her the *Shehehiyanu*, which goes like this: 'Blessed are you, O Lord our God, King of the universe, who has allowed us to live, and sustained us and enabled us to reach this day.' With tear-filled eyes, through the words of an ancient prayer, the two friends embraced, praising God for the wonders he had done."

Perhaps you are wondering whether the recitation of so many blessings might wear thin after a while, degenerating into the kind of prayer that has little connection to the heart. But think about a simple practice you learned as a child. Remember all the times your mother reminded you to use the magic words, "Please" and "Thank you"? She did it because she knew that this small habit has the power to instill attitudes of thankfulness and consideration. Likewise, the habit of continually blessing God teaches us to be ever mindful of how much God loves us and how continually he cares for us.

The writer Lauren Winner comments on what she calls her own most formative prayer lesson. She grew up Jewish and remembers the moment when an older woman by the name of Ruby Lichtenstein took her aside a few days before her *bat mitzvah* and gave her a talking-to. Handing her a present wrapped in a plastic grocery bag, Ruby told her, "Lauren Winner, a mark of being a Jew is praying to your God. This book is the way that Jews pray."[14] Inside the bag was a *siddur*, or prayer book.

After becoming a Christian, Winner still recognizes the value of her prayer book:

> I have sometimes set aside my prayer book for days and weeks on end and I find, at the end of those days and weeks on end, that I have lapsed into narcissism. Though meaning to commune with or reverence or at least acknowledge God, I wind up talking to myself about my emotions *du jour*. I worry about my mother's health, or I stress about money, or (more happily) I bop up and down with excitement about good news or sunshine or life in general, but I never get much further than that.[15]

Like Lauren Winner's prayer book, the habit of blessing God many times a day focuses our attention in the right direction.

A few years ago Lois decided to adopt some of the Jewish customs of praying blessing prayers throughout the day. "It was during a spiritual low time," she says, "when I was feeling disappointed and angry with God. At first the blessings sounded perfunctory, like I was just mouthing them, reciting nice-sounding sentiments. But over time, the sheer number of them peppering my day revealed God's amazing kindness at work in unexpected ways. Even when I felt like shaking my fist over old hurts, God continued to shower his love on me. Whenever I have returned to this habit, I feel a renewed assurance of his love and care."

When you start to make a habit of blessing God, you will discover that daily life can begin to feel like Christmas morning. As your prayer life becomes saturated with *kavanah*, that deep awareness of God's presence and his overwhelming love, you may feel as though you are wading knee-deep through shards of wrapping paper and mountains of bows to enjoy a pile of shiny new gifts.

Jewish prayer is steeped in thankfulness, and nowhere is this habit of thankfulness more enshrined than in the great feasts of Israel. Such feasts offer a continual reminder to the Jewish people that God has provided for them and redeemed them from slavery. In the feasts, they experienced their highest joy and their greatest *kavanah*. It was through these ancient feasts that God hinted at the ultimate blessing he intended for his people, the blessing of the Christ. Let's turn now to the Jewish feasts to discover what they can tell us about our own faith.

AT THE FEET OF THE RABBI

1. Every morning as you wake up this week, consider reciting this prayer: "I am grateful before you, living and eternal King, for returning my soul to me with compassion. You are faithful beyond measure."

2. Try writing your own *berakhah* or blessing for the following:
   - the happiest day of your life
   - the saddest day of your life
   - two things that have happened to you in the last hour

   "Blessed are you, O Lord our God, King of the universe . . ."
   (Remember, the purpose of the blessing is to put God at the center of your prayer.)

3. Look outside. Whether it's sunny or cloudy, snowy or rainy, write a blessing about the weather. Whatever kind of climate you live in, resolve to declare God's greatness when you look up at the sky each day.

CHAPTER 8

A Passover Discovery

*Therefore we are duty-bound to thank, praise, glorify,
honor, exalt, extol, and bless him who did for our
forefathers and for us all these miracles. He brought us
forth from slavery to freedom, anguish to joy, mourning
to festival, darkness to great light, subjugation to
redemption, so we should say before him, Hallelujah!*

PASSOVER LITURGY FROM THE MISHNAH[1]

The full moon of Passover stared down at Jesus, its light filtering through the shivering leaves of the olive trees, their branches trembling in the early April breeze. Despite the evening chill, sweat glistened on his forehead. Still praying, he stood and peered into the darkness, listening to a distant murmur of voices. One of his own *talmidim*, Judas, was approaching. Trailing him was a mob of soldiers, snaking up the hill.

Under a nearby tree, Peter, James, and John were lying in a heap. Twice Jesus had pleaded with them to stay awake, asking them to keep vigil with him on this, the most difficult night of his life. Yet there they were, wrapped in their heavy woolen *tallitot*, mouths agape and snoring softly, oblivious of the approaching threat . . .

"Whenever I used to think back to this scene from Gethsemane," Lois says, "I couldn't help but wonder about Jesus's narcoleptic disciples. How could they have fallen asleep when their beloved rabbi had implored them to stay awake and remain alert? How could they have nodded off when the climax of salvation history was about to take place? I couldn't imagine a satisfactory answer; this was just one of many questions that filled my head whenever I thought back to that fateful week.

"I remembered previous Palm Sunday services I had attended, where only minutes after the children streamed down the aisles, joyously waving palm branches to celebrate Jesus's triumphal entry into Jerusalem, the mood would shift, turning solemn as the gospel account of the passion was read. Why were the crowds in Jerusalem so fickle, adoring Jesus one week and then hating him the next? And why, I wondered, did Jesus choose a Passover Seder to celebrate the last meal of his life?[2]

"Fast forward, now, two thousand years, to the fellowship hall of my church, on the afternoon of the Thursday before Easter, known as Maundy Thursday. We are setting up for a Passover Seder. As Gentile amateurs we are doing our best to recreate the Last Supper, giving ourselves a chance to meditate on its significance. Perfect historical accuracy isn't the point. Our goal is to relive a little of Jesus's final evening with his disciples so that we can better appreciate the Maundy Thursday service.

"All afternoon the church kitchen bustles with the sound of clattering pans and chitchat as we hurry about our tasks, cutting parsley, boiling eggs, and spooning horseradish onto plates. When we finally sit down, I am famished. The time ticks by as I endure the long Seder liturgy, with just a bite of parsley dipped in salt water and dry, cardboard-like *matzah* (unleavened bread) smeared with horseradish to tide me over. When we finally dig into our simple meal of lamb stew, I devour my humble feast. Afterward, I hurriedly help with cleanup and then slip into the back of the service, which has already begun. The liturgy is mournful and solemn.

Tallit

Nowadays, a *tallit* is a prayer shawl, a ceremonial shawl to which tassels are attached. But in Jesus's day, the *tallit* was the outer woolen mantle, a rectangle of heavy cloth that bore tassels on its four corners. It was worn in public at all times and could be used as a blanket for sleeping. Underneath was the *haluk* (hah-LOOK), a linen undergarment. In John 19:23, the soldiers gambled for *haluk*, his linen tunic.

"The events of the day have taken their toll—the nonstop preparations, beginning the Seder feeling famished, and then overeating to compensate. I feel a crushing lethargy sweep over me. Over the next hour, the sanctuary lights gradually dim to complete darkness. I can barely see through shuttering eyelids. As the service rolls on, I rouse with a start. Did someone call my name? I can almost hear the disappointment in Jesus's voice. 'Could you not watch with me just one hour?'

"Suddenly, I understand why the disciples found it so hard to stay awake. And they had an even better excuse than I had. Traditional Passover celebrations involved a huge meal plus four cups of wine, and they started at sunset and didn't end until around midnight. What's more, they took place after several days of exhausting travel and preparation. Certainly everybody in Jerusalem would have wanted to crawl straight into bed after their late-night feast. Aware of this perennial problem, the rabbis ruled that a person who dozed lightly could remain a part of the dinner, but anyone who fell sound asleep could not.[3]

"Our amateurish attempt at reliving the Last Supper has led to other insights on the final hours of Jesus's life. I realized, for instance, why the leaders plotted to arrest Jesus after the Passover meal. A man so wildly popular couldn't have been arrested in broad daylight. To avoid an uprising, the chief priests had to proceed in secret. So they let Judas lead them to Jesus while he was outside the city. Passover evening was the perfect choice because every Jewish family would be celebrating the feast that started at sundown.

"Jesus's arrest and trial proceeded swiftly, occurring during the wee hours, when most of his supporters were in bed. Peter's denials happened as the rooster crowed, around four or five in the morning. According to Mark's gospel, Jesus's final sentence was handed down at sunrise (Mark 15:1). One has to ask, what group of people were around at the crack of dawn on a major Jewish holiday to shout 'Crucify him'? Mostly corrupt priests and Roman soldiers who wanted to kill Jesus.

"But there's more. Jesus was crucified at nine in the morning—the time of the first temple service of the day! The authorities knew they had to finish their secret trial before the crowds reentered the city to come to worship. And indeed, as Jesus was carrying his cross out of town, his supporters reappear, weeping out loud as they see him being led to his death (Luke 23:27). His followers had just learned of the events that had transpired the night before.

"Prior to our Passover Seder, I had always thought the crowds unimaginably fickle, cheering Jesus one day and then shouting for his head the next. But Jesus's supporters never changed their minds. How could they have when they were not even present at his arrest or trial? The entire plot unfolded after the Passover festivities, while most people were sound asleep."[4]

Jesus's Last Passover

Learning about Passover, the first and most important of the Jewish feasts, yields rich insights about Jesus's last week on earth. Passover was a sacred celebration commanded by God himself two thousand years earlier, before the Israelites even left Egypt. It was to become a time of great joy, commemorating the exodus of the Israelites from their slavery in Egypt. Passover marked the beginning of their nation and defined them as God's people.

Today Passover is celebrated at home with a formal evening dinner that includes special food, songs, and liturgy. It is called a "Seder," a word that means "order," because the liturgy follows a certain order that has remained roughly the same as it was in Jesus's time. The focus of the evening is to retell the miraculous story of how God brought his people out of Egypt and to contemplate how God will redeem Israel by sending the Messiah.

In Jesus's time, Passover was one of three pilgrim feasts that brought hundreds of thousands of Jews to Jerusalem. On the afternoon before the meal, each family carried a lamb to the temple to be sacrificed. Afterward it was roasted and shared with a large gathering of extended family and friends. Nowadays, since the temple is not standing, no sacrifice can be made, so in most Jewish traditions lamb is no longer served. Instead, the roasted shank bone of a lamb is placed on a Seder plate along with other ceremonial foods eaten during the evening.

Passover was laden with messianic expectations and filled with prophetic significance, especially in Jesus's time. Just as God had saved his people when the angel of the Lord had "passed over" the homes of the Israelites and afflicted the homes of the Egyptians, it was believed that God would come again at Passover to save his people. A saying of that day was, "In that night they were redeemed, and in that night they will be redeemed."[5] Knowing how the events of Jesus's last week fit into the celebration of Passover shows us the tremendous significance of his death and resurrection.

The book of Exodus said of Passover, "It was a night of vigil for the LORD to bring them out from the land of Egypt, and so on this night all Israel is to keep the vigil to the LORD for generations to come" (Exodus 12:42 NET). The rabbis interpreted this to mean that they should be keeping watch to see what great thing God would do next. Even today, it is traditional for a child to open the door after the Passover supper to see if Elijah might be standing there. Why? Because Malachi said that Elijah would come to herald the Messiah:

> "I will send my messenger, who will prepare the way before me.
> Then suddenly the Lord you are seeking will come to his temple;
> the messenger of the covenant, whom you desire, will come," says
> the LORD Almighty . . .
> "See, I will send the prophet Elijah to you before that great
> and dreadful day of the LORD comes." (Malachi 3:1; 4:5)

So for thousands of years, even up to the present, the Jewish people have believed that God would again send redemption on Passover. Redemption did arrive on the very day they were looking for it, but it took a surprising shape. For God had engineered a far greater liberation than they had imagined—freedom not just for one people but for all people. And it was to be a liberation not from the earthly power of a political enemy but from the sinister power of sin and death.

During the Passover in Egypt, the Israelites had been instructed to mark their doorframes with the blood of a lamb so that the Lord would *pass over* them when judgment came. Interestingly, the rabbis marveled at how the blood of a mere sheep could protect people from God's judgment. They commented that God must have seen the "blood of Isaac" on the doorposts—meaning that God remembered Abraham's willingness to sacrifice his son. Remembering it, he spared his people. How close they were! What they did not realize was that when God saw Abraham's son Isaac, he saw his own Son, Jesus, who would one day sacrifice himself out of loving obedience to his Father.[6]

On the first Passover, God freed his people by taking the life of the firstborn sons of Egypt. Many centuries later, God made salvation possible for all who would accept it by giving the life of his firstborn Son.

The Bread of Passover

Knowing about how Passover coincides with the other two spring feasts, Unleavened Bread (*Matzot*) and Firstfruits (*Bikkurim*), will enlighten us in several more ways about the death and resurrection of Christ. These first three feasts come in rapid succession over the course of a week in early spring, usually falling in late March or early April.

The feasts of Passover and Unleavened Bread begin at almost the same time, and sometimes they are referred to as one (Mark 14:12). The Passover lamb was sacrificed on the afternoon of the fourteenth day of the month Nisan but is eaten after sunset, at the beginning of Nisan 15, when the seven-day Feast of Unleavened Bread began.[7] Remember that in the Jewish calendar each new day begins at sunset.

Why is this feast important? One reason is that it tells us something about the kind of bread Jesus was holding when he broke it and said, "This is my body." Leonardo Da Vinci's masterful painting "The Last Supper" has shaped our imagination of Jesus's last meal. In it, Jesus is depicted with ordinary loaves of bread.[8] But there would not have been a scrap of regular bread on the table or anywhere else in the house because Jews were required to eat the Passover meal using only unleavened bread (Deuteronomy 16:1–3). In fact, leavening of any kind was forbidden for the entire seven days of the Feast of Unleavened Bread, starting with the Passover meal. So Jesus would not have been holding ordinary bread but *matzah*.

Why is this significant, and what's so terrible about yeast anyway? In ancient times leavening was done by adding a blob of old, raw, fermented dough to the new dough. The fresh batch was deliberately infected with microbes that would cause it to rise, but then later to sour, decay, and eventually rot. The puffiness of the leavening reminded the Jews of human pride and hypocrisy. Throughout the year, all grain offerings given to the Lord by fire had to be free of leaven (Leviticus 2:11; 6:17). The ancients saw leavening as a picture of sin and contamination, something God didn't want in his burnt offerings.

So when Jesus held up the bread and said, "This is my body," on the night before his death, he was using a specific kind of bread, made without leaven, unadulterated by decay. Unlike the rest of humanity, Jesus had not been infected with the "rottenness" that was in the rest of humankind. He alone was a fit offering for our sins. When God prohibited his people centuries earlier from eating leaven during Passover, perhaps he was thinking ahead to the night when Jesus would take the bread in his own hands, break it, and then say, "This is my body, given for you."

Paul and other Jewish believers understood exactly what Jesus was saying. Listen to how Paul uses this image to describe how Jesus's sacrifice should enable us to live righteously:

> Don't you know that a little yeast leavens the whole batch of dough? Get rid of the old yeast, so that you may be a new unleavened batch—as you really are. For Christ, our Passover lamb, has been sacrificed. Therefore let us keep the Festival, not with the old bread leavened with malice and wickedness, but with the unleavened bread of sincerity and truth. (1 Corinthians 5:6–8)

Jewish scholar David Daube has pointed out that another significant meaning was given to the bread Jesus broke.[9] He says that Jesus held up a piece of *matzah* and broke off a special piece called the *afikomen*, which was then hidden away. At the end of the meal the *afikomen* was brought out and then broken and eaten by all the participants. Still today this is done, but the explanations vary as to why—commonly it is said to be a way to keep the children awake, because the child who finds it gets a prize. Or, the tradition is said to derive from the Greek word *epikomoi*, meaning "dessert," because it was the last thing eaten after the meal.

But Daube asserts that in Jesus's time, the *afikomen* referred to "the coming one," meaning the longed-for Messiah. The tradition was that the whole piece of *matzah* represented all of Israel, and that the Messiah was "broken off" from the people and hidden away.[10] The appearance of the piece at the end was symbolic of the coming of the Messiah, fervently expected at the time of Jesus. When Jesus held up that particular piece of bread and said, "This is my body," he was making a shocking claim to be the Messiah, the Christ. Daube believes that rabbis later downplayed the messianic nature of this ritual because of the poor relationship that developed between Christians and Jews.

As fascinating as all this is, a question remains. From reading Exodus, you might ask, "Isn't the reason for the unleavened bread on Passover to commemorate the dough the Israelites had to make in haste as they were leaving Egypt?" Yes, that's true too. The bread has multiple layers of imagery. It was also called "the bread of affliction" in Deuteronomy 16:3. As such the unleavened bread represented Israel's suffering in Egypt. So, you could say that it also represents the suffering of Christ for his people. Often multiple ideas are contained in the imagery of the feasts.

The Feast of Firstfruits

As significant as Passover is, another important feast sheds light on the meaning of Christ's death and resurrection. We know he was raised to life on the third day (the first day of the week following the Sabbath after Passover). Remarkably, that day happens to be another feast day, the Feast of Firstfruits. This feast could occur on various dates, some years falling several days after Passover. On the year Jesus died, it exactly coincided with his resurrection.[11] What are the implications?

Firstfruits celebrated the beginning of the barley harvest. On this festival, a sheaf of grain was cut from the field and then offered in thanksgiving to the Lord. Only after that could the rest of the reaping begin. It was a day that represented the people's hope for the future, because the harvest had begun.

But it was more than that. On the Sabbath after Passover, the day immediately preceding the Feast of Firstfruits, a dramatic prophecy was always read in the temple. In it, the Lord instructed Ezekiel to declare to a valley filled with dry bones: "I will make breath enter you, and you will come to life" (Ezekiel 37:5). On Passover God's people had looked for their future redeemer to come. On the following Sabbath they would have read a passage that said God was going to raise the dead when he came.[12] God was promising far more than an earthly harvest. He was saying that he would raise the dead to life!

Now imagine Jesus's followers streaming into the temple on the Sabbath, the day after he died. Still stunned by his brutal execution, they would have listened as a vision was recounted in which God had promised to bring the dead to life. On the very next day, on the Feast of Firstfruits, they would have heard wild rumors sweeping across Jerusalem. Jesus's tomb was empty, and some of his followers claimed to have seen him. Had he really risen from the dead? Could Jesus be the firstfruits of the promised resurrection? Listen to what Paul concluded years later:

> But Christ has indeed been raised from the dead, the firstfruits of those who have fallen asleep. For since death came through a man, the resurrection of the dead comes also through a man. For as in Adam all die, so in Christ all will be made alive. But each in turn: Christ, the firstfruits; then, when he comes, those who belong to him. (1 Corinthians 15:20–23)

Death hangs over the human race as the darkest of shadows. Even the most promising life seems to end in tragedy. But Paul's words assure us that our fear of death can be replaced by an invincible hope. The resurrection stands as a promise of what God will do for each of us. For those who belong to his Son, eternal life is not merely a possibility but an inevitability.

Remembering Our Redemption

What would you say if someone were to ask you to identify the single most important event in the New Testament? Like most of us you would probably respond that it was the death and resurrection of Christ. But what would you say if someone were to ask the same question about the Old Testament? How could you pick from all the possibilities? The creation? The flood? The covenant with Abraham? Entering the Promised Land? Building the temple? Though we might find the question perplexing, the answer would seem obvious to most Jewish people. Their miraculous delivery from Egypt is the event mentioned over and over in the Old Testament—almost every book refers to it. It is the one event they mention in nearly every worship service.

Whenever God wanted to emphasize why his people should obey him, he reminded them of how he had rescued them and forged them into his own people. "I am the God who brought you up out of Egypt," he kept repeating. Many of the laws of the Torah are rooted in the people's deliverance from Egypt:

> The foreigner residing among you must be treated as your native-born. Love them as yourself, *for you were foreigners in Egypt.* (Leviticus 19:34, italics added)
>
> If any of your fellow Israelites become poor and are unable to support themselves among you, help them as you would a foreigner and stranger, so they can continue to live among you . . . *I am the* LORD *your God, who brought you out of Egypt* to give you the land of Canaan and to be your God. (Leviticus 25:35, 38, italics added)
>
> *Remember that you were slaves in Egypt* and that the LORD your God brought you out of there with a mighty hand and an outstretched arm. Therefore the LORD your God has commanded you to observe the Sabbath day. (Deuteronomy 5:15, italics added)

Each of the commands above is directly linked to God's actions on Israel's behalf. His people must not mistreat foreigners. Didn't they remember what it was like to suffer abuse in Egypt before God rescued them? His people must help the poor to live in the land. Hadn't they experienced what it was like to live in poverty in someone else's land before God led them into their own? His people must rest and allow all their servants to rest on the Sabbath. Wasn't this rest what they had longed for as slaves in Egypt before God freed them?

Similarly, as followers of Christ, we can continually remind ourselves of how Jesus, the Passover Lamb, has redeemed us from death. We can forgive, because we have been forgiven. We can serve, because Christ humbled himself for us. We can love, because we have experienced the extravagant love of God in our own lives. We have a new life and a new hope, because Jesus fulfilled the ancient feast of Passover.

It is no coincidence that three important biblical holidays coincided with Jesus's death and resurrection: Passover, Unleavened Bread, and Firstfruits. These annual festivals were filled with new meaning when Jesus died and rose from the dead. But there are yet more biblical feasts that reveal fascinating insights about Rabbi Jesus. We will explore these next.

AT THE FEET OF THE RABBI

1. Consider holding a Christian Passover Seder at your church or with family and friends. (Appendix B provides a list of suggested resources to help you observe the biblical feasts as a Christian.)

2. The Jewish Passover, on Nisan 15, always takes place on a full moon because the Jewish year uses a lunar calendar. Make a point of going outside on the evening of Passover

to ponder Jesus's great battle with evil under the full moon in Gethsemane two thousand years ago. (For the dates of upcoming Passovers, consult Appendix B.)

3. A traditional Passover song is called *Dayeinu*.[13] The word *dayeinu* means "enough for us." In fifteen verses, a long list of God's blessings is recounted with a refrain of *dayeinu* after each verse. The idea is that if God would have stopped at any one, his people would have been completely satisfied. Here is a sample of the verses:

> If he had rescued us from Egypt,
> but not punished the Egyptians,
> it would have been enough! (*Dayeinu*)
> If he had punished the Egyptians,
> but not defeated their gods,
> it would have been enough . . .
> If he had given us the Sabbath
> but not led us to Mount Sinai,
> it would have been enough . . .
> If he had led us to Mount Sinai,
> but not given us the Torah,
> it would have been enough . . .
> If he had given us the Torah,
> but not brought us into the Land of Israel,
> it would have been enough . . .
> How much more, then, are we to be grateful to God
> for all of these good things which he has indeed done
> for all of us!

4. What a wonderful attitude of gratefulness! See if you can write several more stanzas as you consider God's blessings in your own life.

CHAPTER 9

Discovering Jesus in the Jewish Feasts

Judaism teaches us to be attached to holiness in time, to be attached to sacred events, to learn how to consecrate sanctuaries that emerge from the magnificent stream of a year. The Sabbaths are our great cathedrals; and our Holy of Holies is a shrine that neither the Romans nor the Germans were able to burn . . . the Day of Atonement.

RABBI ABRAHAM JOSHUA HESCHEL[1]

Remember Ken Bailey's analogy in the first chapter about spending your life on a beach and then deciding one day to dive into the water to look at what lies beneath? Now imagine diving off Mauna Loa, the volcano on the island of Hawaii. If you trade in your snorkeling mask for deep-sea diving gear to descend into the murky depths, you will discover that Mauna Loa is, in fact, the largest mountain on earth, three-quarters of a mile taller than Mount Everest.[2]

The Passover feast in the light of how Christ fulfilled it is a lot like Mauna Loa. When you begin to explore it, you realize that the hill of Calvary stands much higher than you once thought. Its roots, in fact, lay far back in time, in Israel's earliest history.

If you were to dive into the Pacific Ocean at Mauna Loa, you would discover something else. It connects to an underwater mountain range that forms the rest of the Hawaiian islands. In the same way, Passover is not a solitary island in time. There are yet more "islands" or "mountaintops" to explore. You've already seen how Passover connects to the ancient celebration of Firstfruits, instituted thousands of years earlier. It is also connected to several other biblical feasts.

These ancient feasts, commanded by God on Mount Sinai, created an important rhythm in first-century life, giving shape to the year and linking the Jewish people to their sacred history. Each year, Jesus's own observant family would have traveled several days to and from Jerusalem in order to take part in the feasts. As an adult, Jesus participated, commented on, and employed imagery from the feasts to highlight his role as the Messiah. The seven biblical feasts, still celebrated today, are multilayered and rich in significance, pointing toward the saving work of Christ. What can we learn about them that can transform our lives today?

Celebrating Past, Present, and Future

Because many of the feasts originally focused on agricultural themes, they were celebrated at planting and harvest times. Leviticus 23 provides specific instructions for observing them. (See Appendix B for more.)[3] Modern city dwellers can hardly imagine the joy an ancient farmer would have felt, knowing that a bountiful harvest, eked out of an arid land, would ensure his family's survival for yet another year. Try thinking of it as something like a fat end-of-year bonus check or a big promotion, with God playing the role of your employer. The purpose of the feasts was to give the Jewish people an opportunity to rejoice at the way God had provided and then to offer something back in return. The feasts were a tangible way for them to remember God's faithfulness and care.

Overlaid on these harvest feasts was another message—that the Israelites should remember how God had redeemed them, never forgetting how he had led them out of Egypt into the Promised Land. This theme winds through all seven feasts, with different parts of the story remembered at different times of the year. That way the Jewish people could relive the story each year, focusing on their miraculous escape from Egypt, the covenant on Mount Sinai, and the forty years they spent in the desert sustained by the manna God provided. By remembering what defined them as a people, gratitude and faith would transform the way they lived.

Learning from the Jewish pattern, the church adopted this wise practice by developing a liturgical calendar to remind us of our own redemption. As Christians, we focus on the life of Christ: at Christmas recalling his birth, at Easter remembering his death and resurrection, and at Pentecost celebrating the birth of the church.

When God instructed the Israelites to keep these feasts, he was telling them to celebrate their past by remembering their salvation from slavery in Egypt and also their present by rejoicing at how he was providing food in the harvest. But there was also a future dimension to the feasts. Woven into these ancient festivals were hints of something more and better yet to come.

The Deeper Meaning of Pentecost

We've already learned about the first three feasts of the year, which come in rapid succession. Passover, Unleavened Bread, and Firstfruits all occur within the span of a week. In that fateful last year of Jesus's earthly life, they took on a whole new meaning.

But that's not the end of the story because seven weeks after Firstfruits comes Pentecost, a feast that marked the end of the barley harvest and the beginning of the wheat harvest. In Hebrew this feast is called *Shavuot*, meaning "weeks." In Greek the feast is named for the fifty days of counting after Firstfruits and is called *Pentecost*.

It may surprise you to learn that Christians did not invent Pentecost. We mark it as the day when the first believers received the Holy Spirit, calling it the "birthday of the church," and we celebrate it fifty days after Easter. But at the time of Jesus, Pentecost had already been observed for many centuries. Learning about the Feast of Shavuot adds enormously to our understanding of what transpired. Here's how Acts describes the scene:

When the day of Pentecost came, they were all together in one place. Suddenly a sound like the blowing of a violent wind came from heaven and filled the whole house where they were sitting. They saw what seemed to be tongues of fire that separated and came to rest on each of them. All of them were filled with the Holy Spirit and began to speak in other tongues as the Spirit enabled them . . .

Then Peter stood up with the Eleven, raised his voice and addressed the crowd . . .

Those who accepted his message were baptized, and about three thousand were added to their number that day. (Acts 2:1–4, 14, 41)

If you've ever been to the old city of Jerusalem, you will realize how compact it is. It's hard to imagine three thousand people gathering outside any of the houses inside the walls of that cramped city with its winding, narrow streets; it is harder still to imagine that three thousand people could gather outside a house in the Jerusalem of Jesus's day. But what if the "house" spoken of in the passage above was not the upper room as many of us have imagined but the temple itself, commonly referred to in Scripture as the "house of God"?[4]

Shavuot is one of the three major festivals (along with Passover and Tabernacles) for which attendance is required at the temple. At nine in the morning, Jesus's followers would have been in the temple along with Jewish pilgrims from a host of other countries who had come to celebrate the feast, all speaking various languages from the lands of their origin. So it is likely that the sound of a mighty rushing wind and the vision of tongues of fire described in Acts took place not in an upper room but in front of thousands of people within the temple precincts. It was here that Peter would have had the opportunity to preach to the multitudes about Jesus.

So amazing were the events of that day that three thousand new believers were baptized. No house would have had enough ritual baths to accommodate such a crowd. But right outside the temple were more than a hundred ceremonial pools used for purifying worshippers before they entered the temple, as well as for immersing new converts to Judaism. In fact, this latter ceremony is the forerunner of Christian baptism. This is where three thousand Jewish believers in Jesus would have been baptized.

Remarkably, these baths can still be seen in the temple ruins. Less than forty years ago, dozens were unearthed by archaeologists. Think about it! You can still stand on the spot where God poured out his Spirit on Jesus's followers two thousand years ago.

Clearly the Lord was using the traditions of Shavuot to telegraph a message to his people. But what exactly was he saying? At least two hundred years prior to Christ's birth, the rabbis noted that the Israelites reached Mount Sinai fifty days after they left Egypt (see Exodus 19:1). This led them to conclude that if Passover commemorated the exodus from Egypt, then Shavuot must commemorate the covenant on Mount Sinai.[5] The traditional reading for Shavuot is Exodus 19–20, which recounts the story of what happened when God came down on Mount Sinai to give Moses the Ten Commandments, to seal the giving of the covenant. During this divine encounter the whole mountain seemed consumed by fire.

Just as the divine presence on Sinai was dramatically marked with fire, God was making his presence dramatically known at Pentecost with tongues of fire. But this time there was a vital difference. Instead of carving his law on tablets of stone, he was enshrining it in human hearts through the power of his Spirit. Listen to what Jeremiah prophesied:

> "The days are coming," declares the LORD,
>   "when I will make a new covenant
> with the people of Israel
>   and with the people of Judah . . .
> "I will put my law in their minds
>   and write it on their hearts.
> I will be their God,
>   and they will be my people.

No longer will they teach their neighbor,
    or say to one another, 'Know the LORD,'
because they will all know me,
    from the least of them to the greatest," declares the LORD.
"For I will forgive their wickedness
    and will remember their sins no more."

(JEREMIAH 31:31, 33–34)

On Sinai, God had given his people the covenant of the *Torah*, meaning "law" or "instruction." On Pentecost he gave his Spirit to seal a new covenant of the forgiveness of sin. Like the Torah, the Spirit reveals God's truth, instructs us, and convicts us of sin. But unlike the Torah, the Spirit empowers us to live in communion with God by changing our hearts from within, something that the law could not do (Romans 8:5–7). What a reason to celebrate!

But that's not all, because on the morning of Shavuot, the priests would read aloud a remarkable passage from the book of Ezekiel. The first two chapters of Ezekiel recount his Technicolor vision of a windstorm replete with lightning and fire. Overcome with fear, Ezekiel fell facedown until God commanded him to stand and the Spirit came into him. In this vision, God commissioned Ezekiel to be his prophet, empowering him to take his divine word to his people.

A remarkable similarity exists between Ezekiel's vision and the disciples' experience at Pentecost when the Holy Spirit came with wind, fire, and the gift of tongues, enabling Jesus's disciples to speak God's word to Jews from many nations, regardless of any

Shavuot

Shavuot is the Hebrew word for the feast that in Greek is called *Pentecost*, meaning "fiftieth day." After the Feast of Firstfruits, seven weeks are counted off to arrive at the day. This feast commemorates the anniversary of Moses's meeting with God on Mount Sinai, when he received the law and the covenant. On the first *Shavuot* after Jesus's death, the Holy Spirit was poured out, signifying the new covenant in which God himself would imprint his law on the hearts of believers (see Jeremiah 31:31–34).

language barriers. At Pentecost Christ's followers were being commissioned to take God's message of salvation to his people. The effect was immediate. Peter turned around and preached boldly, and three thousand people became believers.

Once again, we see that the traditions of Shavuot shed new light on the events in Acts 2. Without understanding the context in which they took place, such events may simply seem strange—ghostly winds, floating flames, and ecstatic utterances. The ancient imagery of the feast of Shavuot, or Pentecost, however, sheds light on the birth of the church.

Think about how God was using the ancient feasts to communicate with his people. Many centuries before, on Passover, God had redeemed them from Egypt. Fifty days after their departure, God enacted his covenant on Mount Sinai to form Israel into a nation. The death and resurrection of Christ on Passover brought redemption to all who believe in him. And fifty days later, God poured out his Spirit to seal a new covenant for the forgiveness of sins. Believers were commissioned to make disciples of all nations and empowered by the same Spirit who spoke through the prophets of long ago. Just as Passover and Firstfruits illuminated the meaning of Jesus's death and resurrection, Shavuot communicated what God was accomplishing on the birthday of the church.

Knowing more about the early Jewish church can also help us understand what the gift of the Holy Spirit means to our own lives. Being Spirit-filled in the first century involved more than speaking in tongues, sharing the gospel, and doing miraculous healings, impressive as these were. Acts 2:44–45 tells us that "all the believers were together and had everything in common. They sold property and possessions to give to anyone who had need."

In *Hard Sayings of the Bible*, Peter Davids comments that the Spirit of God "freed people from the spirit of Mammon so that they gave whenever they saw a need, selling property and belongings if necessary. There was no compulsion, no requirement. It was simply a natural response to the presence of the Spirit of the generous God within them."[6] Today some of our churches emphasize spiritual gifts, others evangelism, and still others caring for the poor. But *all three* were essential aspects of the original Spirit-filled church.

The Fall Holy Days

The roots of Christianity lie deep within the biblical feasts. On Passover Jesus became the lamb whose blood redeemed us, on Firstfruits he rose from the dead as the firstborn of the new creation, and on Pentecost he poured out his Spirit to inaugurate the new covenant.

But there are three more holy days commanded on Mount Sinai. These are celebrated in the fall, exactly six months after Passover, in the month of Tishri (late September/ October). Like the spring festivals, they occur close together. What can we learn from them?

On the first day of Tishri comes the Feast of Trumpets. Also called *Rosh Hashanah* (the "head of the year"), it marks the beginning of the civil new year.[7] A *shofar*, or ram's horn, is sounded on that day, in order to herald God as King of the world. In ancient times kings announced their arrival through heralds sounding trumpets. Rosh Hashanah marks the anniversary of the world's creation, so to celebrate, Genesis 1 is read in synagogues throughout the world.

But the mood of Rosh Hashanah is not entirely celebrative. It begins the *yamim noraim*, or the ten Days of Awe. Tradition has it that during those days God opens his books in order to examine the deeds of every person. He then renders judgment in regard to the coming year. As such, these ten days focus on repentance and self-reflection. They

Rosh Hashanah

Rosh Hashanah is the name of the Jewish New Year, also called *Yom Teruah*, the "day of trumpeting."

Yom Kippur

Yom Kippur is the Day of Atonement, the holiest day of the year for Jews. It is a day for prayer, fasting, and repentance. In biblical times the sins of the nation were laid on a scapegoat on Yom Kippur, and it was on Yom Kippur that the high priest entered the Most Holy Place of the temple to make atonement for the sins of the entire nation.

offer a time for examining one's deeds in preparation for *Yom Kippur*, the Day of Atonement, which takes place on the tenth of Tishri.

Yom Kippur is the most holy and solemn day of the year. It is so important that many otherwise nonobservant Jews observe this day. During Yom Kippur people cease from their work and observe a twenty-five-hour fast from both food and water. (An extra hour of fasting is added to "put a fence around the law," to be sure to obey God's command completely.) The day is set aside to "afflict the soul" as a way of asking for atonement for the sins of the past year. Some observant Jews even wear a *kittel*, a white robe in which the dead are buried. They do it to remind themselves and others that life is finite and that everyone must be prepared to stand before the Lord at the time of death. These traditions are rich and moving.

When the temple was standing, Yom Kippur was the only day on which the high priest would dare to enter the Most Holy Place. In that most sacred place he would offer atonement for the sins of the people of Israel. On Yom Kippur he would also lay his hands on a goat (the scapegoat), symbolically transferring the guilt of the nation onto the animal, and then drive it out into the wilderness.

After the temple was destroyed in AD 70, sacrifices ceased, and the rabbis declared that prayer alone was sufficient for the forgiveness of sin. But some Jews still felt the need for sacrifice. Though criticized, some among the ultra-Orthodox still practice a type of sacrifice today, laying their hands (and therefore their sins) on the head of a chicken that is then killed. Afterward, the meat is given to the poor. This ritual is called *kaparot*, which means "covering" or "atoning." Its persistence says something about our human instinct that more than prayer is needed to secure forgiveness. To Christians, the need for atonement by Christ's sacrificial death seems obvious.

The Feast of Tabernacles

Finally, five days after the Day of Atonement comes the most joyous feast of the year—the Feast of Tabernacles, or *Sukkot*. *Sukkot* is the plural of the Hebrew word *sukkah*, meaning "booth" or "hut." During Jesus's day, huge celebrations were held in the temple, lasting for seven days. The Feast of Sukkot is also called the "Feast of Ingathering" because it is the greatest harvest feast of the year—when the fruit was brought in and the rest of the wheat was harvested.

When the feast was inaugurated, God told his people to build booths and live in them for seven days in order to remember how he had brought them out of Egypt and cared for them in the desert. To this day, many Jews observe the tradition of building a *sukkah*. These are supposed to be made from impermanent materials, fashioned so that at least one star is visible through the branches that comprise the roof. The custom is to live in it if possible, or at least to eat your meals in it as if it were your home.

As you sit in one of these rickety little booths, peeking up at the sky through the branches and feeling the wind blowing through the walls, you realize that security comes not from the walls you construct around yourself, but from the Lord who protects you. You also begin to realize the abundance of God's blessings. The Feast of Sukkot offers a potent experience of what following God is like—feeling both insecure and incredibly blessed at the same time. For Jews, it is a time of great joy as they remember the intimacy of those forty years when God "tabernacled" with them in the desert, sustaining them each day with manna from heaven.

Lois recalls when her friends Bruce and Mary Okkema built a *sukkah* in her backyard along with their Bible study group. "Bruce and I," she says, "were busy preparing for a huge worship celebration, a kick-off event for our new ministry, the En-Gedi Resource Center. I'll never forget that brilliant September morning when we drove over to a local radio station to be interviewed about the event. Suddenly, in the middle of the interview, a DJ popped his head into the studio and said: 'We're going to need to break in for a news bulletin about a plane accident in New York.' The World Trade Center had just been struck.

"Our ministry had barely begun when the events of September 11 threatened to sink it. The events of that day paralyzed our country.

So many lives were lost that the nation was plunged into mourning. And there was mounting fear that more terrorist attacks would follow. In the ensuing months, Bruce's business was hard hit by a faltering economy, as were many others. As for myself, I had left a tenure-track professorship to help begin the ministry, confident that people would support us. That fall the strong brick walls of my cozy little house felt as shaky and breezy as the walls of the *sukkah* in my backyard. Those first years with En-Gedi were truly a 'journey through the wilderness,' as we began to discover what it meant to rely on God for our security."

Israel's own journey through the wilderness is brought vividly to mind every summer. For six months, between May and October, not a drop of rain falls, so that by mid-fall, when the Feast of Sukkot is observed, the land is parched and dry. The lush spring greenery has shriveled and died.

No wonder, then, that Sukkot was the time to pray that God would send "living water," or rain, for the coming year. About one out of four years, the rains were late or not plentiful enough for good yields, so rain was a critical need and a common worry. At that time of year, it was easy for people to remember how dependent on God they had been in the desert of Sinai.

How does the Feast of Tabernacles figure into the life of Jesus? On the last day of that feast, the priests performed a water libation ceremony accompanied by impassioned prayers for life-giving water in the form of rain. At that point the joyful voices of thousands of worshippers reached a thunderous intensity.[8] One rabbi commented, "Anyone who has not seen *Simchat Beit Hashoevah* [the water drawing ceremony] has never seen joy in all of his life!"[9]

It was on this last and greatest day of Sukkot that Jesus stood up in the midst of the clamorous crowds and shouted: "Let anyone who is thirsty come to me and drink. Whoever believes in me, as Scripture has said, rivers of living water will flow from within them" (John 7:37–38). Imagine! Jesus was speaking of the living water of the Holy Spirit that he would soon pour out on new believers. This was the water that would fill up their thirst for God and bubble out of them to refresh the whole world. Through him God would give a never-ceasing supply of life-giving water, welling up in them from now until eternity.

As we have seen, in one fateful year, around AD 30, tremendous miracles surrounding the life and death of Jesus redefined the meaning of the first four biblical feasts. What about the last three? Many believe they will only be fulfilled when Christ returns. For Christians, these last three sacred days—the Feast of Trumpets, the Day of Atonement, and the Feast of Tabernacles—can teach us about the future.

Shofar

A *shofar* is a ram's horn that is blown as a trumpet. In biblical times it was sounded for a variety of purposes, but now it is blown on the day of *Rosh Hashanah*, the Jewish New Year, and at the end of *Yom Kippur*, the Day of Atonement.

The *shofar* that sounds on the Feast of Trumpets, or *Rosh Hashanah*, looks forward to Christ's return as King of the new creation. Paul said, "Listen, I tell you a mystery: We will not all sleep, but we will all be changed—in a flash, in the twinkling of an eye, at the last trumpet. For the trumpet will sound, the dead will be raised imperishable, and we will be changed" (1 Corinthians 15:51–52). The trumpet will herald the coming of God's kingdom and the coronation of Christ the King.

But the mood will be mixed, because there will also be judgment, a time when every human being who has ever lived will stand before God to account for their lives. Those who follow Christ will experience it as the ultimate Day of Atonement, when Jesus, their high priest, will be revealed to all as the one who has entered the true Most Holy Place to wipe away sin through the power of his blood. On that day, we will celebrate together the great Feast of Ingathering, the final Sukkot, when believers will dwell with God forever, "tabernacling" with our Savior in heaven.

Temples in Time

When you enter the octagonal Church of the Beatitudes just up the hill from the Sea of Galilee, you may immediately sense that you are in a holy place. The eight stained-glass windows located high on the walls of the church illuminate each beatitude. Sunshine filters down onto the gilded cross on an elegantly draped altar. The place is undisturbed by human voices—small signs request silence from all visitors, out of reverence for the place where Christ once preached.

Similarly, if you visit Jerusalem on a Friday afternoon at sunset, when *Shabbat* ("Sabbath") begins, you'll get that same feeling. During the week the unrelenting din of traffic and construction fills the air, but on Shabbat, you hear only the sound of soft breezes rustling the leaves and birds twittering in the branches. As the sunlight wanes, the bustling streets empty of cars, and a hushed, reverent silence descends.[10] From sunset Friday to sunset Saturday, Jerusalem is transformed. The same sense of holiness is created on the seven great festivals that have been celebrated for thousands of years.

Shabbat

Shabbat is Hebrew for "Sabbath," meaning "to cease." Jews observe Shabbat from Friday sunset until Saturday sunset, during which time they cease from work in order to worship God and enjoy fellowship with each other.

Rabbi Abraham Heschel explains that many religions treat their holy spaces with great reverence, as you can sense in the Church of the Beatitudes. But Jewish worship, he says, sanctifies *time* instead of *space*. Heschel points out that by giving Israel the feasts, God was preparing them for a time after the destruction of the temple. Unlike other gods, Israel's God was not confined to a geographic location, not even to the temple in Jerusalem. Instead of showing reverence for a certain place, the Jewish people have been able, through Sabbaths and other holy days, to sanctify time itself.

In her memoir, *Stranger in the Midst*, Nan Fink says that

> Shabbat is like nothing else. Time as we know it does not exist for these twenty-four hours, and the worries of the week soon fall away. A feeling of joy appears. The smallest object, a leaf or a spoon, shimmers in a soft light, and the heart opens. Shabbat is a meditation of unbelievable beauty.[11]

To protect the Sabbath, the rabbis created a long list of "thou shalt nots," as Lauren Winner observes in her book *Mudhouse Sabbath*. But these seeming negatives have a positive purpose. They are a way of hedging the day, protecting it from all the bustle and responsibility that characterizes every other day of the week.

To explain the positive side effects of some of the restrictions placed on an Orthodox Sabbath, Lauren Winner tells the story of Lis Harris, a secular Jew who spent a Shabbat with a Hasidic family in Crown Heights, New York. Annoyed by the long list of restrictions, Harris challenged her hosts, asking them to explain, "Why would God possibly care whether or not she microwaved a frozen dinner on Friday night?"

"What happens when we stop working and controlling nature?" her host responded. "When we don't operate machines, or pick flowers, or pluck fish from the sea? . . . When we cease interfering in the world we are acknowledging that it is God's world."[12]

Calling the feasts "palaces in time," Abraham Heschel writes:

> While the deities of other peoples were associated with places or things, the God of Israel was the God of events: the Redeemer from slavery, the Revealer of the Torah, manifesting Himself in events of history rather than in things or places . . . We remember the day of the exodus from Egypt, the day when Israel stood at Sinai, and our Messianic hope is the expectation of a day, the end of days.[13]

Jerusalem was built on top of a mountain so that, as the psalmists say, you must go "up" to Jerusalem. Pilgrims ascending Mount Zion on their way to worship at the temple would have felt the muscles in their legs burn with exertion and the anticipation in their hearts grow strong as they ascended the mountain into the presence of the Lord.

The feasts of Israel seem to function much like the Temple Mount once did—a place where a person ascends into God's presence for a time, in order to view things from a divine perspective. From the mountaintop view that the feasts provide, you see far back into remote time, to the dawn of creation, and then far forward into the future when Christ will come again.

You see Abraham ready to plunge a knife into the breast of his son Isaac. You watch with relief as an angel intervenes, providing a ram to take Isaac's place on the altar. You see the Israelites smearing blood on their doorposts in haste as death sweeps Egypt into mournful darkness. You see Jesus—in Gethsemane, betrayed by one of his own, and on the cross in agony, and then standing serenely outside the defeated, empty tomb. Finally you realize something of what God was doing all along, performing the greatest of all wonders by giving us his only Son, the Lamb of God, who is Christ himself.

AT THE FEET OF THE RABBI

1. Ancient people were profoundly aware that God was the giver of every good harvest. To increase your gratitude for God's provision, try celebrating the crop from your vegetable garden by giving some of the firstfruits to your local food bank. Or, if you have a flower garden (or even a bush or two), how about sharing your first bouquet with an elderly neighbor or a single mom?

2. During the Feast of Sukkot in the fall, consider building a *sukkah* on church grounds or in your backyard (or put up a tent). (You can find the dates for upcoming Jewish feasts by consulting Appendix B.) Spend time meditating on the fact that your security comes from God rather than from all the things you own or the house you live in. Think about how long you would have lasted in the desert on a diet of manna and water before you started grumbling.

3. On Yom Kippur, fast for at least part of the day and make a list of your sins from the past year. Pray for God to jog your memory. If you recognize offenses against others that you haven't yet apologized for, do so. Then say a prayer thanking Christ for his atoning death. Celebrate his forgiveness by ripping up the paper.

CHAPTER 10

At Table with the Rabbi

*May the All-merciful One bless this table at which
we have eaten and array it with the choicest
foods. May it be like the table of Abraham our
father; all who are hungry may eat from it
and all who are thirsty may drink from it.*

FROM A TRADITIONAL SEPHARDIC JEWISH LITURGY[1]

Several years ago, friends of Ann's were raving about a memoir entitled *Under the Tuscan Sun*. Intrigued, she picked up a copy. "I don't remember much about it," she remarks, "except the feeling it gave me—that to keep reading this memoir about the sensual pleasures of living in a villa in rural Italy would indelibly mark me as middle-aged, as someone increasingly focused on gustatory pleasures and pursuits. So, despite page after page crammed with sunlight, and vineyards, and rhapsodic descriptions of all variety of Italian food, I put it down, concluding that I was not yet old enough to read it.

"All that has changed.

"With the passage of years, I find that my interest in food has increased—not only in what I consume but in what others eat and how they eat it. Take the Chinese. A few years ago I had the opportunity of visiting the Qing Ping Market in Guangzhou, later identified as ground zero for the SARS epidemic. Sprawled across several city blocks, with more than two thousand stalls, it is a veritable three-ring circus of a grocery store, offering such delectable edibles as snakes, scorpions, seahorses, turtles, monkeys, and more. At one point, as I was wending my way through this enormous open-air market, I heard a small cat meowing. The poor creature was dangling in a mesh bag, slung over the arm of a shopper in front of me. I wanted desperately to believe that he was being toted home to become the family pet.

"My visit to the market confirmed the Chinese saying that tables and chairs are the only four-legged things that the people of this region won't eat, and the Cantonese saying that 'anything that walks, swims, crawls, or flies with its back to heaven is edible.' It also explained why I hadn't seen even a single bird flying over this city of six million people during my visit. At least, I concluded, the people in this region would probably never starve. How could they when they knew how to eat everything imaginable—and unimaginable!

"What a contrast to the Jewish approach to food, with its strict dietary laws and ritual meals. I could not think of two more opposite ways of looking at food."

J. R. R. Tolkien, author of *The Lord of the Rings* trilogy, wrote that "if more of us valued food and cheer and song above hoarded gold, it would be a merrier world."[2] Certainly the Jewish people developed a rich understanding of the place of food in daily life. During the time of Jesus, special meals had already long been part of the cycle of biblical feasts. Many biblical scenes in both the Old and New Testaments take place around meals.

Also, hospitality in this region of the world was considered a sacred obligation. One of the earliest instances of hospitality recorded in the Bible is the one in which Abraham welcomed three complete strangers by immediately killing a fattened calf and then laying out a sumptuous meal (Genesis 18:6–7). Jesus himself was no stranger to hospitality. Think of how often the Gospels portray him as a guest at feasts and banquets. Though his disciples left everything behind to follow him, they certainly must have enjoyed plenty of good meals along the way.

Jesus often told parables about banquets, weaving stories about guests who refused a dinner invitation, who didn't dress appropriately for a banquet, or who chose the wrong seat at the table. Using the meal itself to teach a lesson, he usually told such parables at the table.

Come to think of it, some of his last, most cherished words were uttered at the meal he shared with his disciples the night before his death. How can hearing Jesus's words within their cultural and historical setting give new meaning to the way we live and worship today?

Ancient Hospitality

A visit to Israel will quickly convince you that hospitality in this ancient land must often have been a matter of life and death. Imagine taking a short hike in the middle of the day in summer. It's ninety degrees in the shade—but there is no shade, only an endless rocky landscape dotted by a few scraggly shrubs. Now imagine that you can't climb into an air-conditioned car to get out of the searing heat. Nor can you reach for an ice-cold bottle of water to slake your thirst because grocery stores from which to purchase bottled water haven't yet been invented. Not only that, but the road on which you are walking is frequented by robbers who make their living off vulnerable travelers. But, thank God, there is something in this rugged country that works in your favor. It is hospitality. You can approach any of the residents of this ancient land for food, water, and shelter, and they will gladly provide it.

This same kind of "extreme hospitality" has been the practice around the Middle East and much of Africa for thousands of years. A few years ago when Lois traveled to Uganda with friends, hospitality greeted them at every turn. Whether visiting simple concrete homes, humble congregations, or dirt-floored schools, they were offered the best available food, which might only be bananas, boiled eggs, peanuts, or a bottle of soda. More than once their hosts told their children to run outside and catch dinner. Darting away, the children would return holding a prized chicken that moments earlier had been roaming about in the yard. A feast of roast chicken, plantains, yams, pineapple, and papaya would ensue. Everywhere they went, they feasted, even though at times they were the only ones eating because of the scarcity of food.

When they expressed their awe (and discomfort) at the generosity of their hosts, their African friends explained that hospitality is so highly valued in their culture that they could not possibly consider withholding it. They later discovered that many east Africans end up impoverishing themselves after hosting lavish family celebrations and festive meals. Still, because of the generosity of their African friends, Lois and her friends had the chance to taste the kind of hospitality practiced in Eastern cultures from biblical times until today.

Understanding such customs sheds light on a familiar scene from the Gospels. When Jesus commissioned his disciples to preach in the surrounding villages, he gave them instructions that sound radical to us: "Take nothing for the journey except a staff—no bread, no bag, no money in your belts . . . And if any place will not welcome you or listen to you, leave that place and shake the dust off your feet as a testimony against them" (Mark 6:8, 11). Taking this passage literally, some Christians have gone with little or no money to places that don't have the same high regard for hospitality that existed in Jesus's day. And even though God can provide for them, it seems clear that Jesus wasn't asking his disciples to count on daily miracles to sustain them. Instead, he knew that the *talmidim* of an esteemed rabbi would normally be warmly welcomed. Any community that failed to treat his disciples with honor deserved to be left behind.

In a land without police, social welfare, or insurance agencies to provide for people, mutual dependence was vital to survival. Community was essential, and it was celebrated at mealtime when the whole family gathered together at the end of the day. (A smaller meal, more like a snack, was eaten in the morning.) The main meal took a team of people hours to prepare—collecting wood, hauling water, grinding grain, kneading dough, chopping vegetables, stoking a fire, and stirring the pot.

Imagine for a moment what mealtimes would have been like. When we think of sitting down to dinner, we picture chairs arranged around a dining room table, set with individual plates and silverware. With this image in mind, it's difficult to understand how Jesus and his disciples could have reclined at table. It sounds awkward and uncomfortable.[3]

But ancient people would not have been sitting around the kind of tables that populate our dining rooms because, first of all, they wouldn't have had dining rooms. Neither would they have had large, four-legged tables, which were only found in palaces.[4] During mealtimes, people sat on mats on the floor of a tent or dwelling, and platters or bowls of food were placed in the middle. In New Testament times, they reclined on couches at more formal meals, and food was placed on small three-legged tables with a removable platter for a top.

Neither did people have silverware. Instead, they simply tore a piece of bread from a common loaf, and then dipped it into the same bowl of stew as everyone else. As for the cooking, it was done outside.

When Lois told her Ugandan friends about how biblical meals were eaten, they laughed and said, "Africans still eat the same way."

Though the Israelites didn't have fancy tables or place settings, they had something better. For them, the table was much more than a place to eat. It was a place of mutual trust and vulnerability. Sitting down at the same table with someone meant that you shared a protected relationship with them. Whom you ate with revealed something important about who you were, showing to whom you belonged.

Just as the word "house" could mean your family lineage or the word "bed" could mean your most intimate relationship, the word "table" could stand for family and friends—all those you trusted and on whom you depended. These were the people with whom you enjoyed table fellowship.[5] In fact, table fellowship implied a nearly inviolable relationship. To be a guest at a family's table meant that you were under their protection. As long as you were with the family, they were honor-bound to defend you, even at the cost of their lives.[6]

This approach to hospitality and table fellowship is still honored in some parts of the world. Several years ago, Lois was part of a group that visited a Bedouin family living in the Negev desert, in southern Israel. As they approached, a young boy wearing a *keffiyeh* (an Arab headdress) came riding toward them on his donkey in order to escort them to his goat-hair tent. As they entered, the adults inside welcomed them warmly, motioning for them to sit on the floor. They were served sweet tea, unleavened bread, and coffee roasted with cardamom and boiled over a fire. When it came time to leave, the boy mounted his little donkey once again and rode in front of their bus as it wended its way up the desert road. His presence at their arrival and departure symbolized the family's pledge to protect their guests as long as they were in their territory.

Now try reading the Bible in light of what you have just learned about hospitality and table fellowship.[7] Listen to David's words in Psalm 23:

> Even though I walk
> through the darkest valley,
> I will fear no evil,
> for you are with me;
> your rod and your staff,
> they comfort me.
> You prepare a table before me
> in the presence of my enemies.
> You anoint my head with oil;
> my cup overflows.

The psalm takes on new depth as you realize what David was saying—that even in the most dangerous of circumstances, when enemies lay in wait, he knew he was safe in God's presence. Like a divine host, God was sheltering and protecting him, inviting him to eat at his own table.

How much better life would be if at every moment we shared David's conviction—that even when we feel as if we are alone, walking through a wilderness of some kind, God is with us. When illness, suffering, loss, or anxiety assails us, that is precisely when God offers the protective, sheltering hospitality of his table to nourish and sustain us.

Having Dinner with God

Knowing about ancient biblical traditions of table fellowship sheds light on many other biblical scenes, in both Old and New Testaments. One of the most remarkable dinners in all of Scripture may be one you haven't even heard of. It happened on a mountaintop, thousands of years ago, just after Moses and the people of Israel received the covenant on Mount Sinai.

Before describing the scene, let's take a moment to consider the importance of covenants in the Eastern world. A covenant was much more than a mere business agreement. It signified that a deep relationship existed between all parties to the covenant, bonding people together in friendship, almost like a marriage. When a covenant was made, it was celebrated with a ceremonial meal that represented the peace and mutual acceptance that now existed by virtue of the covenant.

Now let's look at what happened at that ancient feast on Sinai. The covenant between God and his people had just been confirmed. Here's how Exodus 24:9–11 describes the scene:

> Moses and Aaron, Nadab and Abihu, and the seventy elders of Israel went up and saw the God of Israel . . . God did not raise his hand against these leaders of the Israelites; they saw God, and they ate and drank.

Why does the Bible make a point of saying that the elders "saw the God of Israel," noting that God didn't raise his hand against them? Elsewhere the Bible says that no one can see God and live.[8] And yet this scene depicts the leading men of Israel happily eating and drinking in his presence. Like a Middle Eastern host protecting his guests from harm, God had invited them to a ceremonial meal celebrating their covenant with him. Before anything had been done to break it, they had perfect fellowship with God. Moses and the elders sat down at his heavenly table to dine as his close "family," eating and drinking in his presence, without any negative consequences.

This same idea appears to be woven into the Passover meal in Egypt. The Israelites had asked Pharaoh to let them travel outside of Egypt so that they could worship their God. But when Pharaoh forbade them, they worshipped right in the midst of their enemies. The Israelites sacrificed a lamb for their Passover meal and were kept safe from the angel of death while the firstborn of the Egyptians were slain. God's presence at the "table" brought his people protection and their enemies judgment.

This idea of communing with God at his table was a key part of the sacrificial system of the temple. Certain offerings, like the sin and guilt sacrifices, were completely consecrated to God. But others, like the fellowship or peace (*shelem*) offering, were different. In these kinds of offerings, the worshipper and his family, along with the priests, would consume a portion of the sacrifice. When they ate from the altar, it was as if God was sharing some of *his* food with them. By doing so they were affirming that they were dining at God's table. Through the *shelem* offering, they celebrated their *shalom* with God and with each other. The Israelites understood this as true covenantal communion— that they could sit down to a meal with God.

Note that the Passover meal was communal—one lamb could easily feed fifteen people, and none of the meat could be left for another day. Such a meal signified that a state of peace existed between you and God, and between you and everyone present. Perhaps this is also why Jesus told his followers to be reconciled to their brothers and sisters before offering their gifts at the altar. With this in mind, the post–New Testament church forbade members who were quarreling with each other to take part in the Eucharist until they were reconciled. To do otherwise would be to "pollute their sacrifice."[9]

Communion services today are celebrated in a variety of ways within the church throughout the world. Regardless of how our own church understands this act of worship, our faith can be enriched by a deeper understanding of its biblical roots. The next time you receive Communion, take time to reflect on what you've learned about table fellowship, celebrating the peace you enjoy with God and with other believers. If there are any unresolved issues in any of your relationships, especially with other believers, make an effort to work through them before receiving Communion again.

Most of us have probably heard stories of people disagreeing about Communion practices, like the man who argues constantly for a common cup rather than individual glasses, or the elder who is upset that people go up to the sanctuary to receive Communion rather than staying seated. How ironic that Communion, a powerful celebration of our bond with God and other believers, should become a source of division rather than peace!

Table fellowship with God was not restricted to the temple. It was also celebrated in the home. Even now in traditional Jewish homes, the dinner table is considered the family altar, and the home itself is called the *mikdash meyat*, a little sanctuary where God can dwell. Because the family invites God to join them at every meal, all foods must be ritually acceptable. Within the home, the mother and father function as priests, bearing witness of God's presence to their children.

Shabbat Dinner

Nowadays we tend to think of meals merely as times for refueling our bodies. Breakfast is an Egg McMuffin behind the steering wheel, lunch is a vending machine candy bar at our desk, and dinner is a Lean Cuisine entrée in front of the evening news. In our rush-rush world many of us dine alone or while doing something else. Of course we still have our celebrations with family and friends, but the habit of leisurely family mealtimes has almost become extinct. We've lost the close tie that for centuries has existed between food and community. Maybe it's time for us to restore this dimension to our daily lives, sitting down together in order to celebrate our relationship with God and others.

One way to do this is to look closely at the Jewish tradition of the Shabbat evening meal.[10] In an observant Jewish family, Friday mornings are often jammed with housecleaning and cooking. At sunset on Friday (the beginning of the new day) all work ends as the family sits down for dinner. The last act of "work" that can be done on Friday is the lighting of two candles to begin the dinner. Along with a cup of wine, two loaves of beautifully braided *challah*[11] are placed on the table. Lighting the candles, the mother waves her hand over them as though welcoming the Shabbat. Then she covers her eyes and intones this prayer:

> *Barukh atah Adonai, Eloheinu, melekh ha'olam,*
> *asher kidishanu b'mitzvotav*
> *v'tzivanu l'hadlik ner shel Shabbat.*

> Blessed are you, Lord, our God, King of the universe
> who sanctifies us with his commandments,
> and commands us to light the lights of Shabbat.

After more prayers, the father removes the napkins covering the two loaves of bread and then lifts them up while reciting this blessing:

> *Barukh atah Adonai, Eloheinu, melekh ha'olam,*
> *ha-motzi lechem min ha-aretz.*

> Blessed are you, Lord, our God, King of the universe,
> who brings forth bread from the earth.

Then he breaks the bread into pieces and passes it around the table. At one point in the evening, the father reads Proverbs 31 to his wife to extol her virtues and then prays for her and blesses her. Then the father or mother places their lips on the forehead of each child. To a son they recite, "May God make you like Ephraim and Manasseh," and to a daughter, "May God make you like Sarah, Rebecca, Rachel, and Leah." Then to both, "May the Lord bless and protect you, may the Lord bestow his favor upon you and give you peace."[12] Often they follow with a personal prayer and message of encouragement for each child. What a treasured moment for parents and children alike.

Lechem

Lechem is the Hebrew word for "bread." It can also refer to food or nourishment in general.

Every Jewish meal is supposed to be a time for discussing the Scriptures, but this is especially emphasized on Shabbat. The rabbis said, "When three eat at one table and bring up words of Torah, it is as if they ate from the table of God, blessed be He!"[13] Perhaps that was why Jesus was invited to dinner so often—he could always be counted on for a fascinating discussion.

Most people celebrate Shabbat with the best food they can afford. In Jesus's time, fish was commonly served. Those who could afford it would have eaten meat on Shabbat. Wine was usually served only on Shabbat and on some feast days. Today, if a day of fasting falls on the Sabbath, it is delayed.[14] Even mourning is forbidden because the Sabbath is a day of joy.[15]

On Shabbat, the candles are often left burning until they go out on their own. The evening becomes a lovely time for enjoying a fine meal and relaxed conversation. Perhaps we should consider adapting these traditions to restore Sunday as a special time of fellowship and rest.[16]

A Table of Reconciliation

In addition to serving as a place of worship, the table represented a place of peace in biblical times and in many Eastern cultures today. Parties to a covenant of peace celebrated it with a ritual meal. Afterward, neither party was allowed to bring up the grievance again.

Remember the story of Jacob and his tricky father-in-law, Laban? Jacob had fallen in love with his daughter Rachel, but on their wedding day, at the last moment, Laban substituted his older and less attractive daughter, Leah. The hapless Jacob did not discover the switch until the next morning. At that point Laban gave him Rachel to be his second wife, but not until he got Jacob to promise seven more years of labor beyond the seven he had already worked for Leah.

Fed up with Laban's shenanigans and having fulfilled his part of the bargain, Jacob finally fled with his two wives, his flocks, and his children. Ten days later, when Laban finally caught up with him, the two made a covenant of peace in which each agreed that neither would harm the other. Then they shared a meal. Here's how Genesis describes it:

[Jacob] offered a sacrifice there in the hill country and invited his relatives to a meal. After they had eaten, they spent the night there.

Early the next morning Laban kissed his grandchildren and his daughters and blessed them. Then he left and returned home. (Genesis 31:54–55)

By eating together Jacob and Laban were proclaiming that their relationship had been restored. Because the meal was also part of a sacrifice to God, it was understood that the Lord himself was present at the table, partaking of the meal and witnessing their vows. The shared meal signified that Jacob and Laban were at peace with God and with each other.

Such meals still occur. A few years ago a messianic Jew by the name of Ilan Zamir was driving through an Arab village in Israel. Suddenly, a figure darted out from the side of the road. Ilan slammed on his brakes—too late. He had struck and killed a thirteen-year-old Palestinian boy. Ilan couldn't understand why the teenager had ignored the blaring horn and the screeching brakes. Later he learned the reason. The boy was deaf.

Sulha

A *sulha* is a covenantal meal of reconciliation used in Arab cultures. The word *sulha* is the Arabic equivalent of the Hebrew word *shulhan*, which means "table." This practice derives from the ancient belief that eating at the same table with others is the essence of a peaceful, harmonious relationship.

Haunted by the tragedy, Ilan was determined to make amends by seeking the family's forgiveness. Other Jews who heard of his plan thought he was crazy. An Israeli policeman even warned him, saying: "Man, that's dangerous what you want to do. You can get into serious trouble. You're an Israeli Jew and these people you want to meet are Arabs on the West Bank."[17]

The policeman was merely echoing what Ilan already knew. According to Arab tradition, the family could kill Ilan as vengeance for their son's death. But Ilan persisted, enlisting an Arab pastor who suggested he arrange for a *sulha*, a meal of reconciliation.

Here's how Ilan describes what happened when he sat down with the boy's family for the ceremonial meal:

The cups of coffee remained on the table, untouched. According to tradition, the father would be the first to taste from the cup as a sign that he accepted the reconciliation gesture, and had indeed agreed to forgive. The tension in his face had cast a shadow on the proceedings until then, but at that point, he suddenly began to smile. The lines of grief softened. He looked at me squarely and his smile broadened as he moved toward me, opening his arms in a gesture of embrace. As we met and embraced, he kissed me ceremonially three times on the cheeks. Everyone began to shake hands with one another as the father sipped coffee. The whole atmosphere was transformed, the tension at an end.

But then something even more surprising happened. A spokesman for the family turned to Ilan with this remarkable invitation:

Know, O my brother, that you are in place of this son who has died. You have a family and a home somewhere else, but know that here is your second home.

What a picture of reconciliation! A Palestinian family inviting an Israeli Jew into their own family! Come to think of it, this is a striking picture of the way God welcomes us into his family through the death of his Son, inviting us to sit down at his table and partake of the covenant meal.

This practice of eating a meal together as a sign of forgiveness and peace runs from the Old Testament through the New Testament. Remember Jesus's parable of the prodigal son as he is welcomed home by his father, who promptly throws a party to mark his return? Again, the picture is of a festive meal to mark the reconciliation between father and son. The father is ecstatic because his son has rejoined the family.

Wonderful as this story sounds to modern ears, it is even more remarkable than we might imagine. Scholar Kenneth Bailey has asked people all over the Middle East what it would mean if a son were to ask for his inheritance while the father was still alive. The response is universal shock about how unthinkable the request is, because it implies a wish that the father was dead![18] Jesus's story must have offended and shocked many of his listeners because no Middle Eastern father would have been expected to forgive the offense of such a son.

Understanding the story in this light can help us perceive how shocking God's acceptance of us really is. We tend to think of sin as an infraction of rules. But the story Jesus tells makes it clear that our sin is not just an infraction of a set of laws but a terrible offense against God, our loving Father. By taking the good gifts we've been given— our time, money, and talents—and running away to live life our own way, we are acting like the prodigal who turns his back on his father, sells the ancestral lands, and then squanders his inheritance.[19] It is tantamount to wishing God were dead.

Western Christians often describe salvation as a transaction— that we have sinned by breaking God's rules. If we believe in Christ, he will pay the penalty, allowing us to escape punishment for sin when we die. Though there's truth in this explanation, there's so much more to the story. If we reduce salvation to a kind of deal that we make with God, a plea bargain with the Almighty, we run the risk of painting him as an angry judge or an exasperated policeman whose primary purpose is to punish sin. Jesus's parable reveals how shockingly large God's love for us is, for he acts as no self-respecting Middle Eastern father would have, welcoming us with delight back to the family table.

Jesus's story of the prodigal son and the forgiving father also highlights the fact that salvation is not just about our life in heaven but about our relationship with God on earth. By healing our alienation, God enables us to have ongoing daily intimacy with him. Each time we take Communion, we celebrate what Jesus has done for us, enabling us to "sit down to dinner" with God even in this life, which is something that was not possible before.

Dining in Jesus's Day

Some people were offended not only by the stories Jesus told but by the dinner invitations he accepted. They even accused him of being "a glutton and a drunkard." Unable to forgive his promiscuous table fellowship, they could not imagine how any self-respecting rabbi could party with such low-class people! They didn't realize, as Joachim Jeremias has pointed out, that Jesus was living out his own parable, playing the role of the forgiving father welcoming home the prodigal. That's why he welcomed the wayward and ate with tax collectors and sinners.

Jeremias notes that in the East, even today, to invite someone to a meal was to extend an honor, an offering of peace, trust, and forgiveness. Jesus's meals with sinners weren't merely social events or just signs of his empathy for the lowly, though he was compassionate. They represented the very essence of his mission and message. Jeremias points out, "The inclusion of sinners in the community of salvation, achieved in table-fellowship, is the most meaningful expression of the message of the redeeming love of God."[20] Each time Jesus ate with sinners, he was revealing the kingdom of God.

We see these mealtime gatherings at so many key moments in Jesus's ministry. Remember the morning after the resurrection, when Jesus fries up some fish for his disciples for breakfast (John 21:9–19)? Usually depicted as a guest at someone else's table, Jesus now acts as the host, serving his disciples breakfast on the shores of Galilee.

Significantly, the topic of conversation at this meal is Jesus's relationship with Peter. After Jesus's arrest, Peter had betrayed him three times. Now, Jesus asks Peter three times whether he loves him. When Peter answers in the affirmative, Jesus reinstates him as his disciple. The meal beside the sea demonstrates the reconciliation going on between Jesus and Peter. After deserting Jesus and witnessing his agonizing death, how deeply healing it must have been for Peter to dine with his beloved master once again.

The meal of reconciliation also appears in Revelation 3:20. Listen to the familiar promise: "Here I am! I stand at the door and knock. If anyone hears my voice and opens the door, I will come in and eat with that person, and they with me." Have you ever wondered why the Lord talks about dining with us? He is inviting us into an intimate relationship that is to be celebrated by a meal together.

The Banquet of the Messiah

Now you can see why Jesus, at their last supper prior to his death, told his disciples to remember him by enjoying a meal together. The bread and the wine would remind them that his sacrifice made it possible for them to have unbroken communion with God and with each other.

Many groups in Jesus's day had strict rules governing table fellowship. Pharisees would only eat with *haverim* ("friends" who observed their strict rules). Essenes, who would only dine with other Essenes, had purity laws that made the Pharisees look lax by comparison. The early church, however, took the opposite approach, adopting the attitude Jesus had modeled. In fact, their table fellowship quickly expanded to include Gentiles. To many, the idea that God would invite Jewish and Gentile believers in Christ to eat together at his table was shocking. It showed a grace and love beyond comprehension.

The early Christians were beginning to live out the fulfillment of the ancient promise spoken in Isaiah:

> On this mountain the LORD Almighty will prepare
>   a feast of rich food for all peoples,
> a banquet of aged wine—
>   the best of meats and the finest of wines.
> On this mountain he will destroy
>   the shroud that enfolds all peoples,
> the sheet that covers all nations;
>   he will swallow up death forever.
> The Sovereign LORD will wipe away the tears
>   from all faces;
> he will remove his people's disgrace
>   from all the earth.
> The LORD has spoken. (Isaiah 25:6–8)

Once again, like the sacred gathering of the elders on Mount Sinai, Scripture depicts a meal on a mountaintop. But this time it is the meal to end all meals, the greatest of all banquets, to be held at the end of time. Not only will it be safe for human beings to feast in God's presence; no one invited to the meal will ever have to come down from the mountaintop. Instead, we will dwell with God forever. Furthermore, the guest list will include more than just the elders of Israel. Everyone who belongs to God will come to celebrate the feast!

No wonder the New Testament pictures heaven as a wedding feast—the celebration of the union of the Lamb of God with his people. In the meantime, every time we celebrate Communion, not only can we enjoy unbroken fellowship with God and others, we can also get a tiny foretaste of the feast to come.

———————

The ancient biblical traditions of table fellowship are rich and beautiful, offering profound insights into our own relationship with God. But there are other customs, like tying tassels to your garments, that seem odd, even legalistic. Why did the Jews of Jesus's day wear tassels? And if Jesus wore them, why don't we? Let's explore this unusual custom to see what light it might shed on our own faith.

AT THE FEET OF THE RABBI

1. In Matthew 25:35, Jesus said, "I was a stranger and you invited me in." He expected his followers to show hospitality to others. How good are you at this? Ask the Lord to give you an opportunity to invite someone for a meal, or even just coffee or soda.

2. If you've had a falling out with someone, or perhaps if your children have had a fight, try having a *sulha*—a meal of reconciliation. Have a ceremony of apology and then a special

meal. Once you take the first bite, the offense can never be brought up again!

3. What if families apologized for their sins to each other before Communion at church? Then the Communion would become the *sulha*. Everyone would walk out with a clean slate for the new week.

4. Make it a regular practice to enjoy a special meal with family and friends on Saturday night or Sunday afternoon. Place a candle on the table. You might even keep it burning until you go to bed on Sunday night (as long as it's in a safe container). Consider purchasing or baking fresh bread for the occasion. Make the meal leisurely and be sure to discuss a Scripture passage at the table. Before you close the meal, pray a blessing over each child in attendance.

• • •

CHALLAH

Makes two loaves.

2½ cups warm water
1 tablespoon active dry yeast
½ cup honey
4 tablespoons vegetable oil
3 eggs
1 tablespoon salt
8 cups unbleached all-purpose flour

1. In a large bowl, sprinkle yeast over barely warm water. Beat in honey, oil, 2 eggs, and salt. Add the flour one cup at a time, beating after each addition. As dough thickens, begin kneading until it is smooth and elastic and not sticky. Add flour as needed. Cover with a damp clean cloth and let rise for 1½ hours or until dough has

doubled in bulk.

2. Punch down the risen dough and turn it onto a floured board. Divide in half and knead each half for five minutes, adding flour as needed to keep it from getting sticky. Divide each half into thirds and roll into long snake about 1 1/2 inches in diameter. Pinch the ends of the three snakes together firmly and braid from middle. Leave as braid or form into a round braided loaf by bringing ends together, curving the braid into a circle and then pinching the ends together. Grease two baking trays and place a finished braid on each. Cover with towel and let rise about one hour.

3. Preheat oven to 375 degrees F (190 degrees C).

4. Beat the remaining egg and brush a generous amount over each braid. Sprinkle with poppy seeds if desired.

5. Bake at 375 degrees F (190 degrees C) for about 40 minutes. Bread should have a nice hollow sound when thumped on the bottom. Cool on a rack at least one hour prior to serving.

CHAPTER 11

Touching the Rabbi's Fringe

Blessed are You, Lord our God, King of the universe,
who sanctifies us with His commandments,
and commands us to wrap ourselves in tzitzit.

TRADITIONAL PRAYER RECITED WHEN PUTTING ON A *TALLIT* (PRAYER SHAWL)

Maybe it's because I was born in Independence, Iowa," Lois remarks. "Or perhaps it has something to do with growing up in a church that majored on grace versus legalism. Whatever the reason, I have always had a hard time with rules and regulations, like the mountain of lab rules you have to pay attention to when you become a molecular biologist. During graduate school, I spent years running experiments that could identify a person from a single strand of hair, just like on *CSI: Crime Scene Investigation.* Our supersensitive tests could detect infinitesimal substances, but the slightest bit of contamination would yield a false result. Many procedures had to be done with absolute sterility, like in an operating room.

"The regulations were endless: Always wipe down the work surface with alcohol; change your gloves frequently; keep switching to a new sterile pipette tip; always pass the lip of an opened bottle through a flame, etc., etc., etc. . . . Some of the rules seemed almost superstitious, like not walking in the halls with gloved hands, or not bringing personal items into the lab. But I soon discovered that the slightest infraction could ruin a week's worth of work.

"Once in a while my Lutheran background would rear its head and begin to hamper my research. Some of the regulations felt so arbitrary. I needed someone to tell me exactly *why* I should do something a particular way. But experience soon taught me that refusing to observe regulations exactly as written would cause my experiments to punish me for months. Lab work is wonderful for building character.

"This same allergic reaction to rules and regulations carried over into my attitude toward the Bible, especially toward many of the Old Testament laws. Had I been one of the Israelites wandering in the desert after their long sojourn in Egypt, I'm certain I would have been among the first to hoard manna, only to find that it had turned wormy the next day. Maybe there was a reason why Moses instructed the people not to keep it overnight. But if I couldn't understand the reason for a rule, I would probably have ignored it.

"Years later, I realized that my attitude about the law was spilling over into my relationship with God. If someone had asked me whether the God of the Old Testament was a loving God, I would have said, 'Of course he is.' But the way I read the Bible betrayed the fact that I wasn't quite sure. Hadn't God gone out of his way to choose a particular nation and then to burden its people with meaningless regulations, punishing them harshly for their sins? Friends would talk about seeking God's will for their lives, but I hesitated. If I pursued God's will, would he assign me to a job I hated or send me to some backward, lonely place, far from the people I loved? Wasn't that the kind of thing he was always doing to the Israelites in the Old Testament?

"It was an odd schizophrenia, a 'split' in my personality, which derived from my unspoken belief that God himself had a split personality. It was as though I believed the Father to be harsh and uncaring even though his Son was loving and kind. How, I wondered, could Jesus have declared that he and the Father were one, when their personalities seemed worlds apart?"

Discovering Torah

"Fortunately something happened to heal the rift in my perspective," Lois says. "Ironically, it happened when I began to look more closely at the Jewish attitude toward the law. What I discovered surprised and challenged me to rethink my perspective. I had always thought of Judaism as hopelessly legalistic, imagining that its adherents were miserably bound to hundreds of nonsensical laws and regulations. But as I familiarized myself with historical and contemporary Judaism, I began to realize that many Jews do not feel at all oppressed. Though some Jews may fall into legalism just as some Christians do, Judaism itself has displayed an extremely positive attitude toward the law from Jesus's time until today.

"Each year observant Jews read through the five books of the Torah, the 'Law of Moses,' in the synagogue. After the Feast of Sukkot in the fall, when the weighty parchment scrolls are rolled from Deuteronomy back to Genesis, comes a huge celebration called Simchat Torah—'Rejoicing in the Torah.' To express their joy, the people dance around the synagogue with the scrolls in their arms. My Christian brain could hardly imagine 'rejoicing in the law.'"

Simchat Torah

Simchat Torah means "Rejoicing in the Torah." It is a celebration of the completion of the annual cycle of Scripture readings. The scrolls are carried around the synagogue seven times amid singing and dancing. The concluding section of Deuteronomy is read followed by the beginning of Genesis, to celebrate the lifelong study of God's Word.

Why do these Jewish men and women think so differently than we do about the law? To many of us the word "law" evokes the idea of hair-splitting discussions, prosecuting attorneys, speeding tickets, fines, and jail. But the Hebrew word for "law" is torah, and it primarily means "teaching" or "instruction." The word is related to the verb yarah, which means "to aim, point, or shoot an arrow," having the sense of "guidance."

Proverbs 13:14 says, "The teaching [torah] of the wise is a fountain of life, turning a person from the snares of death." And the noble wife of Proverbs 31 "speaks with wisdom, and faithful instruction [torah] is on her tongue" (31:26). These are hardly negative images.

In Jewish Bibles, torah is almost always translated "instruction" or "teaching" rather than "law," as in Christian translations. You can feel the difference as you read. In the NIV, for instance, Psalm 1:1–2 reads:

"Blessed is the one . . . whose delight is in the law of the LORD, and who meditates on his law day and night." But in a Jewish translation it reads, "The teaching of the Lord is his delight, and he studies that teaching day and night."[1] Which sounds more delightful—God's teaching or his law?

Of course, because of God's authority, we are obligated to listen to his teaching and to do what he says. So the word *torah* can indeed mean "law," but that is not its primary intent. To put it simply, the Torah is God's guidance for how we should live. In Jewish parlance, "Torah" often has a reverential sense, meaning "God's Word," and sometimes it refers to the Scriptures as a whole.[2]

To our ears the word "commandment" sounds heavy, even burdensome. But the Hebrew word for "commandment" is *mitzvah* (pl. *mitzvot*), a word that in Jewish usage has a positive connotation. To perform a *mitzvah* is to take hold of an opportunity to do something good that God wants you to do. People say things like, "I had a chance to do a *mitzvah* today when an elderly woman asked for my help." The word is always used positively, suggesting that doing what God asks is a joy and a spiritual opportunity, not a burden.[3]

Believe it or not, Paul had a similar attitude. Just listen: "For it is by grace you have been saved, through faith—and this is not from yourselves, it is the gift of God—not by works, so that no one can boast. For we are God's handiwork, created in Christ Jesus to do *good works*, which God prepared in advance for us to do" (Ephesians 2:8–10, italics added). Ironically, immediately following Paul's classic line about not being saved by obedience to the law, he goes on to say that our very purpose in being created was to "do good works." While salvation only comes by faith in Christ's atoning death on the cross, and not by our own righteous deeds, Paul actually says that we should take joy in doing the good that God has been planning for us since before we were even created.

The Meaning of the Tassels

"Though my attitude toward God's teaching was beginning to change," Lois says, "I still wondered why he had given his people so many seemingly pointless laws. Why, for instance, did he decree that Jewish men were to wear *tzitziyot* (tassels)? They seemed meaningless—and so odd, such a negative fashion statement. What earthly purpose could they serve? But there it was in Scripture: 'Throughout the generations to come you are to make tassels on the corners of your garments, with a blue cord on each tassel. You will have these tassels to look at and so you will remember all the commands of the LORD' (Numbers 15:38–39).

"My questions led me to a partial answer: By wearing *tzitziyot*, a Jewish man was signifying that he was trying to become obedient to all the laws of God. How fitting, I thought—an arbitrary law to symbolize all the arbitrary laws God had given them. And to think that Jesus wore them too!

"My attitude toward the *tzitziyot* and the rest of the law finally began to change when I realized that Jewish scholars posed a far wiser question than I had, asking, 'What good purpose would a loving God have for giving us this command?' I wondered whether I might find deeper answers were I to base my own questions on the solid foundation of God's love rather than on the shifting sands of my own suspicions."

In answer to their question, the rabbis agreed that some laws seemed to lack an obvious purpose, and they called them *hukim* ("decrees"). Obeying such laws, they believed, displayed one's love for God because it showed that you trusted him regardless of whether you understood his intent.

It's fascinating to note that one of these decrees was the command to refrain from breaking the bones of the Passover lamb. People considered the roasted marrow inside the bone a tasty treat, so not breaking the bones meant forgoing the pleasure. It wasn't until centuries later, when Jesus, the Lamb of God, was nailed to a cross, that the reason for this command became apparent. Listen to John's gospel:

> Now it was the day of Preparation, and the next day was to be
> a special Sabbath. Because the Jewish leaders did not want the
> bodies left on the crosses during the Sabbath, they asked Pilate

to have the legs broken and the bodies taken down. The soldiers therefore came and broke the legs of the first man who had been crucified with Jesus, and then those of the other. But when they came to Jesus and found that he was already dead, they did not break his legs . . . These things happened so that the scripture would be fulfilled: "Not one of his bones will be broken." (John 19:31–33, 36)

Some of God's laws contain hidden wisdom that will only later be revealed.

Though the command to wear the *tzitzit* makes no sense to modern people, it made perfect sense to those who first heard it. In ancient times, the garments people wore indicated their status in society. The hem was particularly important because it symbolized the owner's identity and authority. Legal contracts written on clay tablets were "signed" by pressing the corner of one's hem into the clay.[4]

Do you remember the scene in the Old Testament in which David encounters Saul in a cave? It's almost comical because Saul enters the cave in order to relieve himself, unaware that he has just stepped into David's hideout. But instead of seizing the opportunity to kill Saul, David merely sneaks up and slices off a portion of Saul's hem (1 Samuel 24:4–5). Afterward, David is overwhelmed with remorse for what he has done. But why? Hasn't he just spared the life of a power-mad king intent on killing him? However, by cutting the corner of Saul's robe, David was symbolically assaulting the king's authority to reign. His action was tantamount to knocking the crown off Saul's head, a job David believed belonged only to the Almighty.

Tassels were also a sign of nobility; in the ancient world kings and princes decorated their hems with tassels. Remember how the high priest's blue robe was decorated? From it hung an elaborate border of bells and pomegranates (Exodus 28:33). The blue thread in the *tzitzit* that ordinary Jews wore was dyed with the same expensive royal blue dye, called *tekhelet*, as the robe of the high priest.[5] One Jewish scholar, Jacob Milgrom, explains that the blue dye epitomizes the democratic thrust within Judaism because it signals that the entire people of Israel are to become a nation of priests. Milgrom writes:

> In antiquity, the *tzitzit* (and the hem) was the insignia of authority, high breeding and nobility. By adding the blue woolen cord to the *tzitzit*, the Torah combined nobility with priesthood: Israel is not to rule man but to serve God. Furthermore, *tzitzit* is not restricted to Israel's leaders, be they kings, rabbis or scholars. It is the uniform of all Israel.[6]

The *tzitzit* showed that God had chosen to make this one people his representatives—a kingdom of priests to the rest of the world. By wearing the *tzitzit*, every Jew was reminded of the obligation to serve God by obeying his commands. Nowadays, tassels are wound and knotted in a specific pattern to remind the wearer to obey the commandments of God. The pattern of knotting developed after Jesus's time. But then, as now, the tassels were there to remind the Jewish people to continually obey his laws because God himself had put Israel on display as a "light to the nations." Realizing this, the rabbis ruled that the tassels were not to be stuffed inside one's pockets or hidden under a shirt. Numbers 15:39 said, "You will have these tassels *to look at* . . .", so the tassels must dangle visibly for all to see (italics added).

Mitzvah

A *mitzvah* is a commandment, a religious obligation. People commonly use this word to refer to a good deed.

By means of the *tzitzit*, God was encouraging his people to be obvious about their commitment. In a world where other nations prostituted themselves to idols and sacrificed their children to demons, the Jews stood out. The *tzitzit* was a visible reminder that they could not blend into the nations around them because they belonged to God in a special way. Whatever they did, good or evil, was a witness to the God they served. If they fulfilled their calling through obedience, the world would recognize them as a holy nation.

If the *tzitzit* served all these purposes, why did Jesus criticize those who "make their phylacteries wide and the tassels on their garments long" (Matthew 23:5)? Was he saying that we shouldn't stick out because of our faith? That would make little sense in light of the fact that Jesus himself wore tassels and phylacteries. Jesus also told his followers they were a "town built on a hill" that could not be hidden, and that lamps are not lit only to be placed under bowls. And he encouraged his disciples to "let your light shine before others, that they may see your good deeds and glorify your Father in heaven" (Matthew 5:14–16). No, Jesus was criticizing those who exaggerated their piety as a way of enhancing their social status.

What if we, too, had a universal way of showing our faith in Christ? "I have always recoiled at the thought of putting a Christian bumper sticker on my car," Ann admits. "To do so seems like trivializing my faith. But a deeper reason for my reluctance has to do with my driving habits, which are less than angelic. To excuse my bad behavior, I joke with friends, telling them that when I drive I pray for mercy and not justice. But what if I were to slap a bright, bold sticker on my car announcing my faith? Maybe that lead foot of mine would suddenly ease up. Or maybe I'd leave the house a few minutes early so that I wouldn't be so impatient with the slow driver in front of me. Perhaps, over time, I might even become a kinder, gentler driver."

The *tzitzit* was like a bright blue bumper sticker that God had given his people, his way of saying, "Drive well, because everyone is watching you!"

Several years ago Ann was talking to a friend who shared an embarrassing story about himself. A frequent traveler, he had encountered one too many problems with a flight delay. His attempts to get a seat on another airline went nowhere. Exasperated, her friend, the road warrior, kept pushing the gate agent until the two exchanged heated words. When the agent finally asked for his contact information, he slapped his business card on the counter. Suddenly his face flushed. The card he had pulled from his pocket was brand new, identifying him not as any ordinary Joe Shmoe but as the head of a new Christian ministry called—of all things—*Encouraging Words*!

Like this road warrior's business card, the *tzitzit* is a visible sign that offers those who wear it an opportunity to live out their faith in public. Perhaps as Christians we should do something similar, taking the risk of identifying our faith in public, not proudly or self-righteously, but humbly, giving ourselves a little reminder of the *tzitzit* that our Rabbi Jesus wore. "My own practice," Ann says, "is to wear a small gold cross on a chain around my neck. More than once my youngest has asked why I always wear the same necklace. 'Because,' I tell her, 'I need to remember to act like a Christian today.'"

A Call to Holiness

Do you remember the story of the woman in the Gospels who suffered from chronic bleeding? Considered ritually impure, she would have defiled anyone she touched. Here's how Ann imagined the scene of her furtive attempt to reach Jesus in her book, *Women of the Bible*:

> The woman hovered at the edge of the crowd. Nobody watched as she melted into the throng of bodies—just one more bee entering the hive. Her shame faded, quickly replaced by a rush of relief. No one had prevented her from joining in. No one had recoiled at her touch.
>
> She pressed closer, but a noisy swarm of men still blocked her view. She could hear Jairus, a ruler of the synagogue, raising his voice above the others, pleading with Jesus to come and heal his daughter before it was too late.
>
> Suddenly the group in front of her shifted, parting like the waters of the Jordan before the children of promise. It was all she needed. Her arm darted through the opening, fingers brushing the hem of his garment. Instantly, she felt a warmth spread through her, flushing out the pain, clearing out the decay. Her skin prickled and shivered. She felt strong and able, like a young girl coming into her own—so glad and giddy, in fact, that her feet wanted to rush her away before she created a spectacle by laughing out loud at her quiet miracle.

But Jesus blocked her escape and silenced the crowd with a curious question: "Who touched me?"[7]

Now think of this scene in terms of what you have learned about the significance of the hem of a person's garment. The hem would have signified Jesus's identity and authority. What's more, the place where the tassels were attached would have been considered the holiest part of his garment. So it seems likely that the woman knew exactly what she was reaching for.[8] Jesus's purity was so great that instead of becoming defiled by her touch, it healed her impurity. What a beautiful picture of the power of Christ's holiness to heal and to bless.

The Teaching of Mount Sinai

"My earlier assumption," Lois says, "about how arbitrary it was for God to tell his people to wear *tzitzit* soon gave way to feelings of awe as I began to understand the significance of this command in light of the cultural context in which it was given. Such feelings led me to wonder whether some of the other Old Testament laws I had written off as arbitrary might also hide a deeper wisdom." Let's take a closer look at the context in which some of these laws were given.

The best place to begin is at Mount Sinai, where God appeared to Moses and gave him the law. Imagine what it would have been like to have been among those weary Israelite slaves. Until now your life has been lived at the very bottom of Egyptian society. You've been whipped, spat upon, and despised, treated like a machine. Suddenly God himself begins speaking to you through your leader, Moses— telling you to put on a royal robe and to make sure you wear it every day. After years of backbreaking labor, you hear him say that he wants you to celebrate your freedom by ceasing from all labor once a week. Neither should you force anyone else to do your work on that day. Such instructions would be greeted not as new burdens heaped on the backs of slaves but as good news dignifying the lives of free men and women. It may well have sounded too good to be true!

In the ancient world, poor peasants and slaves lived a hopeless, desperate existence, in part because law codes were established to protect the interests of the wealthy and the powerful. The most brutal punishments were meted out even for minor crimes, like theft or property destruction. In one of the most ancient law codes, the Code of Hammurabi, a barmaid who overcharged a nobleman for a beer could be drowned for her offense. But to murder a poor man merely involved paying a fine, the amount of which was determined by the victim's social status.

Ancient laws were not about justice as we know it. They conveyed no sense that rich and poor should be treated equally. The weakest members of society simply had no laws to protect them. In *The Gifts of the Jews*, Thomas Cahill notes that in comparison to the laws of other ancient societies, the laws governing the Israelites were shockingly progressive. He writes:

> The casual cruelty of other ancient law codes—the cutting off of nose, ears, tongue, lower lip (for kissing another man's wife), breasts, and testicles—is seldom matched in the Torah. Rather in the prescriptions of Jewish law we cannot but note a presumption that all people, even slaves, are human and that all human lives are sacred. The constant bias is in favor not of the powerful and their possessions but of the powerless and their poverty.[9]

This was what made the Sinai laws so radically different, challenging the mindset of the age. Through them, God showed his overwhelming concern for the poor, the alien, the widow, and the orphan. His people were commanded to care for the poor with their tithes and to let them glean from their crops. Instead of mistreating an alien (a foreigner or refugee), God's people were told to "love them as themselves." Unlike any other nation, Israel's law code held many laws designed for the protection of the weakest members of society.

Though some of the laws contained in the Torah may appear harsh at first glance (e.g., sacrificing animals or putting to death anyone who curses their parents), a closer look at the context in which they were given often reveals great fairness, compassion, and amazing concern for the sanctity of human life. Our own civilization has been so transformed by these basic moral principles that we take them for granted. We can hardly imagine society without them. The more we recognize the differences between God's ways and the ways of the ancient world, the more we will understand that the love of Christ so evident in the Gospels was also evident in the God who revealed himself on Sinai.

God's Teaching Methods

Instead of transforming his people instantly, God started with what was familiar. Building on what they were accustomed to, he then moved them in a radically different direction. For example, offering sacrifices was a common practice in various cultures in the ancient world. It seems that God had embedded in humanity a universal urge toward worship, a spiritual instinct planted in the human soul. Somehow human beings realized that their sustenance depended on divine power, a power they needed to acknowledge. Many cultures believed, for instance, that meat should never be eaten without first honoring a god for allowing the life of the animal to be taken.[10] But sacrifices often functioned as a kind of bribe, a way of manipulating a god into doing your bidding. If you uttered the correct incantation or performed a ritual sexual act, the god would make your fields fertile and your animals multiply.

In contrast, the God of Israel instructed his people to offer sacrifices, but he radically transformed the way they did it. First, he insisted they refrain from sacrificing to idols. Unlike the "gods" of other nations, Israel's God was utterly beyond human comprehension. He could not be contained in a block of wood or metal or be represented by a lifeless object. Neither were the sacrifices to be accompanied by any kind of incantation or manipulation—Israel was to *serve* him, not try to sway him through magic.

And, unlike other gods, who were thought to reward deviousness and cunning and were themselves immoral, the God of Israel held his people to high moral standards, insisting that they live with integrity. One day, far in the future, God would use the sacrificial system to teach his people about his great love and forgiveness. He would do it, of course, through the sacrifice of Christ on the cross.

In addition to setting the Israelites apart from the world by the way they worshipped him through sacrifice, God also put forth a set of dietary laws to distinguish them from their heathen neighbors. Though certain of these laws held considerable health benefits, like not eating animals that carried diseases, this was not their main purpose. Rather, their primary goal was to remind Israel not to mingle with its Gentile neighbors.[11] Their strict dietary laws prevented them from joining their neighbors' idolatrous worship feasts and from partaking in the intimacy of their table fellowship.

Clearly, God was retraining his people by separating them from the cultures around them. By declaring certain foods clean and others unclean, God was communicating the importance of striving for purity in all things, even those that seemed trivial. Many of the dietary and ceremonial laws that sound so strange to us were intended to enable Israel to fulfill its destiny as God's chosen people, to set them apart as distinctive among the nations of their world.

An Eye for an Eye?

Most of us are familiar with the Old Testament command that the punishment for serious injury was "eye for eye, tooth for tooth" (Exodus 21:24; Leviticus 24:20; Deuteronomy 19:21). Such punishments sound unbelievably cruel. We are horrified by the thought of people limping around with missing appendages or gouged out eyes because of some offense. But the expression was an idiom that wasn't taken literally. "An eye for an eye" was an ancient expression taken from laws originally meant to limit punishment for an injury to no more than the injury itself. It meant equitable punishment that fit the crime. An eye for an eye—not a scolding for an eye, and not a life for an eye. Without it, a victim's clan might demand greater vengeance until a dispute arose that might escalate into an all-out feud. Also, many scholars believe that this command was not followed literally in Israel. Instead, fines were levied for various injuries.[12]

Like a good parent giving one kind of rule to a four-year-old and another to a fourteen-year-old, God was working within the limits of his people's capacity to obey. In Genesis, for instance, God let Jacob marry two sisters, Leah and Rachel. Then in Leviticus, though not prohibiting polygamy, God said that a man should never marry a woman and her sister. Later, Jesus clarified things further. God's ultimate desire, he said, was that one man should marry one woman for a lifetime. Instead of trying to transform his people overnight, God taught them in stages, over the course of many centuries.

If anything, this "go-slow" approach shows God's patience and grace. If a violent felon who was also an inveterate liar were to become a believer, perhaps God would begin by getting him to stop behaving violently. Weeks or months later he might say, "Okay, now it's time to work on the lying." Do we show that same patience with others?

Perhaps the best way to understand the Torah is to see it as something more than an inflexible set of laws. Similar to an archer aiming an arrow toward a target, the Torah offers guidance for how God wants us to live. God began by leading his people out of Egypt physically. Then he led them away from Egypt morally. The Bible speaks about the "path of righteousness" or the "path of life," bidding us to follow God's "way." And it is no coincidence that the early Christians also spoke of their own faith as the "Way."

Scholar William Webb talks about "redemptive movement," meaning that God's law moved the Israelites toward justice and compassion and away from the cruelty of the surrounding cultures.[13] The best way to discover its wisdom for today, he suggests, is not to fixate on individual laws in isolation from their context, but to trace their intended "trajectory," noting their movement through the Old and New Testaments. Then you can ask how the law gives direction within our culture today.

Consider an example. Deuteronomy contains laws allowing slavery. Does this mean that slavery is OK, that Walmart, for instance, would be perfectly within its right to start stocking human beings for sale? We scoff at such a ridiculous idea, but a literal reading of that passage in the Bible could lead to that conclusion. Though the Torah didn't outlaw slavery, which was widely practiced and accepted in the ancient world, it put humanitarian limits on it. For instance, according to the Torah, all slaves were to be exempt from servitude one day a week, and Israelite slaves were to go free after six years. The Torah even went so far as to say: "If a slave has taken refuge with you, do not hand them over to their master. Let them live among you wherever they like and in whatever town they choose. Do not oppress them" (Deuteronomy 23:15–16). This may not strike us as progressive until we realize that in every other culture of that period, the penalty for not returning a slave was death.

The "redemptive movement" of the Torah was always toward releasing the oppressed. Later on, this message is clearly enunciated by the Old Testament prophets and by Jesus himself. The best way to interpret how God is directing us in the present day is to understand the context in which the law first emerged and then to trace its movement throughout Scripture.

What the Torah Can Teach Us

A. J. Jacobs is a journalist who quips that he is officially a Jew in much the same way as Olive Garden is officially an Italian restaurant. That is to say, he is not a religious Jew. Casting about for his next book project, Jacobs hit on the idea of spending an entire year attempting to live out the commands of the Bible literally. The resulting book, *The Year of Living Biblically*, has become a bestseller, regaling its readers with his sometimes hilarious attempts.

To get started, Jacobs decided to read through the Bible, noting every rule or guideline he could find. The result was seventy-two pages of notes, listing more than seven hundred rules. Over the course of the next year, he would do his best to keep every one of those commands, except those that were clearly illegal, like killing magicians or slaughtering oxen for sacrifice.

Reading that the Israelites ate cucumbers in Egypt, for instance, he decided to sow a packet of cucumber seeds in pots under grow lights in his New York apartment, hoping that he could leave cucumber "gleanings." That way he could fulfill Leviticus 19:9–10, "When you reap the harvest of your land, do not reap to the very edges of your field or gather the gleanings of your harvest . . . Leave them for the poor and the foreigner." His harvest was abundant—about a hundred dozen cucumbers, but all were prickly and inedible, about the size of a Good & Plenty candy.

One day, when Jacobs accidentally dropped a five-dollar bill, he decided to leave it on the ground for someone else to "glean." But the person behind him scooped it up and ran after him, saying, "You dropped this!" to which he stammered back, "No—it wasn't mine." To his dismay, Jacobs realized that he had just broken the command not to lie![14] Strict literalism didn't seem to work.

Of course we laugh at such antics. But what if we took a less literal approach? What might the ancient gleaning laws teach us? Think about the last time you dined out. How generous was that tip you left behind? Lois still remembers the paltry wage she made at her first job as an A&W carhop—$1.75 an hour when minimum wage was $3.35. To her, tips weren't just about the money, much as she needed it. They were about experiencing people's care as they left behind some of their "harvest" out of consideration for a "gleaner" like her.

Perhaps you saw the episode of *The Simpsons* in which the nuclear reactor where Homer Simpson works is beginning to have a meltdown. In a panic, his wife Marge prays: "Dear Lord, if you spare this town from becoming a smoking hole in the ground, I'll try to be a better Christian. I don't know what I can do. Ummm . . . oh, the next time there's a canned food drive, I'll give the poor something they actually like, instead of old lima beans and pumpkin mix."[15] Maybe we can avoid Marge's mistake by taking inventory of our own cupboards on a regular basis. Instead of extracting what we least like, we could bag up a few of our favorite foods for the local food pantry.

Look around your neighborhood, your church, your community.

Surely there is someone with little resources who could "glean" from the overflowing abundance of God's blessings to you. Performing these kinds of *mitzvot* will help you become more generous, and a little more like your Rabbi Jesus.

The Goal of the Torah

Paul tells us in Romans 10:4 that the "*telos*" of the law is Christ, which we traditionally translate, "Christ is the end of the law" (see NIV 1984). If the Torah is God's teaching for how to live as his people, in what sense did the law come to an end? Let's look more deeply into Paul's words.

As Christians, we believe that Jesus took upon himself the punishment we deserve for our inability to keep all of God's commands. As such, he brought the law to the end of its ability to separate us from God because of our sin. And for that we rejoice.

Jesus was also the "end" of the law in another way. For thousands of years, God's policy had been to separate Israel from the influence of its pagan neighbors. He did this, as we said, so that he could train his people properly, like a parent teaching a small child. But Christ gave a new command that went in the opposite direction. Now, instead of maintaining their distance from nonbelievers, his followers were to go out into the world and make disciples of all nations (Matthew 28:19). No longer would the law keep Gentiles apart from God.

The instant Peter made his first visit to a Gentile house, the old policy of separation collided with the new policy of outreach. According to Jewish law, Peter could not accept Cornelius's hospitality because Gentiles were "unclean."[16] But God released him from the ancient purity laws by giving him a vision in which unclean animals were declared "clean." With the guidance of the Spirit, the church later ruled in Acts 15 that Gentile believers did not need to take on the covenant of the Torah given to the Jews on Mount Sinai. The "dividing wall of hostility" that the ceremonial laws put up in order to keep the Gentiles away was suddenly torn down (Ephesians 2:14).

But while *telos* can mean "end" or "termination," it can also mean "goal," "perfection," or "culmination." Paul's wording here is deliberately vague, conveying two ideas at once.[17] He was also proclaiming that Christ is the climactic *goal* of the law of Moses, the living embodiment of the holiness and compassion toward which the Torah is aiming. Jesus is the "Word made flesh." He is the only one who has ever perfectly lived out the Torah.

As Gentiles we are not obligated to keep the ceremonial laws given on Mount Sinai, but we can still discover great wisdom within the Torah because Christ himself was the goal toward which the Torah was aiming. And this is our goal too—to be filled with the love and goodness of our Lord and Rabbi, Jesus.

We've talked about how the Jewish people understood the law. But how did Jesus himself understand it? Did his approach differ radically from the rabbis of his day? How can understanding Jesus's relationship to the law transform our own attitudes and actions? In the next chapter, we'll learn more.

AT THE FEET OF THE RABBI

1. Think of ways to be more up front about your faith. Try wearing or carrying something that can function as a *tzitzit* for a week—perhaps a piece of jewelry or a spiritual book to read at lunchtime. Remind yourself that you are representing Christ to everyone around you.

2. Unlike other ancient law codes, the Torah emphasizes caring for widows and orphans. Because of how difficult it was for single-parent families to survive in that age, an "orphan" could mean either a child bereft of parents or a child without a father.[18] Think of "orphans" you know and find ways to befriend them either as a "big brother" or "big sister," or by enfolding them in the warmth of your family.

3. Leviticus 19:16 says, "Do not go about spreading slander among your people." See if you can go a week (perhaps only a day?) without saying something negative about someone. Then aim even higher by speaking positively about someone you dislike.

4. Ask God to show you at least one *mitzvah* (popularly defined as a "good deed") that you can perform every day this week.

CHAPTER 12

Jesus and the Torah

O put into our hearts to understand and to discern,
to mark, learn and teach, to heed, to do and to fulfill
in love all the words of instruction in Thy Torah.

FROM THE TRADITIONAL PRAYER RECITED BEFORE SAYING THE SHEMA

As dawn spreads over the Sea of Galilee, the grey-blue silhouette of the surrounding mountain ridge grows distinct against the brightening sky. All is quiet except for the soft thumping of waves lapping against the wooden hulls of boats moored close to shore, and the squawk of birds flitting about in the rustling reeds along the rocky edge. Linen nets are laid out to dry on the beach, their delicate layers carefully disentangled from the night's catch of fish. Just up the bank lies Capernaum, a quaint fishing village, rising to greet another day.

This is the Cove of the Sower, a rounded inlet on the western edge of the lake. Matthew's gospel tells us that this was the setting for Jesus's parable about the farmer casting seeds in different types of soil. It is also the likely setting for the world's most famous sermon—the Sermon on the Mount. If you hike to the top of the hill above the cove, you will find the Church of the Beatitudes, marking the traditional site. As you stand, facing the Sea of Galilee, you realize what that hillside must have looked like two thousand years ago when Jesus was preaching—a great multicolored quilt of people packed together and listening intently. You wonder what it would have been like to have been part of that crowd, to have heard that most extraordinary of rabbis.

> Blessed are the poor in spirit . . .
> Blessed are the meek . . .
> Blessed are the merciful . . .

Jesus's preaching seems effortless, his words so clear, as though he is speaking directly to you.

But how is it possible that Jesus could have been heard by thousands of people without a megaphone to amplify his voice? A number of years ago, biblical scholar B. Cobbey Crisler discovered the answer in the land itself. He found that the hillside near this rounded shoreline forms a natural amphitheater.[1] Because of the acoustical properties of the surrounding land, a person could stand at the bottom of the hill or sit in a boat just offshore and be heard by someone far up the side of the hill. So good are the acoustics that the speaker could talk in a normal voice and be heard. Crisler estimates that eight to ten thousand people could have sat within listening distance of Jesus.

Knowing about the acoustics of the land solves one mystery about Jesus's preaching. But others linger, especially questions about the sermon itself, which contains some of his most challenging words.

Imagine yourself as a first-century resident of Capernaum. You have heard Jesus speak and seen him heal people, but you have also heard a lot of criticism. Some have accused him of being soft on the law, saying that Jesus is undermining the Torah and leading people astray. So now, as you sit on the hillside with thousands of others, you listen carefully to what Jesus is telling the crowd:

> Do not think that I have come to abolish the Law or the Prophets; I have not come to abolish them but to fulfill them. For truly I tell you, until heaven and earth disappear, not the smallest letter, not the least stroke of a pen, will by any means disappear from the Law until everything is accomplished. (Matthew 5:17–18)
>
> . . . unless your righteousness surpasses that of the Pharisees and the teachers of the law, you will certainly not enter the kingdom of heaven. (5:20)

You have heard that it was said, "You shall not commit

adultery." But I tell you that anyone who looks at a woman lustfully has already committed adultery with her in his heart. If your right eye causes you to stumble, gouge it out and throw it away. (5:27–29)

Instead of loosening things up, Jesus seems to be tightening the screw. Rather than merely repeating the stricture against adultery, for instance, he tells you that a mere lustful glance makes one guilty of adultery. And then he links anger to the sin of murder. Ouch!

Modern Christians cherish the notion that Jesus came to free us from the unbearable burden of laws we cannot keep, but here Jesus seems to be saying the exact opposite. So is the good news really as good as we think it is? Realizing that Jesus sets the bar higher and not lower *is* good news, once you understand what he was saying.

Perhaps listening to this famous sermon once again, this time with the ears of a first-century Jew, will help us grasp the true brilliance of his message. Perhaps it will also help unravel some of the "knots" in Matthew 5–7, the passage that contains the Sermon on the Mount.

Catching Jesus's Drift

The first thing you notice is that Jesus wastes no time putting the crowd on the alert. He makes it clear that he has no intention of weakening the Torah, which has shaped and guided the Jewish people for many centuries:

> For truly I tell you, until heaven and earth disappear, not the smallest letter, not the least stroke of a pen, will by any means disappear from the Law until everything is accomplished. Therefore anyone who sets aside one of the least of these commands and teaches others accordingly will be called least in the kingdom of heaven, but whoever practices and teaches these commands will be called great in the kingdom of heaven. (Matthew 5:18–19)

As a first-century Jew, you pick up the rabbinic lingo immediately.

When Jesus speaks about "the least stroke of a pen" ("one jot or one tittle" in the King James Version), you recognize that this is an idiom meaning "to the most microscopic detail."

The *yod* is the smallest Hebrew letter, and it looks like a large apostrophe: י Calligraphers embellish it with a tiny hook, or a "thorn," called a *kots*. Remarkably, this Hebrew idiom is still in use today. Former Israeli Defense Minister Shaul Mufaz declared that he would hold the Palestinian leadership accountable for fighting terror *al kotso shel yod*, "to the thorn of a *yod*."[2]

Jesus is using this idiom to emphatically declare that not one word or letter will be removed from God's Torah. Even the decorations on the letters will last forever. What an incredible statement from the One who has himself come to be known as the Alpha and Omega, or the A to Z!

You also recognize another Jewish idiom concerning "abolishing" and "fulfilling" the law. To "fulfill" a law could simply mean doing what it says. But when Jesus contrasts "fulfilling" with "abolishing" the law, you know he is employing a rabbinic idiom. In this case, to "fulfill the Law" means *to properly interpret the Torah*. In contrast, the phrase "abolish the Law" means the opposite—to *cancel or nullify the Torah* by misinterpreting it. Both of these idioms arise from the assigned task of every rabbi—to interpret just how the Torah applies to daily life. When rabbis disagreed, they would accuse each other of "nullifying" the Torah.[3]

Imagine, for a moment, that a new pastor comes to town with a shocking set of sermons. One week he preaches that underestimating your income on your taxes is fine as long as it allows you to give more to the church. The next week he says that watching adult videos is OK, as long as you don't have an affair. The pastor's interpretation of the laws against lying and adultery undermine your ability to live by God's Word. He has "abolished" God's laws by misinterpreting them.

On at least one occasion, Jesus leveled this charge against the Pharisees, accusing them of nullifying the law to honor one's mother and father by saying that possessions declared *corban* (dedicated to God) could not be released to support one's elderly parents (Mark 7:11–12).

But the religious leaders made the same accusation against him, saying that his teaching was undermining the Torah. Jesus responded in the Sermon on the Mount by saying that he was not misinterpreting God's law, but bringing it to its best understanding. Furthermore, he said, if any of his disciples twisted or misinterpreted its least command, they would be considered "least" in his kingdom. Jesus's entire ministry as a rabbi was devoted to getting to the heart of God's Torah through what he said and how he lived.

Certainly Jesus fulfilled the law by obeying it perfectly. But as a rabbi, he also "fulfilled" it by clarifying its meaning and enlightening people about how God truly wanted them to live.

Jesus, the Rabbis, and the Law

How did Jesus's teachings about the law compare to the teachings of other rabbis? As we have said, rabbinic rulings on how to apply the Written Torah to daily life were referred to as "Oral Torah." Such interpretations of the Written Torah were circulated by word of mouth for several centuries before they were written down about AD 200. The Oral Torah was developed in response to the need to apply the law in different circumstances and cultural contexts. For instance, the Written Torah forbade working on the Sabbath. But what exactly constituted work? And what did it mean to "keep the Sabbath holy"? The rabbis' legal decisions for how the Torah should be obeyed were called halakhah (ha-lah-KAH), which can be translated "the path that one walks." By their rulings, the rabbis were trying to show people how to walk in the ways of God's commands.

One important principle of rabbinic

Halakhah and Haggadah

Halakhah comes from the Hebrew word for "walking" and refers to how the Torah is applied to your "walk" in life. It refers to rabbinic legal interpretation of the Torah. (Notice that "Torah" is not understood this way, but as "instruction" or "teaching.") Rabbis, including Jesus, taught both *halakhah* (ethics and law) and *haggadah* (stories to explain the Scriptures). (The *Haggadah* is also the name of the book of liturgy traditionally read at a Passover Seder.)

interpretation involved "putting a fence around the Torah."[4] The rabbis reasoned that it would be easier for people to live within God's laws if they enacted rulings that prevented them from even getting close to breaking them. For instance, no one was to handle tools on the Sabbath lest the temptation to work become too strong to resist.

The rabbis were like worried parents intent on protecting their children from straying into the road by building a fence three hundred yards away from another fence constructed at the edge of a busy highway. And though the rabbis' intentions were good, this practice opened the door to rigidity and legalism, making it easy to understand Jesus's scathing criticism of some of their hairsplitting decisions:

> "You say, 'If anyone swears by the temple, it means nothing; but anyone who swears by the gold of the temple is bound by that oath.' You blind fools! Which is greater: the gold, or the temple that makes the gold sacred?" (Matthew 23:16–17)

Jesus was not speaking against God's law but against perverting the law, something to which many of the Pharisees would also have objected.[5]

Contrary to popular misconception, the rabbis were not teaching "works righteousness"—that you need to earn your salvation by observing laws. They assumed that Jews would be saved, not because of anything they did, but because of their election as God's chosen people. The Mishnah said, "All Israel has a share in the world to come."[6] This is why some Jews insisted that Gentile Christians convert to Judaism and observe the law; they felt that *only* Israel could be saved. Paul's letters revolve around this controversy.

Elsewhere in Matthew 23 Jesus lists seven "woes" against the errors of the Pharisees. You may be surprised to learn that the rabbis themselves had formulated a nearly identical list! Their list included seven types of Pharisees, each one caricatured as falling into an error: legalism, pride, hypocrisy, and so on. Only the last Pharisee, who serves God out of love, escapes criticism. Obviously, the Pharisees weren't afraid to recognize the flaws in their own movement. As David Stern points out, Jesus was leveling a "within-the-family" criticism aimed at making his Jewish brothers live up to their high calling, an aim in which he partly succeeded.[7]

It's important to realize that not all Pharisees thought alike, just as not all Episcopalians, Presbyterians, or Baptists think alike. There were, however, two predominant groups of Pharisees during Jesus's time: the disciples of Shammai, known for their strictness, and the disciples of Hillel, known for their greater leniency. Jesus's criticisms were often leveled against the more stringent policies of Shammai.[8] Jesus sided with them on at least one occasion, however, when asked whose side he took in the case of divorce (Matthew 19:1–9).

Far from rejecting the rabbinic discussions swirling around him, Jesus actively engaged in them. He could hardly have ignored the debates since people were always asking his opinion on key issues of the day. Though he didn't closely associate with the Pharisees, he declared their rulings authoritative, saying, "The teachers of the law and the Pharisees sit in Moses' seat. So you must be careful to do everything they tell you. But do not do what they do, for they do not practice what they preach" (Matthew 23:2–3).[9] In this case, Jesus was not objecting to their rulings but to their failure to live by them. Like any idealistic group or movement, the Pharisees were not immune to the personal failings of its members. Jesus must have thought the Pharisees close enough to the truth to want to correct their errors. Why else would he have accepted their supper invitations and engaged them in debate?

Let's return to the Sermon on the Mount. Imagine for a moment that you are packed into the hillside along with the rest of the crowd,

Pharisees

The Pharisees were one of the most influential groups in the New Testament period. Most were common laborers who devoted their spare time to study and teaching. They carefully studied the Torah, the first five books of the Scriptures, to discover how best to live according to the law. It was the Pharisees, not the Sadducees, Zealots, or Essenes, who determined the character of rabbinic Judaism after the fall of the temple in AD 70.

above the glittering waters of the Sea of Galilee. The longer you listen, the more uncomfortable you become. The crowd is hushed, as though everyone is holding their breath, listening as Jesus compares lustful thoughts to adultery and anger to murder. His examples are hitting a little too close to home. Then it dawns on you that Jesus is himself employing the rabbinic method of "fencing in" the Torah by telling the crowd that small sins lead to greater sins, advocating that you set up boundaries against great evils by avoiding small ones.

This idea of linking small sins to greater ones was common among the rabbis. Listen to a rabbinic comment on laws from Leviticus: "He who violates, 'Love your neighbor as yourself,' will ultimately violate, 'You shall not hate your brother in your heart,' and 'You shall not take vengeance nor bear any grudge,' until in the end he will come to shedding blood."[10] The rabbis wisely noted that the consequences of sin slope ever downward:

> Not loving your neighbor ⅂
> Hating him in your heart ⅂
> Taking revenge on him ⅂
> Taking your neighbor's life!

Both Jesus and the rabbis were preaching that the time to avoid sin is when it is small, before we slip any further down the slope. Like Cain, sin crouches at the door of our hearts. It only takes one click to open a porn site, and a few visits to get addicted. One flirtatious exchange with an attractive coworker can open the door to an affair. The rabbis said, "At first the evil inclination is like the thread of a spider's web, and in the end it is like the ropes of a wagon."[11]

Later rabbis also preached about sin by comparing small sins to greater ones. Listen to what they had to say about gossip:

"To which is gossip more similar, robbery or murder?"

"Murder, because robbers can always give back what they've stolen, but gossips can never repair the damage they've done."

To them, humiliating someone publicly was also like murder, because "the pain of humiliation is more bitter than death." The rabbis called such sin "whitening the face" because when a person's face pales with shame, it's as if the pallor of death has overtaken him or her. "Therefore," they said, "one should rather fling himself into a fiery furnace than humiliate someone in public."[12]

Such comments remind us of Jesus's striking exhortations to cut off your hand or pluck out your eye should they cause you to sin (also in the Sermon on the Mount, Matthew 5:29–30). The rabbis knew the great damage that even tiny sins can do. A little bit of gossip can ruin a reputation. One sharp retort can ignite a war. The goal of their exaggerations was to impress upon their listeners the dire consequences of sin. Jesus, too, was urging his listeners to avoid evil at all costs. His strong warnings express his anguish at the destruction that ensues when we do not resist temptation at the very beginning.

A Different Kind of Rabbi

As we have pointed out, Jesus's teaching style was similar to that of other rabbis. He employed many of the same idioms and methods of logic. But there was a critical difference.

Imagine once again that you are sitting on that hillside above the Sea of Galilee. As Jesus concludes his great sermon, you hear the excited murmur of the crowd. People are buzzing with the same question: Just who is this extraordinary rabbi? Matthew sums up the crowd's response, saying that the people "were amazed at his teaching, because he taught as one who had authority, and not as their teachers of the law" (Matthew 7:28–29). Unlike other rabbis, this rabbi spoke with great authority, as though he knew the mind of God—and this was the essential difference.

Hillel and Shammai

Hillel and Shammai were famous Jewish scholars who lived just prior to the time of Jesus. Shammai was active in the first century BC and was known for his strict approach to interpreting the laws of the Torah. Hillel lived slightly later and was active between 30 BC and AD 10. He was known for his gentleness and moderation in the interpretation of the law. His school of disciples often debated the disciples of Shammai over their stricter interpretations of Jewish law. These debates shed light on the context of Jesus's sayings.

Many of the other rabbis tended to focus on defining the minimum requirements of the law. They tried to outline exactly what you should and should not do to stay within the law. This approach makes sense, since by nature, laws are limited to defining the least good thing you can do and still stay within the boundaries: don't murder, don't steal, don't work on the Sabbath. The rabbis lacked the authority to say, "This is what God *really* meant when he told us to keep the Sabbath holy." Who could know that but God himself? So their strategy was to keep tightening the minimums, hoping that doing so would bring people closer and closer to holiness.

While others worked on defining the boundaries, Jesus took the opposite approach. Instead of focusing on minimums, he focused on maximums, speaking about the ultimate *aims* of the law. As the author of the Torah, Jesus alone was able to explain its true intention. Like other rabbis, Jesus's goal was to teach his followers how to do God's will. But he did it by bringing the Torah to its greatest expression.[13]

Case in point: compare the way Hillel summarized the Torah to the way Jesus summarized it forty years later. One day, an impatient Gentile asked Hillel to explain the entire Torah while standing on one foot. Hillel's response was brilliant: "Whatever is hateful to you, do not do to your fellow. This is the whole Torah and the rest is commentary, go and learn it."[14]

Hillel clearly summarized the law. Indeed, you could even repeat his formulation while standing on one foot! Those who followed this teaching could achieve a minimum standard of conduct, keeping them safely within the boundaries of the Torah.

But listen to Jesus's answer. He says: "Love your neighbor as yourself." By flipping Hillel's formulation, Jesus compels us to focus on the maximum, pointing out the goal of following God's will.[15] The difference between Hillel's approach and Jesus's seems subtle, but it is revolutionary. Most of us can find it in our power to avoid being hateful. But how hard it can be to love our neighbors as ourselves!

Let's look at how this might play out in our own lives:

When there's a snowstorm . . .

Hillel says—shovel your sidewalk so no one will slip and hurt themselves.

Jesus says—shovel your sidewalk and then shovel your neighbor's sidewalk too.

When your little sister borrows your clothes . . .

Hillel says—don't ransack her closet.

Jesus says—open your closet door and see what else she might like to wear.

When you are pinched financially . . .

Hillel says—don't steal.

Jesus says—look around to see who's worse off than you and find a way to help.

When someone annoys you . . .

Hillel says—don't bad-mouth that person.

Jesus says—find something kind to say to such a person.

If someone forces you to go one mile . . .

Hillel says—go with him.

Jesus says—go with him two miles.

The Challenge to Go Beyond

Ultimately, Jesus is not handing out a list of tougher rules and regulations, nor is he raising the bar to make life miserable. The intent of the Sermon on the Mount is not to make us run harder and jump higher, but to help us redirect our aim. Jesus is saying, "Don't live by the minimum!" Don't say to yourself, as long as I don't commit adultery, it's fine to lust. Don't say that as long as I don't kill anyone, I can be furious with them. If you want to be part of God's redemptive kingdom on earth, don't ask how little you can do, but ask how much you can do to please your Father in heaven. By changing our aim we are released from the burden of paying attention to infinitesimal rules designed to keep us out of trouble so that we can use our energy to love God more passionately.

Imagine for a moment that you have a date with someone you've admired for a long time. You really want the evening to go well, so you solicit information from her younger brother. He passes on several suggestions to prevent you from fouling things up:

Don't suggest an Italian restaurant, because she hates pasta.
Don't mention that you love boxing, because she thinks it's barbaric.
Don't wear baggy pants or an oversize T-shirt, because she'll write you off.
Let her pick the movie.

The list goes on and on. You do your best to avoid every single pitfall, fearful lest you offend your date. But the evening is a dud and no wonder! Focusing on minimums is no way to spark a passionate relationship. Jesus wants us to passionately pursue the maximum in our relationship with God.

This idea of "going beyond the minimum" is actually the predominant theme of the Sermon on the Mount. Over and over Jesus uses a formula to make his point: "You have heard that it was said . . . But I tell you . . ."

You have heard that you can take vows in God's name, but I tell you to be a person with so much integrity that your yes and no are as good as an oath. You have heard that you can punish people in the measure they have hurt you, but I tell you to turn the other cheek. You have heard that you are to love your neighbor and hate your enemy, but I tell you to love your enemies. Loan people your money, carry their burdens, go the extra mile. Do everything you can to show that you are just like your Father in heaven.

No one can legislate what can be done purely out of love. So what did Jesus mean by exhorting his followers to display a "righteousness

[that] surpasses that of the Pharisees and the teachers of the law" (Matthew 5:20)? He may not have been speaking about outdoing particular individuals in their observance of the law, but about *going beyond* what the official interpreters of the law said you should do. The passage could then be read, "Do *more* than what the finest interpreters of the law say you must do."

This idea of "going beyond the minimum" was one for which the rabbis later formulated a name. They called it *hasidut* (ha-see-DOOT), which is often translated "piety." It means to walk closely with God and to be utterly obedient to him. A *hasid* (ha-SEED), or pious person, eagerly asks the question, "What more can I do to please you?" An Orthodox rabbi describes the idea of being a *hasid* as someone who "does not do only what he is told, but looks for ways to fulfill G-d's will. This requires intelligence and planning; one must anticipate just what G-d wants of him and how he can best use his talents and abilities in service of his Creator." This rabbi is quick to distinguish real piety from "mock" piety, which involves showy displays of fasting or prayer. Real piety is "careful, planned and responsible service of G-d. We are not to sacrifice ourselves for G-d with self-destructive acts of devotion; we are to *live* for Him."[16] (Note that substituting the "o" in God with a hyphen is out of reverence for the name of God, to not use it in vain.)

Salvation Is Only the First Step

The Sermon on the Mount was not a revolution against the Torah, but a revolution in understanding how to live out the Torah. How might you have responded, sitting on that ancient hillside? Perhaps you would have felt both challenged and thrilled by what you heard, realizing that Jesus was probing the Torah even more deeply than the great Hillel. This rabbi seemed to have a remarkable grasp of the heart and mind of God. Furthermore, he was not exhorting you to become stricter than the strictest but to model your life on the character of God himself by living in a way that reflected his extravagant goodness.

The Sermon on the Mount not only redirects our aim in life, it tells us something else—that we are not to live as though we have a ticket to heaven tucked snugly inside our pockets, as though we merely need to sit back and enjoy the ride. "Accepting Christ" is only the beginning, not the ultimate goal. Likewise, evangelism is vital, but so is discipleship. To go no deeper is to risk being like the seed that fell not on good soil but on rocky ground, sprouting up but bearing little or no fruit. Focusing solely on God's free gift of salvation is focusing on the minimum.

It is thrilling to see a person come to Christ, but that isn't the whole story. People who don't exhibit the fruit of a Christian life are like a couple who longs for a child, but once that child is born can't wait for her to grow up so that they can regain their freedom. Parenting is for the long haul—it's a twenty-four-hour-a-day calling that often asks you to deny your own desires for the sake of your child. You give it everything you've got, even if you know you'll never be perfect. That's what it's like to walk with Christ.

Hasidut

Hasidut is Hebrew for "piety." It comes from the word hesed, meaning "loving-kindness." In Hebrew, a person who is pious is a hasid (hasidim, plural). Hasidic is an adjective describing ultra-Orthodox Jews, often in reference to a Jewish movement that began in the 1700s, which emphasized mysticism and piety.

Saying yes to Christ is the first step of a great adventure with plenty of surprises and challenges along the way. Because of Christ's enabling grace, we can make love the central aim and great fulfillment of our lives. Ultimately, God's love is what frees us from rigidity and legalism. And God's Spirit is what enables us to pattern our life on Christ's.

What might such a passionate life look like? It might look like a million different things, but here's the story of what it looks like in the life of one man, a Vietnamese Christian by the name of Tong Phuoc Phuc. A forty-one-year-old building contractor, Phuc lives in a country with one of the highest abortion rates on earth. A few years ago, he decided to purchase a plot of land in which to bury the tiny bodies of unborn children, whose tragedies he keenly felt. Everyone who heard about his plan, including doctors, neighbors, and even his own wife, thought he was crazy. Why would anyone spend his savings to purchase a cemetery? But Phuc's determination to honor these unborn children produced an unexpected result. When word got around about his efforts, women who had themselves undergone abortions began visiting the cemetery in order to pray and burn incense. They must have wondered whether the graves of their own children were among the seven thousand that had already been dug.

Phuc spoke to the women, urging them to tell others who were considering an abortion to talk to him first. Since then he and his family have sheltered several women with unwanted pregnancies. Thus far, sixty babies have been born and twenty-seven have gone home with their mothers. "I will continue this job until the last breath of my life," he says. "I will encourage my children to take over to help other people who are underprivileged."[17]

You can't manufacture the kind of passion so evident in this man's voice. Only the love of Christ can compel a person to respond to a need with so much generosity.

Love, the Essence of the Torah

Both before and after Jesus, the rabbis were fascinated by one important question: "What is the greatest principle of the Torah?"[18] They were looking for the one abiding principle that would embody all the rest. Hillel's answer—"Whatever is hateful to you, do not do to your fellow"—was one response. About a hundred years after Jesus, Rabbi Akiva said: "You shall love your neighbor as yourself—this is the great principle [clal gadol] of the Torah."

Later, the Talmud records a conversation in which the rabbis used key Scriptures to summarize the 613 commandments of the law (as they counted them) into fewer and fewer precepts, and finally into only one.[19] Micah, they said, reduced the law to just three things: "To act justly . . . to love mercy, and to walk humbly with your God" (Micah 6:8); Isaiah reduced it to two: "Maintain justice and do what

Shema

To pray the *Shema* is to commit one's self to loving God and obeying his laws. *Shema* is the Hebrew word that begins this famous passage from Deuteronomy: "Hear, O Israel: The LORD our God, the LORD is one." *Shema* means "hear," but it implies action, also meaning "take heed" and "obey." The entire Shema is composed of three Bible passages: Deuteronomy 6:4–9; 11:13–21; and Numbers 15:37–41.

is right" (Isaiah 56:1); and, finally, Amos and Habakkuk reduced it to one: "Seek the LORD and live" (Amos 5:6), or "The righteous person will live by his faithfulness" (Habakkuk 2:4).

Hearing these conversations tells us that when Jesus was asked, "Which is the greatest commandment in the Law?" (Matthew 22:36), he was faced with the burning question of his age: What was the one abiding principle of the Torah? His answer was to quote not one but two passages, beginning with the *Shema*: "Love the LORD your God with all your heart and with all your soul and with all your strength" (Deuteronomy 6:5). Then he quoted from Leviticus 19:18: "'Do not seek revenge or bear a grudge against anyone among your people, but love your neighbor as yourself. I am the LORD.'"

But why two commandments, and not one? Jesus was being typically Jewish in setting two truths in tension with each other. Remember Tevye, in *Fiddler on the Roof*, who used to say, "on the one hand . . . but on the other hand"? In his book, *The Gospel According to Moses: What My Jewish Friends Taught Me about Jesus*, Christian novelist Athol Dickson points out how both are essential:

> If I try to love God with all my heart and soul and mind to the exclusion of everything else, I exclude the love of my neighbor and risk viewing her as a distraction, a *thing* that interferes with my devotion to God. This is the mistake of pious hermits and those of us who prefer churches or synagogues to soup kitchens. But if I center all of my attention on loving my neighbor as myself and forget about loving God, I find it impossible to maintain that neighborly love because I am no longer connected to the Source

of love itself. This is the mistake of secular humanists. True love must flow from God through me to everyone else . . . So is "love the Lord" the greatest commandment or is "love my neighbor"? The answer is "yes." And "yes."[20]

Several years ago, Ann was part of a group of Christians that split down the middle. Like most such divisions, it was messy, hurtful, and prolonged. Accusations flew through the air thick as mosquitoes in July. Sometimes it was difficult to know who or what to believe, especially when people she admired started acting like backroom politicians jockeying for position. The whole thing was depressing and bewildering. She felt surrounded by a cloud of confusion.

Then, in the midst of it, she remembered something vital. The words popped into her head like a message from God: *Just remember the two great commandments. That's all you need.* Those simple words put everything to rest for her, clearing away the fog. As she steered a course through that difficult time, she knew what her guiding principles needed to be: to love God and to love her neighbor. Come to think of it, the two commands that Jesus singled out can help us navigate any dispute. Wherever we are and whatever we face—at home, at church, or in the workplace—we can rely on the counsel of the wisest of rabbis.

Jesus was saying that love is the best possible interpretation of the laws of the Torah—the ultimate summation of everything that God has taught in the Scriptures. In rabbinic lingo, you might even say that "love *fulfills* the law." In fact, Paul said exactly that: "For the whole Law is *fulfilled* in one word . . . 'You shall love your neighbor as yourself'" (Galatians 5:14 NASB, italics added). Not only is love the best interpretation of the law, Paul says that loving your neighbor is also the ultimate way to live it out:

Let no debt remain outstanding, except the continuing debt to love one another, for whoever loves others has *fulfilled the law.* The commandments, "You shall not commit adultery," "You shall not murder," "You shall not steal," "You shall not covet," and whatever other command there may be, are summed up in this one command: "Love your neighbor as yourself." Love does no harm to a neighbor. Therefore *love is the fulfillment of the law.* (Romans 13:8–10, italics added)

Paul took Jesus's message to the world, telling us that when we love our neighbor, we have truly achieved the goal of every single commandment. We have done what God has asked.

Ultimately, for both Jews and Gentiles, love of God and love of neighbor is what fulfills the Torah. And as John so eloquently tells us:

This is love: not that we loved God, but that he loved us and sent his Son as an atoning sacrifice for our sins. Dear friends, since God so loved us, we also ought to love one another. No one has ever seen God; but if we love one another, God lives in us and his love is made complete in us. (1 John 4:10–12)

AT THE FEET OF THE RABBI

1. Read the Sermon on the Mount in Matthew 5–7. Try to picture yourself in the setting in which it was preached. Imagine that you are sitting on the hillside above the Sea of Galilee, listening carefully to what Jesus is saying. What are your questions? What is your prayer? Let the Holy Spirit pierce your heart with the words of this extraordinary rabbi.

2. What temptations do you tend to brush off as tiny and inconsequential? Write them down and then ask God to help you see where these might lead you. Then ask for wisdom to eliminate each from your life.

3. Rabbi Joseph Telushkin tells of a wealthy man who cursed frequently. In an effort to eliminate this bad habit, he made a deal with his rabbi, promising to donate $180 to a Jewish cause every time he cursed. What about making a similar deal with a friend you trust, promising to fine yourself whenever you lose your temper? "If you find this technique too expensive for your liking," Telushkin remarks, "do nothing at all to curb your temper. In the course of a few years, this approach will not cost you any money—but it might cost you your friends, your spouse, and your relationship with your children."[21]

CHAPTER 13

The Mysterious Kingdom of God

Let his name be glorified and sanctified throughout
the universe which he created according to his
purpose. May he bring about the reign of his kingdom
in your lifetime, in your days, and in the lifetime
of all of the house of Israel, speedily and soon![1]

FROM THE KADDISH, AN ANCIENT JEWISH PRAYER

In the back seat of her family's station wagon, Lois used to pass the time on the four-hour rides through the rolling, wooded hills of Wisconsin to her family's cabin by playing "Twenty Questions." Is it animal, vegetable, or mineral? Is it bigger than a deck of cards, smaller than an elephant, larger than an aardvark? With each yes or no answer her confidence would grow. She could feel herself honing in on the mystery object. But occasionally, just as she was about to declare the mystery solved, a surprising yes or no would get tossed back at her and she would realize she had been heading down the wrong track all along.

Sometimes it sounds as if Jesus was playing a kind of "Twenty Questions" with his disciples to pass the hours on their long walks from town to town discussing his mysterious kingdom.

It's like a mustard seed.
It's like a fisherman's net.
It's like a farmer who had a weedy field.

Jesus seemed always to be dropping clues rather than providing a flat-out definition for his disciples. Reading these, you may wonder whether there isn't a key, something simple to help us understand what Jesus was saying. Perhaps you've heard sermons that say, "The kingdom is the church," or "It's heaven," or "It's the reign of Christ when he returns," or "It's already but not yet." But then along comes another of Jesus's parables that makes no sense in light of the latest hypothesis— just like "Twenty Questions."

Honestly, many of Jesus's sayings about the kingdom have been head-scratchers for Christians over the centuries. What does it mean to "receive" the kingdom, or what does it mean that the kingdom comes "upon" someone? Is the kingdom something right now, or something in the future, or both? Why does it even matter?

For one thing, some interpretations of the kingdom have caused considerable anxiety among Christians. In *The Jesus I Never Knew*, Philip Yancey tells about the annual prophecy conferences he attended at his childhood church, in which silver-haired men would stand up and preach about the end times. Yancey writes:

> I listened in fear and fascination as they drew a straight line
> south from Moscow to Jerusalem and sketched in the movements
> of million-strong armies who would soon converge on Israel. I
> learned that the ten members of Europe's Common Market had
> recently fulfilled Daniel's prophecy about the beast with ten horns.
> Soon all of us would wear a number stamped on our foreheads, the
> mark of the beast, and be registered in a computer somewhere in
> Belgium. Nuclear war would break out and the planet would teeter
> on the brink of annihilation, until at the last second Jesus himself
> would return to lead the armies of righteousness.[2]

In high school Yancey took courses in Chinese while his brother studied Russian so that one of them could communicate with whatever army invaded. Over the years that followed, his views of the kingdom changed profoundly as he realized that "God is working not primarily through nations, but through a kingdom that transcends nations."[3]

Reading what Jesus has to say about the kingdom doesn't always clear things up. Take this well-known passage: "It is easier for a camel to go through the eye of a needle than for someone who is rich to enter the kingdom of God" (Mark 10:25). If Jesus is defining the entry requirements for heaven, it's hard to see how any rich person can ever be saved. Since most people in the developed world would be considered "rich" compared to the rest of the world, it sounds as though we are all headed toward an uncomfortably hot eternity. But is that what Jesus is saying?

Talk of kings and kingdoms can often seem irrelevant and archaic, conjuring pictures of autocrats and dictators or of the fairytales we read as children. Why can't we be content to simply think of God as a loving father or as a good friend? Because, even though the phrase "kingdom of God" may sound outdated to us, it was of the utmost importance to Jesus. In fact it was at the very heart of his mission, the reason he came to earth.

Modern readers find Jesus's words confusing precisely because his way of talking about the kingdom is so thoroughly *Jewish*. In fact, Jesus was not the only one talking about the kingdom. A larger discussion about it was taking place around him. Without access to what was being said, we are like people who overhear only one side of a telephone conversation trying to piece together the rest of it through guesswork. Tuning in to this two-thousand-year-old Jewish conversation will bring us greater clarity. It may even transform our understanding of Jesus's ministry and of the nature and character of God himself.

Let's listen to the kingdom sayings again through the ears of first-century Jews. As we do, we will begin to connect the dots, realizing that Jesus was building on certain Jewish ideas while rejecting others. We will also see just why he was so driven to share his message. As we join the conversation, we may even find that it speaks to our lives today.

Another Look at the Words

First, let's look at the words themselves. The Gospels use two different phrases—the "kingdom of heaven" and the "kingdom of God."

"Kingdom of heaven" is the phrase most often used in Matthew's gospel while "kingdom of God" is the phrase used in Mark, Luke, and John. Why the difference? Because in Jesus's day, and even now, Jewish people show their reverence for God's name by not pronouncing it. Instead they substitute a respectful euphemism like "heaven."[4]

Jesus did this too. For example, in his parable about the prodigal, the son says, "Father, I have sinned against *heaven* and against you" (Luke 15:21). We do the same thing when we say, "thank heavens" or "goodness knows." By using "kingdom of heaven," Matthew's gospel was preserving the culturally correct expression. The rest of the gospel writers used "kingdom of God" in order to communicate more clearly with their Greek audiences, who would not have understood that "heaven" meant "God."[5]

But there is yet more to be learned by looking beyond the English translation and examining the Hebrew phrase that Jesus probably used: *malkhut shamayim* (mahl-KOOT shah-MY-eem), an idiom common in rabbinic teaching in his day.[6] *Malkhut*, which we translate as "kingdom," sounds like a place or a government of some sort. But it really refers to an ancient sense of the word that describes the actions and dominion of a king—his reign and authority, and anyone who is under his authority. *Shamayim* is Hebrew for "sky" or "heavens." "Heaven," in "kingdom of heaven," always refers to God, not to a place.

In other words, a simple way of translating "kingdom of God" or "kingdom of heaven" would be *God's reign*, or *how God reigns*, or *those whom God reigns over*. This Hebrew phrase is a rich, multifaceted idiom that the rabbis used in ways we might find surprising, even though many of their ideas were similar to what Jesus himself taught about the kingdom.

It's enormously helpful to realize that the rabbis used this idiom in several different ways, just as Jesus did.[7] At times, Jesus agreed with and built on certain ideas that were already in circulation. At other times, he disagreed with prevailing ideas. At such times, his parables and sayings about the kingdom would have surprised or even shocked his Jewish listeners, designed as they were to reorient and expand their thinking.

Though the Jewish people believed God was going to redeem the world by bringing it under his reign, most didn't understand what kind of king he would be. That was the essence of Jesus's message—to explain that God was different than any king they had ever seen or imagined and that his Messiah was different as well.

Thy Kingdom Come

One of the most familiar phrases in the Lord's Prayer is this: "Thy kingdom come" (KJV). But what did Jesus mean by it? You might be surprised to learn that Jews have been praying in a similar way for thousands of years. Listen to the words of the *Alenu*, an ancient prayer that is still on the lips of Jews today.

> Therefore do we wait for you, O Lord our God, soon to behold your glory, when you will remove the abominations from the earth and idols shall be exterminated; when the world shall be regenerated by the kingdom of the Almighty, and all humankind invoke your name; when all the wicked of the earth shall return to you. Then all the inhabitants of the world shall perceive and confess that unto you every knee must bend, and every tongue swear . . . So will they accept the yoke of your kingdom, and you will be King over them speedily forever and ever. For yours is the kingdom, and to all eternity you will reign in glory, as it is written in your Torah: "The Lord shall reign forever and ever." And it is also said: "And the Lord shall be King over all the earth; on that day the Lord shall be One and His name be One."[8]

Even though ancient Jews believed that God already reigned over them, they prayed that the whole world would one day know and honor God. They wanted every nation on earth to repent and worship the true God of heaven.

This can help us understand the Lord's Prayer. To many of us, "thy kingdom come" sounds as if it's about Christ's second coming. But the *Alenu* shows us what it's really about—that all the world will come to worship God. The first three lines of the Lord's Prayer, then, voice our desire for God to expand his loving reign, bringing all people into relationship with him so that they might revere him and do his will. In effect, we are praying for the gospel to go forth. Instead of passively waiting for Jesus to return, we are asking God's help in making disciples of all nations.

Still, Jesus's prayer as well as many other Jewish prayers point out a gap between the ideal reign of God and the way he actually reigns in the present. They seem to be saying that God isn't king of the world just yet. Of course as creator, God is ultimately sovereign. But in rabbinic thinking, evil still fills the earth because the world has refused to acknowledge that God is its true King.

The Kingdom Is Here

Yet Jesus claimed that God's reign had definitely come to earth in his ministry. Jesus healed or cast out demons and then declared that the kingdom of God was "near" or "at hand" (Luke 10:9). This way of speaking of God's kingdom was unique to Jesus and essential to his message.[9]

One thing might confuse you—the English word "near" can be misleading, because it sounds as though Jesus is telling his friends that the kingdom is "close, but not quite." But it is likely that Jesus was using the Hebrew verb *karav*, which means intimately close. The prophet Isaiah, for instance, "came near" (*karav*) to his wife in Isaiah 8:3, and she conceived a son. How much nearer could the prophet get than that?

To make the point another way, some of Lois's Danish friends used to write her, warmly inviting her to "come stay by them." It sounded as though they wanted her to fly all the way to Denmark just to pitch a tent in their backyard. On the contrary, her friends were really inviting her into their home. In a similar way, nuances of language can make it sound as if Jesus is talking about God's reign being "not quite yet," when he is actually stating that it is already revealing itself on earth through his ministry.

But what exactly does it mean to say that God's "kingdom" had arrived in Jesus's ministry? It means that through Jesus, God was revealing his sovereignty. He was stepping into history and taking charge, defeating the gods of this world through the life, death, and resurrection of his Son.

Every week in their Sabbath liturgy, Jews recall Israel's miraculous redemption from Egypt with these words: "Your people saw your kingdom as you cleaved the sea before Moses." By this they are saying that when the Red Sea parted, God's power burst in upon creation in an astonishing way. It was as though a giant hand had suddenly reached out of the sky and parted the waves, allowing God's people to walk across while their enemies were swallowed up. By performing this great miracle of deliverance, God was showing his people (and his enemies) who is really in charge of the universe.[10]

Similarly, when Jesus walked through the land healing and delivering people, God's kingdom was visibly breaking into history, just as it had in Exodus. But now God's reign was revealing itself in a greater way than ever before as people experienced his saving, redeeming love.

After one dramatic incident of deliverance, Jesus's opponents accused him of using demonic powers to cast out demons. Listen closely to his response: "If I drive out demons by the *finger of God*, then the kingdom of God has come upon you" (Luke 11:20, italics added). Jesus was making a not-so-subtle reference to Exodus, to the scene in which the Egyptian magicians, after witnessing God's power in the plagues, exclaim, "This is the *finger of God*" (Exodus 8:19). It is at this moment that Pharaoh's hirelings realize they have been beaten. God's power is utterly beyond any demonic force they can conjure. In the same way, Jesus is saying that now is the moment when people should realize that his own power over demonic forces reveals his spiritual authority.[11]

Already Christ has stormed the beaches of Satan's kingdom, initiating his great defeat. Jesus is taking back prisoners, setting them free one life at a time. No wonder Jesus's words were so shocking to his accusers.

Let's go back for a moment to that scene at the Red Sea. Imagine that enormous crowd of people beginning to panic as they realize their peril. They are trapped between Pharaoh's advancing army and the roiling waters of the sea. With no way out, they know they are about to be slaughtered. Suddenly, everything changes. The winners become the losers and the losers the winners. For one dramatic moment the curtain is parted and everyone sees who is really on the throne.

Something similar can happen to us, though on a far smaller scale. For a time we may feel threatened by some kind of darkness, and life may seem to be swirling out of control. Then something happens to show us that God is with us. Ann remembers having that sensation when her father finally stopped drinking after living most of his life as an alcoholic. "Along with other family members," she says, "I had begged God for years to help him. If only God would reveal himself in some unmistakable way. If only he would give my father the desire to quit drinking. But the more I prayed, the worse he got, until he nearly died from alcohol poisoning. Then, when it was nearly too late, something remarkable did happen and my father stopped drinking. In the years that followed, as I saw a life in ruins being graciously rebuilt, I knew who was really in charge of the universe."

The Messiah and the Kingdom

Why was Jesus so focused on proclaiming that the kingdom of God had arrived on earth, and why did he link it to his ministry of physical healing and spiritual liberation? Jesus did this because *everyone expected the Messiah to bring God's kingdom to earth.*

Remarkably, some theologians have completely missed this point, mistakenly concluding that Jesus never claimed to be the Messiah. But Jesus's audience would have immediately recognized what he was saying—that he was making the shocking claim to be the fulfillment of God's great promises. Jesus employed a Jewish way of saying that he was the Christ, the Anointed King whom God had promised.[12]

From the very beginning, in Genesis, God had promised to anoint a king from the people of Israel to reign over the whole world (see Genesis 49:10). Listen to this beautiful messianic passage from the prophet Isaiah:

> For to us a child is born,
>> to us a son is given,
>> and the government will be on his shoulders.
> And he will be called
>> Wonderful Counselor, Mighty God,
>> Everlasting Father, Prince of Peace.
> Of the greatness of his government and peace
>> there will be no end.
> He will reign on David's throne
>> and over his kingdom,
> establishing and upholding it
>> with justice and righteousness
>> from that time on and forever. (Isaiah 9:6–7)

Jesus is all of the things Isaiah prophesied even though he is not yet reigning in his full glory. Though he is the Mighty God, the Gospels introduce him to us as the humble Prince of Peace. One day, though, he will be revealed as the King of kings and Lord of lords.

How can Jesus both bring God's reign to earth and yet speak of it as coming in the future? Listen to how Charles Colson explains it:

Probably the most significant event in Europe during World War II was D-Day, June 6, 1944, when the Allied armies stormed the beaches of Normandy. That attack guaranteed the eventual destruction of the Axis powers in Europe. Though the war continued with seeming uncertainties along the way, the outcome was in fact determined. But it wasn't until May 8, 1945—VE Day—that the results of the forces set in motion eleven months earlier were realized.

Colson goes on to write:

Christ's death and resurrection—the D-Day of human history—assure His ultimate victory. But we are still on the beaches. The enemy has not yet been vanquished, and the fighting is still ugly. Christ's invasion has assured the ultimate outcome, however—victory for God and His people at some future date. The second stage, which will take place when Christ returns, will complete God's rule over all the universe; His Kingdom will be visible without imperfection.[13]

A Different Kind of Kingdom

One after another, Jesus fulfilled the Old Testament promises about the Messiah. Why, then, didn't everyone immediately recognize him as such? Part of the reason was that Jesus disagreed with his contemporaries in significant ways. The Zealots and the Essenes expected the Messiah to be a military conqueror who would swiftly establish God's kingdom on earth. They were looking for a mighty king who would not only defeat Israel's enemies but who would destroy sinners within the nation itself. Even Jesus's disciples were convinced that his goal was to defeat Israel's enemies. After his resurrection, they asked him "Lord, are you at this time going to restore the kingdom to Israel?" (Acts 1:6).

It is not hard to understand the people's longing for God's judgment to fall on their enemies. Faithful Jews found many passages in their Scriptures about the great and dreadful "day of the Lord," a day in which he would come to judge their enemies.[14] They longed for that day as any oppressed people might. Of course there were hints of a "suffering servant" and a "Prince of Peace" in the prophetic thread, but a mighty king who judged the wicked and defeated Israel's enemies was the image that captured their imagination and fired their hopes.

Under Herod's rule, public crucifixion and torture were commonplace and taxes were oppressive. The only Jews who prospered were the tax collectors and the corrupt priests, who had sold out to the Romans. James Carroll,

Essenes

The Essenes were an ascetic group that existed during the time of Christ. Some withdrew into the Judean wilderness, where they lived with great ceremonial purity. Many of their first-century writings were discovered among the Dead Sea Scrolls. Some believe John the Baptist may have associated with an Essene community.

the author of *Constantine's Sword*, describes the Roman Empire as "the world's first totalitarian regime," asserting that "Jesus and his movement were born in the shadow of what would stand as the most grievous violence against the Jewish people until Hitler's attempt at a Final Solution."[15]

In their anguish, many Jews yearned for God to establish a kingdom of justice by purifying their nation from corruption and by freeing it from their Roman overlords. Jesus's message must have offended many of his listeners; how hard it would have been to hear that only by giving up vengeance could they enter God's true kingdom. No wonder so many failed to follow him.

We shouldn't, however, make the mistake of assuming that all Jews thought this way. The desire for God's judgment to come was characteristic of the Zealots and the Essenes, who longed for war. The teachings of Pharisees and later rabbis about the kingdom of God seem to be intended to refute their ideas.[16] Like Jesus, they saw God's reign as something here and now, and yet coming in the future. But they said the Messiah would only arrive when Israel lived according to God's law. Jesus used their ideas and built on them, yet said a new thing— that God's reign *had* come through his ministry of healing and his atoning work on the cross.[17]

Jesus's Teaching about the Kingdom

Even John the Baptist echoed the understanding that the Messiah would bring God's judgment when he said: "The ax is already at the root of the trees, and every tree that does not produce good fruit will be cut down and thrown into the fire" (Luke 3:9). John was saying that the ax is no longer lying idle in the shed; it's about to begin swinging and woe to the person who has not been living for God. John portrays Christ as coming with "fire" to destroy the wicked.

Apparently Jesus surprised John by not coming in the way that he and others had foreseen. In fact, some of Jesus's parables seem intended to redirect these expectations. Jesus told one parable in particular that seems like a response to John's prophetic words. While John spoke of an ax that was ready to chop down all the fruitless trees, Jesus said this:

> "A man had a fig tree growing in his vineyard, and he went to look for fruit on it but did not find any. So he said to the man who took care of the vineyard, 'For three years now I've been coming to look for fruit on this fig tree and haven't found any. Cut it down! Why should it use up the soil?'
>
> "'Sir,' the man replied, 'leave it alone for one more year, and I'll dig around it and fertilize it. If it bears fruit next year, fine! If not, then cut it down.'" (Luke 13:6–9)

Like John, Jesus describes a tree facing judgment. But unlike John's tree, the one Jesus speaks of will not be immediately chopped down but will be given another chance. Judgment will not come then, but later. Other parables of Jesus's about the kingdom have a similar theme, about the kingdom growing and prospering, but then judgment coming at the very end.[18]

Seeing the difference between how John and Jesus understood God's timeline reveals why John sent his disciples to ask, "Are you the one who is to come, or should we expect someone else?" (Matthew 11:3). Jesus responded by quoting Scripture after Scripture to reassure John that he was the one, but he was completing God's mission in a very different way from what John had ever imagined.

Was John the Baptist wrong, then, about Jesus? Not at all. His timing was just premature, as was the case with Jesus's own disciples. John knew that Jesus was the Christ, and that he would come in judgment. He just didn't know when. Jesus confirmed his role as judge when he spoke of his second coming, saying that at that time he would separate the sheep from the goats, judging the world for eternity (Matthew 25:31–46).

Transforming Our Understanding of God

Not only did Jesus's teaching about the kingdom change expectations regarding the Messiah, it also transformed his followers' understanding of God. Instead of a wrathful God intent on annihilating the opposition, Jesus revealed a compassionate God who was eager for mercy. The appeal to judgment would have seemed right by human standards—a logical response to the problem of evil. Of course, those who were most looking forward to God's judgment assumed that *they* were the righteous ones who would survive the judgment.

Jesus utterly disagreed with this point of view. Instead of linking God's reign to the violent overthrow of the Romans and to the destruction of sinners within the nation of Israel, he linked the kingdom to his works of healing and forgiveness. His would be a kingdom built up not by destroying the impure but by forgiving and atoning for their sins himself. In that way he would gain a kingdom of pure-hearted followers.

Once we understand the kingdom Jesus was describing, many of his sayings begin to fall into line. His kingdom is composed of the "poor in spirit," those who admit their guilt and ask forgiveness. "Blessed are the merciful" because they do not want to see God's judgment come on others and are shown mercy themselves. Though Christ's kingdom would at first seem hidden, like a tiny mustard seed it would grow to an enormous size, sheltering all kinds of people in its welcoming branches.

Ironically, some of the most faithful Jews had the most trouble embracing Jesus. They wanted a Messiah who would offer relief from their enemies, not one who would expose their own need for forgiveness and then demand that they extend forgiveness to their oppressors. Little wonder that the "sinners"—the prostitutes and tax collectors—flocked to Jesus, drawn by his message of mercy.

It would be easy to look at the evil that still disfigures our world and conclude that Jesus was merely a dreamer. But that would mean misunderstanding both his strategy and his mission. Instead of using the blunt instrument of judgment, Jesus inaugurated his kingdom with mercy. And mercy can have its own side effects, one of which is that it allows evil to grow right alongside goodness. But mercy is also what makes possible the greatest of all victories, defeating God's enemies not through the use of outside force but by the inward power of grace, transforming our hearts from within. In the end, it is God's mercy that determines the timetable for the final judgment.

Listen to what the rabbis said about the relationship between God's mercy and his justice: "Greater is the day of rain than the resurrection of the dead, because the resurrection of the dead benefits only the righteous, but rain benefits both the righteous and the unrighteous."[19] Every day that God sends rain to provide food for people who hate him shows his great love for humanity. His mercy is even greater than his justice!

Jesus tells his own followers that they should share God's love for sinners, and he does this also by pointing to the gift of rain: "Love your enemies and pray for those who persecute you, that you may be children of your Father in heaven. He causes his sun to rise on the evil and the good, and sends rain on the righteous and the unrighteous" (Matthew 5:44–45).

How to Enter the Kingdom

But the kingdom is not inevitable for everyone. Because he is a merciful king, Jesus issues an invitation, not a command. He will never force anyone to join but waits patiently for us to repent and follow him. When Jesus spoke about receiving the kingdom of God (Luke 18:17) or entering the kingdom of heaven (Matthew 7:21), he wasn't talking about how to get into heaven after we die, as many people have thought. He was speaking about having the greatest life possible. How? By living under his reign through the power of his grace. And, once again, he was using a Jewish idiom to communicate his message.

One of the earliest and best-known sayings about the "kingdom of heaven" is one that commented on the *Shema*—the prayer of every faithful Jew, uttered morning and evening. As we have seen, the *Shema* begins with Deuteronomy 6:4–5: "Hear [*Shema*], O Israel: The LORD our God, the LORD is one. Love the LORD your God with all your heart and with all your soul and with all your strength." The rabbis taught that anyone who prays this prayer with a sincere heart "receives upon himself the kingdom of heaven."[20]

Why did the rabbis associate the "kingdom of heaven" with this particular prayer? They understood that people who made this daily commitment were mentally bowing down before God, "enthroning" him as their king. Such people were proclaiming their faith in God and pledging to live under his reign. To make this commitment had nothing to do with taking part in a political movement but everything to do with making an individual, spiritual decision. This understanding fits completely with Jesus's words that "the kingdom of God is within you" (Luke 17:21 NIV 1984).

So for both Jesus and the rabbis, to "receive" or to "enter the kingdom of heaven" could describe making a personal commitment to loving God with all your heart. The rabbis understood it as worshipping God the Father as one's king, but Jesus expanded it to mean worshipping God in light of the authority Christ was given to rule over it. That was why he spoke of it as "my" kingdom.

No wonder Jesus spent so much of his ministry proclaiming the kingdom. This is why he came into the world: to open the way for all people to come back to God by atoning for their sins. Entering into that relationship can be described as "entering into God's reign." We use similar language when we talk about "accepting Christ as Lord"—a phrase that captures the idea of enthroning Christ as our king.

Jesus's teachings about the kingdom become so much clearer when we understand this. Listen to his words, "Blessed are the poor in spirit, for theirs is the kingdom of heaven" (Matthew 5:3). People who are "poor in spirit" are those who feel crushed by circumstances beyond their control, or those who are sick and tired of their lives under their own bad management. Hungry for God's leadership, they accept his guidance with humility, realizing the impossibility of life without Christ.

Jesus also declared that "anyone who will not receive the kingdom of God like a little child will never enter it" (Luke 18:17). Notice that he didn't say we are to receive it like teenagers testing the boundaries and pushing the envelope. Nor are we to receive it like self-reliant adults, people who think they have it together. No, we are to have the attitude of a small child responding with trust, dependence, delight, and a desire to please.

Remember what Jesus said of the wealthy young man who turned down a chance to become one of his disciples: "How hard it is for the rich to enter the kingdom of God!" (Luke 18:24). Jesus wasn't talking about what the man needed to do to get into heaven after he died. He was saying that the proud young ruler was refusing to accept God's kingship over his life right then. How difficult it is to choose God's will over our own.

Of course, belonging to the kingdom means pledging our obedience to the king. Jesus himself, who was hardly a legalist, said: "Not everyone who says to me, 'Lord, Lord,' will enter the kingdom of heaven, but only the one who does the will of my Father who is in heaven" (Matthew 7:21).[21] Once again, Jesus wasn't speaking about a heavenly afterlife. He was talking about enthroning God here and now, showing our love by doing what he asks.

Many of us long to experience God in deeper ways. But we forget that obedience is the key to spiritual vitality. Ann has a friend who is the mother of two young boys who are on opposite ends of the obedience spectrum. The eldest loves to help his mother whenever he can, while the youngest has to be dragged kicking and screaming to do the simplest task. Her friend loves both of her boys but admits that her youngest is a constant source of frustration. This mother understands completely why Jesus once said to his disciples: "If you love me, keep my commands" (John 14:15). In fact she finds herself saying something similar, asking, "Why do you say you love me but don't do what I say?" Like most mothers, my friend cherishes all the kisses and hugs her young son showers on her, but what she treasures most is his obedience. It's the same in our relationship with the Lord.

If you recognize yourself in that story, take heart. Disobedience is a problem, but it can also be an opportunity. If half-heartedness has been stunting your growth, you can reverse its downward pull by repenting and asking God to help you respond to him with renewed trust and obedience. As you do, you may find yourself enjoying unprecedented spiritual growth as God opens up new channels for grace to flow into your life.

The way we understand Jesus's words about the kingdom is critical to the kind of life we will live. If we think that the "kingdom of heaven" is simply about Christ's second coming or about going to heaven when we die, we'll be tempted to become passive and complacent. But if Jesus's kingdom is a living, dynamic reality—a reality that is right now steadily advancing against the kingdom of darkness—that's a different story. As followers of Christ, our obedience is vital because it is a cat-alyst for the Spirit's work, making us more like Jesus so that his reign can spread across the whole earth.

Jesus's message of the kingdom is Jewish to the core. It is also at the very heart of the gospel, revealing a God of tenderness and mercy, who postpones final judgment until as many people as possible can be gathered into the kingdom of his Son.

———————•———————

Having learned so much about the Jewishness of Jesus and the Jewish roots of our faith, it seems right to ask ourselves some important ques-tions. How much of Jesus's Jewishness should we take on? Which aspects can enrich our Christian faith, and which should we resist? Furthermore, how can we maintain balance and discernment as we seek to learn from the Jewishness of Jesus? Let's explore these questions together.

AT THE FEET OF THE RABBI

1. Try to pray these words from the *Kaddish* every day this week: "Let his name be glorified and sanctified throughout the universe that he created according to his purpose. May he bring about the reign of his kingdom in your lifetime, in your days, and in the lifetime of all of the house of Israel, speedily and soon!"

2. The Lord's Prayer should sound utterly different to you in light of what you've learned about the kingdom and about Jewish prayer in chapter 6. Write out a modern version based on how you hear it now, in light of all you've learned.

3. Think of a time in your life or in the life of someone you know when you saw "the finger of God" at work redeeming someone in an unmistakable way. Spend some time blessing God for the way he is building up his kingdom right here and right now.

CHAPTER 14

Becoming True Disciples
of Our Jewish Lord

Wisdom begetteth humility.

RABBI ABRAHAM IBN EZRA (AROUND 1100)

Ahhh, the feeling of setting foot inside your own home again after a two-week trek through the summer heat and dust of the parched Middle East. Teeming with the evidence of its three faiths—Judaism, Christianity, and Islam—Israel is fascinating but overwhelming. Full of ancient ruins, cultural ferment, and religious fervor, it is like no other place on earth. You have learned so much that you will never read your Bible in quite the same way. The story has come to life before your eyes.

Now you are slumped into your own easy chair, breathing in the familiar fragrance of home. The wonderful adventure you had prayed about and prepared for is over, and "normal life" is beckoning with its own sharp sense of urgency. As you try to resist its pull, you begin to feel a bit weary, a little deflated. The whole trip seems like nothing more than a dream.

But then you glance at your suitcases, still covered with Israeli security stickers. As you begin to empty your luggage, you realize that your swimsuit still carries a faint scent of the Sea of Galilee and that the treads of your hiking boots are still packed with soil that a Judean farmer would have tilled thousands of years ago. Then a treasured pottery shard falls out of an unwashed sock. Just imagine—an Israelite woman may have stumbled on her way to the well, shattering a favorite water pitcher, leaving its fragments in the dust for you to find centuries later.

It may only take minutes to unpack your suitcases, but it will take years to unpack your memories. You remember the thrill of seeing Jerusalem's limestone walls for the first time, gleaming in the sunlight as your bus ascended the Judean mountains. Your nose still braces to the memory of the strange, piquant scent of the Old City markets. Your legs still feel the ache and itch of hiking through thorns and sun-baked grass as you explored the biblical sites.

Though more than two thousand years have elapsed since Jesus was born, you no longer have difficulty imagining him walking with his disciples across the length and breadth of Israel's rugged terrain. Familiar Scripture passages now burst with new life. You will never forget your trip to that ancient land.

Our hope is that the whirlwind tour of first-century Israel that you've encountered in this book has been a little like this for you. You've been strolling the ancient streets with your Rabbi, absorbing the different customs and traditions of this ancient place. By looking intently into the cultural setting in which Jesus lived, you may have discovered many new things about him, like the way he . . .

- used the Scriptures to make powerful claims in a subtle Jewish way
- joined the conversation of other rabbis around him
- celebrated the ancient Jewish feasts and was indeed their supreme fulfillment
- brought the Torah to its greatest expression
- made it his primary goal while living on earth to raise up *talmidim*—disciples

But how should learning about the Jewishness of Jesus impact your own life? What are the implications for you, living as you do thousands of years later in an entirely different cultural setting?

By now, you've probably realized that Jesus's Jewish context is *really* important. As you read the Bible, new questions may begin haunting your thoughts: *Was that an idiom? I wonder what the significance of that was in Jewish culture. Was Jesus quoting an Old Testament verse when he said . . . ?* Now that you know more about the Jewish background of Jesus, there's no going back. We hope this book has ignited in you a curiosity that will help you grow deeper in God's Word.

If you are anything like us, your faith has grown stronger as you have learned about the Jewish roots of Christianity. As the historical reality of Jesus comes into clearer focus, so too do his words and his claims. Over the past fifty years, archaeologists and biblical scholars have unearthed important texts and ancient clues to help us understand Jesus better. Indeed, we now have access to information about the first-century Jewish world that theologians in previous centuries hardly dreamed possible. Much of it reaffirms the reliability of the ancient documents, making many biblical scholars less skeptical today about the historical accuracy of the Bible than they've been in previous decades.

As you learn more about the customs and religious beliefs of first-century Israel, events and stories that previously seemed unrelated will suddenly become connected in fascinating ways.

Rethinking Our Attitude toward the Jewish People

Lois describes how her attitude toward the Jewish people, especially in Jesus's day, has been transformed by all that she has learned. "With the advantage of hindsight," she says, "I can see how I used to paint the Jewish backdrop of the Gospels with a dark brush, as though a deeply shaded background would make Jesus shine more brightly. If he affirmed women, I assumed that his contemporaries despised them. If he spoke out against the love of money, I thought it was because everyone around him was grasping for wealth. I remember how uncomfortable I felt when I began to realize that things were not always as I had imagined. Gradually, as my faith grew stronger, I gained the confidence to reexamine my own suppositions.

"It occurred to me," she goes on, "that disparaging Jesus's Jewish audience was also a way of letting myself off the hook. I wanted to picture Jesus as being invariably loving and gentle, so I cringed at the strong words he directed at his first-century audience. Certainly he wouldn't talk that way to me. His listeners must have been foolish, obstinate people—I'm so glad I'm not like them! But what if they were people like myself? Worse yet, what if their faith was even *more* dedicated and earnest than mine? Suddenly, Jesus's stern words became an enormous challenge, calling me to a righteousness far beyond what I had imagined."

Though Christians have often portrayed first-century Jews in negative ways, we owe much to them as well as to their Jewish forebears, through whom God worked to bring us a Savior. (We shouldn't forget how many, even among the priests and Pharisees, became Jesus's avid followers; cf. Acts 21:20.) Still, just as it's a mistake to paint all first-century Jews as villains, it's equally mistaken to assume they were all saints. Jesus's first listeners struggled with sin and faith and the difficulties of life, just as we do today. We can be grateful for how God has worked through the Jewish people, but we should avoid idealizing Judaism for its own sake.

Learning more about the Jewishness of Jesus raises acutely painful questions. Why haven't Christians been schooled in the Judaic background of their faith? Could it have something to do with the tragic history between Christians and Jews? Barely a hundred years after the birth of the church, Marcion, a bishop in Turkey, argued that the God of the Old Testament was cruel and evil and that the true God was revealed in Christ. He even advocated that the Old Testament be purged from the Bible along with any New Testament book that showed undue Jewish influence. Sadly, though Marcion was excommunicated for heresy in AD 144, his ideas have persisted throughout Christian history.[1] If you wonder why Christians haven't known more about Jesus's Jewishness before now, this is a large part of the reason.

But listen to how Paul warns Gentile believers not to boast about their standing with God:

> If some of the branches have been broken off, and you, though a
> wild olive shoot, have been grafted in among the others and now
> share in the nourishing sap from the olive root, do not consider
> yourself to be superior to those other branches. If you do, con-
> sider this: You do not support the root, but the root supports you.
> (Romans 11:17–18)

Paul is saying that the Gentiles have been grafted into the "olive
tree" that God planted thousands of years earlier in his covenantal
promises to Abraham. The truth is that we are but branches grafted
into a Jewish tree, nourished by the words God gave to Jewish prophets,
apostles, and even a Jewish Messiah. Of all people, Christians should
be the most humble. How different the story of our relationship with
the Jewish people might have been had we heeded this warning. But
for much of our history, the church has paid little attention to Paul's
important admonition.

After World War II, many Christian scholars began to realize that
the monstrous tragedy of the Holocaust had grown out of centuries
of rampant anti-Semitism in the church throughout Europe. A new
openness developed toward examining the Jewishness of Jesus and the
New Testament. Some Christian scholars began to study with Jewish
scholars in order to learn more about the traditions out of which the
Bible grew. As we reconnect with the Jewish background of our faith,
we must realize that we, too, have a lot of soul-searching and repenting
to do for the sins of our forebears. Rather than merely casting blame
on "those people back then," it is better for each of us to ask what our
own responsibility is right now.

A New Perspective

After reading *Sitting at the Feet of Rabbi Jesus*, you may notice that the
way you read the Bible has changed. It can be disconcerting to view
Scripture from a somewhat different perspective. But think of it like
watching a football game on TV. A pass has just been completed, but

the receiver is down; did he fumble the ball when he was tackled, or did he manage to hang on to it? Through the magic of instant replay, you can watch the action unfold in slow motion, this time from another angle. Reality hasn't changed, but details that you missed at first suddenly become clear.

Or, try this experiment. As you hold this book in your hand, close one eye. Notice the details of where the book is, relative to the objects behind it. Then close the other eye and note the relative position of the book. The two views are similar, yet different. From one eye things are hidden, but from the other they are visible. Edges recede at slightly different angles. Your brain is receiving two sets of conflicting data, two slightly different pictures, and merging them into one. In fact, your brain needs both pictures in order to provide depth perception. Neither eye alone can enable you to distinguish three dimensions. Similarly, viewing Christianity and Jesus from a Jewish perspective can add depth and dimensionality to our own faith.

Let's take the "eye" analogy a bit further. The reason your brain can merge the two pictures is because one eye is dominant—it sets the perspective that your brain ultimately considers "authoritative." With both eyes open, point your index finger at something across the room. Now close one eye. Then close the other. From your dominant eye's perspective, your finger stays in the same place. From the other eye's perspective, it "jumps." If neither eye were dominant, your brain wouldn't be able to process the hopeless jumble of conflicting information it receives from both eyes.

In the same way, it's important that you have a "dominant eye" when it comes to learning about the Jewish roots of your faith. The people who grow most with this kind of study are those who start out with a solid knowledge of Scripture and a strong faith in Christ. Such people are not "brittle," afraid that their faith might fall apart whenever they are faced with new information. They can revise their understanding as necessary but reject ideas that are truly incompatible with faith. A person without this "dominant eye" will be confused when presented with two conflicting portrayals of reality.

It is also important to treat the sources you read with caution. Traditional Jewish sources, by definition, do not assume that Jesus is the Messiah. Heated debate has gone on for two thousand years between Jews and Christians, and both sides have reacted by distancing themselves from each other. Just as Christianity has ignored and distanced itself from its Jewish background, Judaism has sometimes done the same, downplaying earlier practices and beliefs that led large numbers of first-century Jews to believe in Jesus as the Messiah.

One example is found in a classic commentary on the Torah called the *Chumash* (hoo-MAHSH) written by Rashi, a source widely used by Orthodox Jews today. Rashi lived in France during the First Crusade in 1096. Since some of his close friends and family members died at the hands of Christians, it is hardly surprising that his commentaries on the Torah and Psalms often refute Christian beliefs, either openly or indirectly.[2] Modern Christians interested in studying the Torah often try using the *Chumash*, not realizing that it was reacting against Christian ways of reading the biblical text. It is important to realize that Judaism is not a static religion. It has been influenced by its own need to respond to the forceful claims of Christianity.

Seder

The *Seder* is the name of the ritual meal eaten on Passover. The word can be translated "order" and refers to the fact that the Passover Seder follows a traditional order of liturgy and includes certain ceremonial foods that commemorate the suffering of the ancient Israelites and their exodus from Egypt.

Christian sources, too, should be treated with care. All sorts of odd theories pop up in books and on the Internet. Because interest in Jesus's Jewishness is a fairly recent development among laypeople, the field is open to all kinds of voices. Scholarly sources may also challenge traditional ways of reading Scripture, sometimes legitimately, sometimes not. Prayerful discernment is an absolute must.

If traditional Christianity is like a well-manicured garden, studying the Bible from a Hebraic perspective is like a wilderness of untamed trails and rocky pathways. Sometimes you turn a corner and encounter a beautiful vista, or you dig deeper and unearth a brilliant jewel. But there are potholes and thorns, as well as ways to get lost. You need to have strong legs for the journey and the wisdom to carefully choose your trails.

Remember Lois's attempt to recreate a first-century Passover with other members of her church? Their Seder instructions indicated that Jesus and his disciples ate while reclining around the outside of a low, squared-off, U-shaped table called a *triclinium*. To be as authentic as possible, they laid some folded-up rectangular folding tables on the floor in a U shape. Then everyone reclined around the makeshift *triclinium* by lying on the floor and propping themselves up by one arm. It was an uncomfortable way to eat. Still, they felt enlightened, because they had avoided the "mistake" of celebrating Passover sitting in chairs around a modern table, as Leonardo Da Vinci depicted Jesus and his disciples doing in his painting of the Last Supper.

Ten years later, while on a trip to Israel, Lois learned that their Passover instructions (which many other groups use) had misunderstood what a *triclinium* was. Jesus and his disciples had not been uncomfortably arrayed around a U-shaped table. A *triclinium*, it seems, is not a table after all. The word means "three couches" put together in a U-shape. People reclined on the couches, and the food was served from the fourth side, placed on a small round table in the middle.[3] A *triclinium* is also the name for the dining room where this ancient "sectional couch" was located. Often the three-sided platform was built against the walls. There's no place behind it to sit or to lie down— people laid on top of it.

What's more, Dr. Steve Notley, the scholar who led Lois's trip, doubted that there was a *triclinium* at the Last Supper.[4] He thought it much more likely that Jesus and his disciples simply sat on mats or reclined on cushions on the floor. The food was probably served on platters placed on stands that formed small tables.

Does it really matter how people sat at the Last Supper? Of course not. But details have a way of making the ancient scenes come to life. So as we seek to understand more about the Jewishness of Jesus, it is important to realize that we may need to revise our theories later on.

Meanwhile, it is good to stay humble and open to correction. As Rabbi Ibn Ezra says, "Wisdom begetteth humility."

Our Calling as Talmidim

Discovering new insights about the historical reality of Jesus is fascinating, and it can greatly enrich our understanding. But what should we *do* with our newfound knowledge? One of the most important things we can do is to realize that Jesus is calling us to be his disciples, his *talmidim*. Millions of Christians throughout the world and throughout the ages have viewed Jesus primarily through the lens of the Apostles' Creed, which begins this way:

> I believe in God, the Father Almighty, the Creator of heaven and earth, and in Jesus Christ, his only Son, our Lord: who was conceived of the Holy Spirit, born of the Virgin Mary, suffered under Pontius Pilate, was crucified, died, and was buried . . .

They understand Jesus as Savior and Son of God, believing in his atoning death and resurrection. Vital as these beliefs are to our faith, many of us still do not realize that there's more to Christianity than assenting to a creed. We are also called to be in daily, living relationship with Rabbi Jesus, becoming his *talmidim* and then sharing our lives with others so that they, too, can become his disciples. To emphasize salvation and neglect discipleship is to miss the point of why Jesus came to earth and lived as a rabbi.[5]

Jesus doesn't expect perfection from his disciples anytime soon. If you doubt it, just look at his first *talmidim*! But Christ does expect us to follow him, to "sit at his feet" so that we can learn how to live. Remember when Jesus said: "Why do you call me, 'Lord, Lord,' and do not do what I say?" (Luke 6:46). Perhaps Jesus is speaking the same words to us today, calling Christians to greater obedience and deeper faithfulness.

Since any good disciple needs to understand what the master is saying, clarifying Jesus's words is a necessary preliminary step to living out his commands. Christians today have an unprecedented opportunity to understand the historical and religious context in which Jesus lived and ministered. Let's take full advantage of these discoveries, deepening our discipleship by exploring what life and faith were like in the first century.

Experiencing Jewish traditions—like praying blessings, observing a Sabbath, or hosting a Seder—can enrich our understanding of Christ. Those who have done so have discovered how meaningful these practices are. With every experience, they grow deeper in their understanding of Scripture and God's ways. To the extent that Jewish customs and traditions draw us closer to our Rabbi, changing us into more faithful and wiser *talmidim*, we should do them.

But there are cautions. Many Jewish traditions are lovely but have little to do with Jesus since they arose much later than the first century. Customs of dress and traditional foods mostly date back only a few hundred years, typically to the culture of the countries where Jews have lived. It also can be interesting to learn how later Jews have understood many of the same Scriptures we read, but they may or may not reflect the reality of how these texts were understood in Jesus's time.[6]

We should also ask ourselves whether adopting a particular practice makes us a better witness to others. We live in a community, and we cannot ignore the impact of our actions on others. Also, our respect for the faith practices of Judaism should not turn us into relativists, as though all ways lead equally to God. Nor should we ignore cautions about falling into legalism as we explore the Hebraic roots of Christianity.

It's important to realize that new insights can sometimes lead to pride and division. If, in our excitement about what we are learning, we start speaking a Jewish "lingo" that no one else understands or find ourselves irritated by our less-enlightened friends, spiritual pride is likely the problem. Of all people, we should be the most humble, because we are just beginning to understand how much more there is to learn.

In the end, what matters most is observing the two greatest commandments. Jesus, the greatest of all rabbis, calls us to love God with all our hearts and to love our neighbors as ourselves. These two summarize *all* of God's law, indeed the entire Torah. Everything we do or learn or say must be evaluated in light of how it helps us stay faithful to these commands.

Consider a simple example. Say that you are thinking about attaching a *mezuzah* to the doorframe of your home. For those who don't know, a *mezuzah* is a small, oblong box that contains a copy of the Shema written on a tiny scroll. It is placed beside a door to fulfill the command from Deuteronomy 6:9, referring to God's laws, "Write them on the doorframes of your houses and on your gates." *Shaddai*, one of God's names, is often inscribed in Hebrew letters on the front of the *mezuzah*. All Jewish buildings have them, and they are found by the door to every room except the bathroom. A *mezuzah* is a simple reminder to keep God's Word in your thoughts at all times. It is a practice that predates Jesus. In fact, an ancient *mezuzah* was found with the Dead Sea Scrolls, and the first-century Jewish scholar Josephus mentions them.[7]

Tzitzit, Tzitziyot

Tzitzit or *tzitziyot* (plural) are tassels placed at the four corners of a garment in accordance with the command to wear tassels in Numbers 15:37–39. In the early first century they were worn on the outer woolen garment, but today they are worn on a ceremonial shawl during prayer. Hasidic Jews and some Orthodox Jews still wear *tzitziyot* all the time by putting on a small *tallit* (a rectangular cloth carrying the tassels, with a hole for the head) underneath their shirts.

As a Christian, you have freedom in Christ. You don't have to put a *mezuzah* on your doorframe, but you can if you want to. The *mezuzah* tradition is lovely and meaningful, a useful reminder about the roots of our Christian faith. Affixing one to your doorpost might spark some interesting conversations with neighbors and friends, forcing you to be up front about your faith, kind of like wearing *tzitzit*. A Jewish person who observes your *mezuzah* might see it as a gesture of kindness and understanding, an effort to move away from the anti-Semitism of the past.

But on the other hand (as Tevye would say), a *mezuzah* might not be a great idea. Perhaps some Jewish people will find it offensive, thinking it a misappropriation of their religious symbols. Or maybe someone else will conclude that you believe all religions are equivalent. Of course, these things might not happen. In many ways a *mezuzah* may help you fulfill the command to love God and your neighbor. But without wisdom, it might be a hindrance. *Everything* we do should be evaluated in light of the supreme commands of Rabbi Jesus: love God and love your neighbor.

New Tools for Breaking Ground

Few contrasts are as striking as the landscape of En-Gedi in southern Israel, near the Dead Sea. The undulating hills around En-Gedi seem barren and lifeless, utterly bald under the blistering, searing heat of the sun. But the scene changes as soon as you look down into the ravine. There you can see springs bubbling up, transforming the sun-caked soil into a lush oasis teeming with life. The only difference between the vibrant growth of the ravine and the surrounding desolation of the hillsides is water. Indeed, the entire country of Israel is that way. Just about any plant on earth can be grown there, as long as the land is irrigated. With a little water it is intensely fertile, but without it, there is only dust and dirt.

Learning about the Bible in its cultural context can be a lot like this. This most ancient of texts can at times seem dry. The long lists of names and the archaic imagery often are like untilled, parched ground, tough to plow into deeply. But discovering how to probe deeper into the Bible's culture and context is like being given a sharp new spade that allows you to break through to the richness below. With the living water of the Spirit, gardens of understanding and application spring to life and grow up where nothing grew before. Every new experience leads to somewhere better, and the "aha" moments never come to an end.

SITTING AT THE FEET OF RABBI JESUS

Study and Discussion Guide for Individuals or Groups

ELISA STANFORD, BASED ON THE WORK OF ANN SPANGLER AND LOIS TVERBERG

Welcome to the study and discussion guide for *Sitting at the Feet of Rabbi Jesus*. Jesus loved to talk about God and God's Word with others. If you are reading the book in a group or with a prayer partner, we are excited that you are continuing that tradition of becoming *haverim* by digging into this book with other people. If you are reading the book alone, we pray that your experience will enrich your personal faith in new ways.

However you choose to use this study guide, be open to how God is directing your reading and study. Feel free to spend more time on questions that particularly resonate with you or your group. We trust that this chapter-by-chapter exploration of the book will help you take the next step toward understanding Jesus's Jewish world. As we have discovered, it is a never-ending, fascinating journey!

Introduction

Understanding more about the culture and language of Jesus's time helps us know more of Christ himself. When we honor the Jewish people by learning about their heritage, God blesses us with a deeper understanding of our Jewish Messiah.

1. Describe your experience with Jewish people, culture, and practices (if any).

2. The archaeologist Gabi Barkai once said, "Every day in Jerusalem is a day of discovery" (p. 11). What do you want to discover through reading this book?

Chapter 1: Joining Mary at the Feet of Jesus

Although we meet God through Scripture, sometimes the difference in culture, time, and language makes the Bible seem distant or confusing. Studying Jesus's Jewish culture helps us "fine-tune our hearing" (p. 17) so we can know the same power, controversy, and spiritual meaning that Jesus's original listeners experienced.

1. Describe a time when you had difficulty communicating across a cultural or language barrier.

2. Rather than undermining our faith, "looking at the Jewish background of the Bible deepens our understanding of Jesus" (p. 23). What fears do you have, if any, about learning more about Jewish culture? How might a better understanding of Jesus's times deepen your faith?

3. Give an example of a passage, verse, or concept in the Gospels that you find especially confusing.

4. What is your first thought or emotion when you come across something Jesus said that you don't understand?

5. If you were literally sitting at Jesus's feet with Mary, what is the first thing you would ask him?

Chapter 2: Why a Jewish Rabbi?

As we learn more about the life of a rabbi, we can see why being a rabbi was a perfect vocation for Jesus. As the greatest of all rabbis, Jesus followed the rabbinic tradition of studying Scripture, using debate as a way of learning, teaching by telling parables, and raising up disciples.

More than that, he was the promised Messiah, the Savior whom the oppressed Jewish people longed for.

1. When you were growing up, what was your image of Jesus?
2. In what ways do you personally identify with the excitement over biblical study that Lois describes (p. 30–31)? In what ways do you struggle to engage with the Bible?
3. What does it mean on a practical level to study the Bible with "a deep reverence for God's Word" (p. 31)? In what ways does a sense of reverence motivate us to study the Bible more?
4. Debate was a significant part of learning in Jesus's day (p. 33). When have you seen healthy debate foster greater understanding of a subject? How do people in today's church debate issues?
5. The authors write that the mission of Jesus, and of those who follow him, was to "become a living example of what it means to apply God's Word to one's life" (p. 38). Whom do you know who fulfills this call to be a living example of God's Word? What impact does that person have on your faith?
6. In what ways does a greater appreciation of Jesus's role as a rabbi help you understand his words and actions more? For example, how does knowing that rabbis used parables influence your reading of Jesus's parables? How might an awareness of the rabbinic emphasis on debate, discipleship, and study change your perception of your relationships and daily priorities?

Chapter 3: Stringing Pearls

Like other Jews of his day (and today), Jesus studied the Law of Moses, the Prophets, and the Psalms. As Christians, we recognize these books as our Old Testament (note that Roman Catholic and Orthodox churches recognize additional books as part of the Old Testament canon in contrast to the smaller canon accepted by Protestant churches). Jesus used the Jewish love of Scripture to teach others about himself and to show how the Scriptures point to Jesus as their fulfillment. Today, some of Jesus's words may seem perplexing, but often they reflect a rabbi's way of communicating within the framework of Scripture. The more we understand the Old Testament, the more meaningful Jesus's words become.

1. If you had to choose a favorite book of the Bible, which one would it be? Why?

2. What is your experience with the Old Testament? Do you identify with Lois's surprise over learning how important the Old Testament is to understanding the New Testament? Why or why not?

3. The study of Scripture was vitally important in Jesus's day and is still considered a high form of worship for Jewish people. Would you say the Christian church today (and your local church in particular) has a similar reverence for God's Word? Why or why not?

4. Can you identify with Ben Azzai's words about Scripture passages coming together so perfectly that the words "burst into flames" (p. 48)? Describe a time when a biblical passage came to life for you.

5. What images come to mind when you think of a shepherd? How might the image of Jesus as shepherd be meaningful in your life right now?

6. Why was it important for Jesus to tell his followers—including us—that he was the Son of Man?

Chapter 4: Following the Rabbi

In Jesus's day, a rabbi's disciples learned not only from what a rabbi said in times of teaching but also from what he did in everyday life. Just as Elisha learned from Elijah, so a disciple's task was to become as much like the rabbi as possible. This was a long yet fulfilling process. Our goal as disciples of Jesus is the same today: to become transformed into the likeness of Christ.

1. How did you learn your current vocation? Have you ever experienced a formal apprenticeship, as Ange Sabin Peter did? What was the experience like?

2. The master craftsman told Ange, "You cannot separate life from work" (p. 56). In what ways does today's Western culture reflect the opposite belief?

3. Why do you think our culture places more emphasis on information than on transformation?

4. Describe a specific sacrifice you've made to follow Jesus. Was the fulfillment in such a choice worth the cost? Why or why not?

5. What is one "ugly habit" (p. 61) in your life right now that you would like Jesus to heal? What fears or discouragements do you have as you wait for God's inner transformation?

6. Describe a time when your spiritual life deepened because you were absorbing truth from someone around you—perhaps attending to someone as Elisha attended Elijah or simply watching someone's daily life. In what ways did the person you were following serve you? In what ways did you need to be obedient and humble in order to learn?

7. Who is learning from you by watching your life right now? In what ways can you serve that person? In what ways might you be tempted to be self-important in your leadership? Does living transparently come easily to you, or is it a struggle?

Chapter 5: Get Yourself Some Haverim

Following his Jewish tradition, Jesus considered it vital to learn about God in the presence of other people. His instructions to his disciples and his own daily life affirmed his followers' need for community. As Christians, we can honor this tradition of *haverim* through intentional relationships with others and an awareness of our connectedness with the Jewish community in the Bible. God calls us to learn, love, study, forgive, and encourage others in community, just as Jesus did.

1. When have you learned something more deeply because you were studying or working with someone else?

2. Consider the story of Passover (see p. 75). How does your understanding or appreciation of this pivotal event in Jewish history change when you think of the Jewish people as your spiritual ancestors?

3. Briefly describe your past experiences with spiritual community and spiritual solitude. Do you usually get emotional energy from being with people or from being alone? How does this influence your spiritual life?

4. How do you usually handle conflict or disagreement in relationships?

5. Do you view disciple-making as something that happens mainly at the "fence," to get people into the pasture (p. 81)? Why or why not?

6. Though many of us have a circle of friends, few of us have anyone who really pushes us in our spiritual life or energizes us to study the Bible more. Do you have a spiritual "jogging partner" (p. 80) who challenges you to grapple with the Bible and helps to refine you? Describe how that relationship developed. If you don't have that kind of influence in your life, what is one practical thing you could do to develop a *haver* relationship with someone or with a group of people?

Chapter 6: Rabbi, Teach Us to Pray

The Jewish customs of the day, including the rich customs of Jewish prayer, were a significant part of Jesus's everyday experience. In the Lord's Prayer, Jesus relied on classic Jewish themes to illustrate what the essence of prayer, then and now, should be. Jesus is the ultimate model for us of *kavanah*, a sense of the presence of God.

1. Consider the Jewish practices, such as wearing phylacteries and prayer shawls, that Ann encountered on her flight to Tel Aviv. What rituals do Christians use to study the Bible, pray, and worship God? What spiritual practice or tradition is especially meaningful to you?

2. What is your current experience with prayer? Would you say that, for you, prayer is usually a time of joy? Confusion? Guilt? Encouragement? Answers?

3. What does it look like to approach God with reverence but also as a trusting child?

4. Why do you think prayers such as the Shema and the *Amidah* (pp. 87–89) involve so much repetition? What does Jesus's use of such prayers suggest about our need to remember our commitment to God?

5. The "daily bread" of the Lord's Prayer is a reference to God's sustenance as a whole. What is one thing you would like to ask God to provide for you this week as a way of sustaining you spiritually, physically, or emotionally?

6. The Jewish theologian Abraham Heschel says that *kavanah* is to "sense the preciousness of being able to pray, to be perceptive of the supreme significance of worshipping God" (p. 95). How would a deeper sense of the preciousness of prayer, and God's presence with you when you pray, affect the way you relate to God?

7. Think of a task you do every day. What is one way in which your increased understanding of the Jewish view of prayer might change the way you do that task?

Chapter 7: For Everything a Blessing

Jesus modeled the Jewish tradition of blessing God for events, small and large, throughout the day. This habit of blessing God can transform our spiritual lives as we continually acknowledge his presence with us.

1. What is the first thing you thought about when you woke up this morning?

2. When has intentionally developing a habit changed your actions or thoughts permanently, even though you simply went through the motions of the habit at first?

3. Describe a time when your attitude toward a situation changed as you expressed thanks. Describe a time when you realized you'd forgotten God's involvement in your life because you had forgotten to thank him for being with you.

4. What does it mean to "give thanks in all circumstances" (1 Thessalonians 5:18)?

5. Loving God with all our hearts means loving him not just with "the part of our heart that is happy, but with the angry, sad, mourning part of our heart as well" (p. 101). What would it look like to love God with all your heart—including all your anger, grief, and questions—right now? When is it most difficult for you to express your emotions to God?

6. Describe a recent time when you were filled with a desire to bless God.

Chapter 8: A Passover Discovery

Passover—the most important Jewish feast—is a time to remember how God brought his people out of Egypt and how he will redeem his people again. Learning about Passover and two coinciding spring feasts, Unleavened Bread and Firstfruits, yields insights into Jesus's final week on earth.

1. What family stories do you talk about with your children or at a family gathering? Why do you think such stories get passed around in your family?

2. The Jewish people celebrated Passover as a way of remembering God's provision during a time of change. Why is it important to commemorate past events? In what ways can such celebrations bring us closer to God?

3. Do you think we should memorialize times of past suffering as well as joy? Why or why not? How can we allow pain to have a positive influence in our spiritual lives?

4. Passover is a time of expectation as well as a time of remembrance for the Jewish people. When has living with hopeful expectation changed the way you act or think?

5. What difference does it make to you spiritually to consider that God knew about Jesus's redemption when he brought the Israelites out of Egypt?

6. Think about a time of difficulty in your life, a time of dramatic change, or a time when you saw God's deliverance. What could you do to commemorate that time? What would it look like to consider that commemoration a reminder of God's "invincible hope" (p. 116)?

Chapter 9: Discovering Jesus in the Jewish Feasts

The seven biblical feasts of Leviticus 23 were observed in Jesus's time and are still celebrated today. Rich in significance, they point to the redemption of Christ; Jesus used their imagery to highlight his role as the Messiah. The feasts were tangible symbols of God's faithfulness and reminders of how God led the Israelites into the Promised Land. Today, feasts are a way to celebrate the past, to acknowledge God's provision in the present, and to hope for the future. Through feasts and traditions, we can get a glimpse of God's plan for eternity.

1. What is the most joyful celebration you remember, either as an adult or as a child? What made it such a joyful experience?

2. We all have different beliefs about what it means to be "Spirit-filled." What does that phrase mean to you? How have you seen the Holy Spirit at work in your life recently?

3. How does our knowledge of Jesus's life and death affect how we confess our sins to God? Describe a time when asking for God's forgiveness freed your mind and heart. (Note: If you are in a group, be respectful of those who would prefer to think about this question in silence.) Is it ever hard for you to accept God's forgiveness? Why or why not?

4. In what ways does our culture teach us to forget "that life is finite and that everyone must be prepared to stand before the Lord at the time of death" (p. 128)? How can the Jewish understanding of mortality and God's judgment enrich our spiritual lives?

5. What is your experience with fasting? Have you ever considered making it a part of your spiritual disciplines? Why or why not?

6. Would you rather receive two hours of free time or twenty dollars? Why? How does keeping space in our lives for Sabbath turn our focus away from time and money and toward God?

7. Taste, hunger, sight, clothing, and other sensory experiences are important parts of Jewish commemorations. What are some things Christians do to make prayers, worship, and church experience encompass all of the senses? What could you do to bring more sensory experiences into your spiritual life?

Chapter 10: At Table with the Rabbi

Since ancient times, the Jewish people have considered the table a place of community, worship, joy, and reconciliation. A deeper understanding of this biblical tradition of table fellowship and hospitality can strengthen our own relationship with God and others. (Note: If you are reading this book as a group, consider discussing this chapter around a meal.)

1. What were meals like at your home when you grew up? What are most meals like at your home today?

2. Hospitality was often a matter of life and death in Israel. How might our Western self-sufficiency, geography, and typical work life affect our attitude toward welcoming others? What rewards are there for a culture, church, or family that places an emphasis on hospitality? Would you say hospitality is a strength or a challenge for you?

3. Why is sharing a meal together a sign of mutual vulnerability?

4. In what ways has taking Communion enriched your life spiritually? Have you ever intentionally reconciled with someone before taking Communion? If you have never taken Communion, what are your thoughts on this idea of "sitting down to dinner" with God (p. 142–43)?

5. When have you seen a meal bring people closer together? On a more personal level, have you ever found yourself more willing to accept or forgive someone after sharing food with that person?

6. Why was it significant for Jesus's Jewish disciples to share a meal with him? What would your first response be if Jesus asked you to have dinner with him tonight?

7. Considering Jesus's emphasis on sharing food with us, how does a deeper understanding of what "table" means in Jewish culture draw you closer to God?

Chapter 11: Touching the Rabbi's Fringe

God provided the law, or Torah, to the Israelites to guide them in the best way to live. We see Christ's love in these Jewish laws— laws that honor human life, offer patience to wayward followers, and call God's people to stand out as his children. When we view God's commandments in light of his love, even when we don't completely understand them, we know the joy of obeying him.

1. When have you seen a seemingly small choice to do good make a big difference in a relationship, a business decision, or your spiritual life?

2. What is one spiritual rule or commandment that you have a particularly hard time following? How might it change your perspective to consider that commandment as a reflection of God's love rather than as a guilt-inducing trap or limitation?

3. Why do you think Jewish people consider performing a mitzvah—a good deed—to be a joy rather than a burden?

4. When have you asked someone to do something even though the person did not understand your intent?

5. Have you ever obeyed God while not knowing why he was asking you to do something? If so, did you find out later why he wanted you to obey—that "hidden wisdom that will only later be revealed" (p. 159)? If not, are you still glad you obeyed? Why or why not?

6. By instructing his people to wear tassels, God was encouraging them to be obvious about their spiritual commitment. What makes you stand out as a Christian—whether at home, in the workplace, or at a grocery store?

7. Jesus told his followers to stand out but also criticized those who exaggerated their piety. On a practical level, what makes the difference between standing out because you follow God and standing out because you judge people who don't follow God?

8. God provided dietary laws to keep his people separate from the cultures around them. How can you be separate in your actions and words this week but still reach out to people who need to know God?

Chapter 12: Jesus and the Torah

Jesus had no intention of weakening the Torah that had shaped generations of Jewish people. In fact, he came to perfectly obey and perfectly fulfill the Torah. But Rabbi Jesus taught that we are not to follow rules for the sake of following rules but rather to obey them out of a desire to model our lives on the character of God. All his actions and words were directed toward getting at the heart of God's laws—the one most important commandment that the Jewish people were seeking. As Jesus modeled, God's love frees us from legalism and invites us to love him with all our heart, soul, mind, and strength and to love our neighbors as ourselves.

1. We usually think of laws as limiting. When have you seen laws or boundaries as freeing?

2. Describe (a) a time when a decision to resist a small temptation kept you from falling into sin, or (b) a time when giving in to a small temptation led to a greater sin.

3. After reading this chapter, are you surprised at how much Jesus's words reflected the teachings of the Pharisees? Why was it important for Jesus to use the speaking styles of the Jewish people and rabbinic traditions? What does this suggest about how we talk to others about God?

4. Jesus spoke with authority about the mind of God because he was God. When have you seen an author, painter, musician, or other artist speak more passionately about the work he or she created than others could?

5. What does it mean to "go beyond the minimum" (p. 184) in loving God? With this in mind, what would loving God with all your heart, soul, mind, and strength look like in your life today?

6. What does it mean to "go beyond the minimum" in loving your neighbor? With this in mind, what would loving your neighbor as yourself look like in your life today?

7. Why is love "the best interpretation of the law" (p. 189)?

8. In light of this chapter, why would you say the Torah matters to Christians?

Chapter 13: The Mysterious Kingdom of God

The kingdom of God was at the heart of Jesus's mission on earth. This kingdom—or reign—of God is based on forgiveness and atonement. Many Jews of Jesus's day were uncomfortable with this merciful view of God, but Jesus's life and ministry remind us that God's mercy is greater than his wrath. Through the sacrifice of Jesus, we can enthrone God right now in the kingdom of God within us.

1. Jesus fulfilled God's mission in a different way from what people expected. When has God surprised you with how he delivered you from a situation or answered a prayer?

2. The Jewish people had a passionate desire for the entire world to worship God. How does a desire for others to follow God influence your life? What triggers that desire more than anything else?

3. Why would building a kingdom on forgiveness and atonement result in "pure-hearted followers" (p. 204)?

4. Jesus revealed a compassionate God rather than a wrathful God. When have you seen compassion change someone's attitude or actions? Why is compassion powerful?

5. Why is it hard to forgive someone who has wronged you? Why is it hard to accept someone's forgiveness?

6. How do you respond to the idea that "Jesus's kingdom is a living, dynamic reality . . . Our obedience is vital because it is a catalyst for the Spirit's work" (p. 208)? In other words, what does it mean to you right now that "the kingdom of God is within you" (p. 206)?

Chapter 14: Becoming True Disciples of Our Jewish Lord

When we approach Scripture and reputable historical information with humility, we can discover remarkable connections between Jesus, the Old Testament, and the rich Jewish culture. As Rabbi Jesus taught, we are called to be in daily, living relationship with him and then live our lives in such a way that others want to be his disciples as well.

1. What has surprised you the most about Rabbi Jesus as you read *Sitting at the Feet of Rabbi Jesus?*

2. In what ways, if any, do you think you have been judgmental, elitist, or apathetic in your view of the Jewish people? How do you feel about the idea that as Christians "we are but branches grafted into a Jewish tree" (p. 214)?

3. Why does humility influence the way we learn?

4. In what ways has *Sitting at the Feet of Rabbi Jesus* made you more curious about the Jewish roots of Jesus's words?

5. How has this book changed the way you read the Bible?

6. In what ways has this book strengthened your faith as you discovered more about the connections between Jesus, the Old Testament, and God's timeless plan for his children? How has this book enlarged your understanding of who God is and what he thinks of you?

Prayers Jesus Prayed

The Shema

The *Shema* (pronounced "shmah") is not actually a prayer, but a set of Scriptures that are recited morning and evening each day as a declaration of loyalty to God's covenant. It is a commitment to love God and be obedient to him, to teach the Scriptures to your children, and to keep them in your thoughts at all times.

> Hear, O Israel: The LORD our God, the LORD is one. Love the LORD your God with all your heart and with all your soul and with all your strength. These commandments that I give you today are to be on your hearts. Impress them on your children. Talk about them when you sit at home and when you walk along the road, when you lie down and when you get up. Tie them as symbols on your hands and bind them on your foreheads. Write them on the doorframes of your houses and on your gates. (Deuteronomy 6:4–9)
>
> So if you faithfully obey the commands I am giving you today—to love the LORD your God and to serve him with all your heart and with all your soul—then I will send rain on your land in its season, both autumn and spring rains, so that you may gather in your grain, new wine and olive oil. I will provide grass in the fields for your cattle, and you will eat and be satisfied.
>
> Be careful, or you will be enticed to turn away and worship other gods and bow down to them. Then the LORD's anger will burn against you, and he will shut up the heavens so that it will

not rain and the ground will yield no produce, and you will soon perish from the good land the LORD is giving you. Fix these words of mine in your hearts and minds; tie them as symbols on your hands and bind them on your foreheads. Teach them to your children, talking about them when you sit at home and when you walk along the road, when you lie down and when you get up. Write them on the doorframes of your houses and on your gates, so that your days and the days of your children may be many in the land the LORD swore to give your ancestors, as many as the days that the heavens are above the earth. (Deuteronomy 11:13–21)

(The last section, below, is repeated only in the morning, because the tallit, *which carries the tassels, is only worn during daylight hours.)*

The LORD said to Moses, "Speak to the Israelites and say to them: 'Throughout the generations to come you are to make tassels on the corners of your garments, with a blue cord on each tassel. You will have these tassels to look at and so you will remember all the commands of the LORD, that you may obey them and not prostitute yourselves by chasing after the lusts of your own hearts and eyes. Then you will remember to obey all my commands and will be consecrated to your God. I am the LORD your God, who brought you out of Egypt to be your God. I am the LORD your God.'" (Numbers 15:37–41)

The Amidah

The *Amidah* has been the central prayer of Jewish liturgy for well over two thousand years. The version used today was formalized around AD 70, except for one blessing added later. Some variations of the prayer existed in Jesus's time, but he certainly would have known a version of this prayer quite well. See chapter 6 (pp. 84–97) for more.

(1) Blessed are you, O Lord, our God and God of our fathers— God of Abraham, God of Isaac, and God of Jacob. The great, the

mighty, and the awesome God, God Most High, who bestows loving-kindness and is the creator of all. Who remembers the love of our fathers, and will lovingly send a redeemer for their children's children, for the sake of your name. O King, Helper, Savior, and Shield, blessed are you, Shield of Abraham.

(2) You are mighty forever, O Lord, you resurrect the dead, you are great to save. Sustaining the living in loving-kindness, resurrecting the dead in abundant mercy, you support the falling and heal the sick, set free the captives, and keep faith with those who sleep in the dust. Who is like you, Master of mighty deeds, and who may be compared unto you? O King, who sends death and revives again, and causes salvation to sprout forth. You are surely believed to resurrect the dead. Blessed are you, O Lord, who revives the dead.

(3) You are holy and your name is holy, and the holy ones praise you every day. Blessed are you, O Lord, the holy God.[1]

(4) You graciously give knowledge to man, and teach mortals understanding. Favor us with your knowledge, understanding, and intelligence. Blessed are you, O Lord, who graciously gives understanding.

(5) Lead us back, our Father, to your Torah; bring us near, our King, to your service, and cause us to return in perfect repentance before you. Blessed are you, O Lord, who accepts repentance.

(6) Forgive us, our Father, for we have sinned; pardon us, our King, for we have transgressed, for you pardon and forgive. Blessed are you, O gracious one, who multiplies forgiveness.

(7) Look upon our affliction and fight our fight, and redeem us speedily for the sake of your name, for you are a strong redeemer. Blessed are you, O Lord, the Redeemer of Israel.

(8) Heal us and we shall be healed, help us and we shall be helped, for you are our joy. Grant full healing for all our wounds,

---

1   When recited publicly, a liturgy is inserted here.

for you, O God and King, are a true and merciful physician. Blessed are you, O Lord, who heals the sick of his people Israel.

(9) Bless for us, O Lord our God, this year and all of its yield for good, and shower down a blessing upon the face of the earth. Fill us with your bounty and bless our year that it be as the good years. Blessed are you, O Lord, who blesses the years.

(10) Blow the great trumpet for our liberation, and lift a banner to gather our exiles, and gather us into one body from the four corners of the earth. Blessed are you, O Lord, who gathers the dispersed of your people Israel.

(11) Restore our judges as before, and our counselors as in the beginning, and remove from us grief and sighing. Reign over us, O Lord, you alone, in loving-kindness and compassion, and clear us in judgment. Blessed are you, O Lord the King, who loves righteousness and justice.

(12) May no hope be left to the slanderers, but may wickedness perish in a moment. May all your enemies be soon cut off, and speedily uproot the arrogant. Shatter and humble them speedily in our days. Blessed are you, O Lord, who strikes down enemies and humbles the arrogant.[2]

(13) May your compassion, O Lord our God, be stirred over the righteous and over the pious and over the elders of your people, the House of Israel; over the remnant of their scribes, over the proselytes, and over us. Grant a good reward upon them who truly trust in your name, and assign our portion with them forever. May we not come to shame because we have trusted in you. Blessed are you, O Lord, the stronghold and assurance of the righteous.

(14) To Jerusalem, your city, return in mercy, and dwell in her midst as you have promised. Build her speedily in our days as an everlasting structure, and quickly establish there the throne of David. Blessed are you, O Lord, the builder of Jerusalem.

---

2   This blessing was inserted about 100 years later.

(15) May the descendant of David, your servant, be brought forth speedily, and may he be exalted through your salvation, for we hope for your salvation every day. Blessed are you, O Lord, who brings forth the horn of salvation.

(16) Hear our voice, O Lord our God, spare and have mercy on us, and accept in mercy and favor our prayer. For you are a God who hears prayers and supplications. Do not turn us away empty-handed, O our King, when we come before you. For you listen to the prayer of your people Israel in mercy. Blessed are you, O Lord, who hears prayer.

(17) Be pleased, O Lord our God, with your people Israel and their prayer, and reestablish the sacrificial service to the altar of your House. May you accept the fire-offerings of Israel and their prayer offered in love with favor, and may the sacrificial service of Israel your people be ever acceptable to you. And may our eyes behold your merciful return to Zion. Blessed are you who restores your Shekinah to Zion.

(18) We acknowledge to you, O Lord, that you are our God as you were the God of our fathers, forever and ever. Rock of our life, Shield of our salvation, you are unchanging from age to age. We thank you and declare your praise, for our lives that are in your hands and for our souls that are entrusted to you. Your miracles are with us every day, and your benefits are with us at all times, evening and morning and midday. You are good, for your mercies are endless; you are merciful, for your kindnesses are never complete; from everlasting we have hoped in you. And for all these things may your name be blessed and exalted, always and forevermore. Let every living thing give thanks to you and praise your name in truth, O God, our salvation and our help. Blessed are you, O Lord, your name is good, and to you it is right to give thanks.

(19) Grant peace, happiness, and blessing, grace, loving-kindness, and mercy to us and all Israel, your people. Bless us, our Father, every one of us, by the light of your countenance, for

by this light of your countenance you gave us, O Lord our God, the law of life, loving-kindness, and righteousness, and blessing and mercy, life and peace. May it be good in your eyes to bless your people Israel in every time and at every hour with your peace. Blessed are you, O Lord, who blesses your people Israel with peace.

This text, with minor modernizations, is adapted from the article "Shemoneh 'Esreh," by Cyrus Adler and Emil Hirsch at www.jewishencyclopedia.com/articles/13561-shemoneh-esreh (public domain).

A Selection of Blessings (Berakhot)

Since about AD 400, prayers of blessing have always started with the words, "Blessed are you, Lord our God, King of the universe." In the first century they were much shorter, simply beginning with the words "Blessed is he." The first book of the Mishnah (*Berakhot*) lists dozens of blessings and when they were used. Below are some of them in the form they would have had in the first century.

When you first open your eyes in the morning, you say,
Blessed is he who gives sight to the blind.

When getting out of bed, you say,
Blessed is he who sets the captives free.

When putting on clothes, you say,
Blessed is he who clothes the naked.

When putting on your shoes, you say,
Blessed is he who provides for all my needs.

When you eat a meal where bread is at the table, you hold up the bread and say,
Blessed is he who brings forth bread from the earth.

When you eat a festive meal where wine is served, you say,

Blessed is he, Creator of the fruit of the vine.

When you eat other types of food, you say,
Blessed is he through whose word all things come to exist.

(There are several other specific blessings for various kinds of food.)

When you see the first budding tree in springtime, you say,
Blessed is he who did not omit anything from the world,
and created within it good creations and good trees for people to
enjoy!

When you see lightning, falling stars, lofty mountains, great
deserts, or the sky in all its beauty, you say,
Blessed is he who has made the creation.

When you hear thunder or feel an earthquake, you say,
Blessed is he whose strength and power fill the world.

When you see a beautiful person, animal, or tree, you say,
Blessed is he who has such as these in the world.

When you see a friend after a year's separation, you say,
Blessed is he who revives the dead.

When it rains (or something else good happens), you say,
Blessed is he who is good and gives good things!

When something terrible happens, you say,
Blessed is he who is the true judge.

When you are saved from an accident or serious illness, you
say,
Blessed is he who does good to the undeserving and has
rendered every kindness to me!

When you encounter a place where God has done a miracle,
you say,

> *Blessed is he who has done miracles in this place.*

When you've reached some long awaited joyous occasion, you say,

> *Blessed is he who has given us life, and preserved us, and brought us to this season.*

For more on these and other blessings, see the article "Benedictions" by Cyrus Adler and Kaufmann Kohler, at www.jewishencyclopedia.com/articles/2931-benedictions.

The Feasts

Yearly Calendar and Feasts

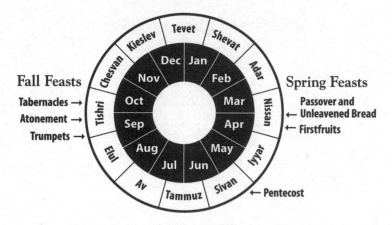

Fall Feasts

Tabernacles →
Atonement →
Trumpets →

Spring Feasts

Passover and
← Unleavened Bread
← Firstfruits

← Pentecost

Some Suggested Resources on the Feasts for Christians

Howard, Kevin, and Marvin Rosenthal. *The Feasts of the Lord*. Nashville, TN: Nelson, 1997. Beautifully illustrated guide to the biblical feasts and their fulfillment by Christ.

Kasdan, Barney. *God's Appointed Times*. Baltimore: Messianic Jewish Publications, 1993. Nice overview of the feasts in Jewish tradition and the New Testament, with ideas for Christian observance today.

Moffic, Evan. *What Every Christian Needs to Know about Passover*. Nashville: Abingdon Press, 2014. Very good discussion of the significance of Passover from a Jewish point of view.

Sampson, Robin, and Linda Pierce. *A Family Guide to the Biblical Holidays*. Woodbridge, VA: Heart of Wisdom, 2001. Comprehensive guide for Christian celebrations of the biblical holidays. A good resource for families.

Smith, Michael, and Rami Shapiro. *Let Us Break Bread Together: A Passover Haggadah for Christians.* Brewster, MA: Paraclete, 2005. Coauthored by a rabbi and a pastor, this pamphlet guides Christian groups and families through a Passover Seder.

Van Loon, Michelle. *Moments & Days: How Our Holy Celebrations Shape Our Faith.* Colorado Springs: Navpress, 2016. Balanced, well-researched guide to the origins of Jewish and Christian festivals and how they relate to each other.

Dates for Some Upcoming Feasts

2018

Passover (*Pesach*)	March 31 (starts sundown March 30)
Pentecost (Shavuot)	May 20 (starts sundown May 19)
Trumpets (Rosh Hashanah)	September 10 (starts sundown September 9)
Day of Atonement (Yom Kippur)	September 19 (starts sundown September 18)
Tabernacles (Sukkot)	September 24 (starts sundown September 23)

2019

Passover (*Pesach*)	April 20 (starts sundown April 19)
Pentecost (Shavuot)	June 9 (starts sundown June 8)
Trumpets (Rosh Hashanah)	September 30 (starts sundown September 29)
Day of Atonement (Yom Kippur)	October 9 (starts sundown October 8)
Tabernacles (Sukkot)	October 14 (starts sundown October 13)

2020

Passover (*Pesach*)	April 9 (starts sundown April 8)
Pentecost (Shavuot)	May 29 (starts sundown May 28)
Trumpets (Rosh Hashanah)	September 19 (starts sundown September 18)
Day of Atonement (Yom Kippur)	September 28 (starts sundown September 27)
Tabernacles (Sukkot)	October 3 (starts sundown October 2)

Biblical Feasts

COMMON NAME	HEBREW NAME	DATE	ACTIVITIES	THEME	FULFILLMENT
*Passover	Pesach	14th day of Nisan (spring)	Sacrificing Passover lamb	Protection from Angel of Death Deliverance from slavery in Egypt	Jesus dies on Passover as the lamb whose blood protects believers from God's judgment. Jesus delivers us from slavery to sin and death.
Unleavened Bread	Matzot	15th day of Nisan (spring)	Remove leaven Live without leaven for seven days	Getting rid of sin (leaven)	Jesus's body is without sin, a perfect sacrifice. Believers live "unleavened" lives in response.
Firstfruits	Bikkurim	1st Sunday after Passover (spring)	Bring firstfruit offering of barley to temple	Celebrating first fruit of barley harvest	Jesus's resurrection was on Firstfruits. He is the firstfruits of those risen from the dead.
*Pentecost	Shavuot	50 days after Passover (late spring)	Celebration in temple Bringing sacrifices of wheat Read Ezek. 1–2	First of wheat harvest Celebration of covenant of law on Mount Sinai	The Spirit is given and first harvest of souls takes place. Holy Spirit writes law on believers' hearts.
Feast of Trumpets	Rosh Hashanah	1st day of Tishri (early fall)	Blowing of shofar Confess sin for ten days	Celebration of New Year Anointing God as King	Dead shall rise at final trumpet. Christ returns to reign as King.
Day of Atonement	Yom Kippur	10th day of Tishri (early fall)	High priest atones for sin	Atonement for sin Scapegoat	Jesus becomes our atoning sacrifice at the final judgment.
*Feast of Tabernacles (Ingathering)	Sukkot	15th day of Tishri (early fall)	Living in booths Dwelling with God in wilderness	Celebration of harvest Water pouring ceremony (last day)	All God's people are gathered into new heaven and new earth to dwell with him forever. Jesus promises living water of the Spirit.

* Passover, Pentecost, and Tabernacles are all pilgrim feasts. All people of Israel were encouraged to journey to Jerusalem to celebrate as a community on these days/weeks.

**The Bible mentions two additional holidays that are still celebrated but are not commanded in the Torah: Hanukkah and Purim. Hanukkah (called the "Feast of Dedication" in John 10:22) is celebrated in December and commemorates the victory of Judas Maccabeus and purification of the temple in 168 BC. Purim takes place in late winter and remembers the deliverance of the people of Israel during the time of Queen Esther. The Sabbath is also considered a holy day, as important as the yearly feast days.

Celebrating Passover:
A Simple Seder

Now that you've gotten an understanding of the tremendous importance of Passover to both Jews and Christians, you may like to try celebrating it yourself. While you can set up a Seder at your church like Lois did, the most appropriate setting is the home, around the family dinner table, as it is celebrated by Jews today. The overall theme of the Seder meal is that of a father and mother telling their children the wonderful story of how God himself saved their family long ago. For this reason, we include here instructions for a family celebration of a Passover meal. The preparations for a traditional dinner are quite involved, and the liturgy can be long. Here is a very simplified Seder to give you a taste of Passover. Afterward are resources for learning more.

Remember that during the Passover celebration, each person is supposed to imagine him or herself on that very last night of slavery before being set free. The special foods that are eaten are a multisensory, experiential way of teaching about that wonderful event. Being hungry and having only dry bread and bitter herbs to eat is a way to have a tiny taste of the deprivation and affliction of slavery. The great pleasure we get when we take our first bite of a mouth-watering feast is like the joy of being set free. As each food enters your lips, ask yourself what God can teach you through it.

Note: The prayers below are based on traditional Jewish prayers, and don't expressly mention Jesus as the fulfillment of Passover. But the point of the meal is to discuss and explore the meaning of God's redemption. You should feel free to meditate as Christians on both pictures—of God's loving liberation of his people from the suffering and hopelessness of slavery, and Christ's salvation of us from sin and death. Make it your goal that the Passover meal is filled with *kavanah*—a sense of the presence of God. It doesn't need to be solemn and overly formal, however. It is supposed to be a feast to celebrate God's victory!

Preparation

Traditionally, each home is thoroughly cleaned to remove all traces of leavened food, and this can take days or weeks. During that time people examine themselves, asking how the physical act of cleansing can parallel the spiritual, moral cleansing of the "leaven" from their hearts. As you prepare, ask the Lord what cleansing he wants you to do in your own heart for this time.

For the meal, set the table with the following:

A nice tablecloth and place settings for an elegant dinner for your family

Two candles, with matches or a lighter nearby.

A plate with three pieces of *matzah* (available at many grocery stores), covered with a napkin. More *matzah* can be eaten during the meal, but no leavened bread may be present.

A goblet full of wine or grape juice at each setting, plus one extra for Elijah. Instead of four cups, take four sips from this cup during the meal. We'll refer to it as "wine" even though it may be juice.

A *haggadah* on each plate. This is a booklet with all the prayers and liturgy of the evening. You can copy the prayers in this guide onto a sheet of paper for each person, if needed.

In the center of the table, place the following items on a nice dinner plate. (If you can buy or borrow a traditional Seder plate, all the better):

A roasted lamb bone (beef or chicken is fine too)

An egg

A small bowl of salt water

Several sprigs of parsley (enough for each person)

A few spoonfuls of ground horseradish

A mound of *haroset* (recipe below)

Haroset

2 cups peeled, finely chopped apples

1/2 cup chopped pecans

1 tablespoon honey

1/4 teaspoon cinnamon

2 tablespoons grape juice (approx.)

Mix apples, pecans, honey, and cinnamon together until well blended. Add grape juice slowly, until texture is a thick paste, like mortar. Taste and adjust the cinnamon and juice accordingly.

Seder Liturgy

This liturgy assumes that a mother, father, and school-age children are present. Feel free to reassign parts as needed.

1. The mother lights the candles and prays the following:

> Blessed are you, Lord our God, King of the universe, who teaches us to be holy through his commandments, and commanded us to light these Seder lights.
>
> Blessed are you, Lord our God, King of the universe, who has preserved us and sustained us, and brought us to this season.

Everyone else says, "Amen." (In Jewish prayer, the one saying the prayer does not say "amen," but everyone else does, in order to voice their agreement with the prayer.)

2. The father holds up his wine or juice, and he and everyone leans back slightly, as if reclining at a royal banquet. The father prays the blessing for the first cup:

> Blessed are you, Lord our God, King of the universe, Creator of the fruit of the vine. Blessed are you, Lord our God, King of the universe, who has chosen us from among all people, and with love given us solemn days for joy, festivals and seasons for gladness, this day of the Feast of Unleavened Bread, the season of our redemption, a holy celebration, a memorial of the departure from Egypt, and your festivals which you have caused us to inherit with joy and gladness.
>
> Blessed are you, O Lord, who sanctifies Israel and the seasons. (The family responds, "Amen.")

All take their first of four sips.

3. Everyone takes a sprig of parsley and dips it into the salt water. This is to represent the tears that the Israelites shed in slavery in Egypt. The mother prays the following blessing:

> Blessed are you, Lord our God, King of the universe, Creator of the fruit of the earth. (Amen.)

All eat their parsley and salt water.

4. The father picks up the plate of three *matzah* pieces and says the following:

> Lo! This is the bread of affliction, which our fathers ate in their need. Let us, whom God's mercy has freed, now remember those who are still oppressed and resolve to aid them with all our means. Let those who are hungry come

and eat! Let those who are in want come and celebrate the Passover with us! God grant that next year at this time, the whole house of Israel may be free.

He takes the middle piece, breaks it in half and wraps the larger half in a napkin and hides it to be brought back at the end. This is the *afikomen*.

5. One of the children recites the Four Questions:

> Why is this night different from all other nights? On all nights we may eat either leavened or unleavened bread, but on this night, only unleavened bread. On all other nights we may eat any species of herbs, but on this night, only bitter herbs. On all other nights we do not dip even once, but on this night twice. On all other nights we eat and drink sitting, but on this night we are leaning.

6. The father responds by saying:

> It is both a duty and a privilege to answer the Four Questions of Passover and to recite the mighty works of our faithful God. Once we were slaves to Pharaoh in Egypt, and the Lord, in his goodness and mercy, brought us forth from that land with a mighty hand and an outstretched arm. Had he not rescued us from the hand of Pharaoh, we and our children would still be enslaved, deprived of liberty and human dignity. We therefore gather year after year to retell this ancient story, for it is not ancient but eternal in its message and its spirit.
>
> Why is this night different from all other nights? On this night we eat unleavened bread to remember that our ancestors, in their haste to leave Egypt, could not wait for bread to rise.
>
> On this night why do we eat only bitter herbs? We

partake of the bitter herbs on this night so that we might taste of some bitterness to remind ourselves how bitter is the lot of one caught in the grip of slavery.

On this night why do we dip the herbs twice? We dip twice, parsley in salt water and bitter herbs in *haroset*, once to replace tears with gratefulness, and once to sweeten bitterness and suffering.

On this night we eat in a reclining position. To recline at mealtimes in ancient days was a sign of freedom. On this night of Passover, we demonstrate our sense of freedom by reclining as we drink from each cup of wine, symbolizing our joy.

7. Members of the family take turns reading the story of the first Passover in Exodus 12:21–39 and 14:5–31.

8. The mother says,

> In order to free us from Egypt, God parted the waters and drowned the Egyptians. He sent ten plagues upon Egypt to punish their gods and release us from bondage. But our joy is lessened by knowing about the suffering that the Egyptians endured. As I call out the name of each plague, let us dip our little finger in our wine and drip it out onto our plates. The wine, symbolizing our joy, is lessened by the tears the Egyptians shed.
>
> These are the ten plagues which the Most Holy, blessed be He, brought upon the Egyptians in Egypt, and these they are:

Blood!	Boils!
Frogs!	Hail!
Gnats!	Locusts!
Biting Flies!	Darkness!
Cattle Disease!	Death of the Firstborn!

9. The father then raises his glass for the second cup of wine for the Cup of Remembrance, saying,

> How numerous are the gifts which the Lord has bestowed on us. He brought us forth from Egypt, executed judgment on the Egyptians, slew their gods, slew their first-born, gave us their wealth, divided the sea for us, caused us to pass through on dry land, supplied us with everything in the wilderness for forty years, gave us the Sabbath, led us to Mt. Sinai, gave us his law, led us to the land of Israel, and built the Temple for us.
>
> Blessed are you, Lord our God, King of the universe, Creator of the fruit of the vine. (Amen.)

Everyone leans back and takes another sip.

10. The family recites the ancient Dayeinu liturgy, which dates back to before AD 200. *Dayeinu* means "Enough for us," and each verse ends with "Dayeinu":

> If he had rescued us from Egypt,
> but not punished the Egyptians,
> It would have been enough! (*Dayeinu*)
> If he had punished the Egyptians,
> but not defeated their gods,
> It would have been enough! (*Dayeinu*)
> If he had given us the Sabbath
> But not led us to Mount Sinai,
> It would have been enough! (*Dayeinu*)
> If he had led us to Mount Sinai,
> But not given us the Torah,
> It would have been enough! (*Dayeinu*)
> If he would have given us the Torah,
> but not brought us into the land of Israel,
> It would have been enough! (*Dayeinu*)

How much more, then, are we to be grateful to God
for all of these good things which he has indeed done
for all of us!

11. The father picks up a piece of unleavened bread, breaks it, and says:

    Blessed are you, Lord our God, King of the universe, who
    brings forth bread from the earth. Blessed are you, Lord our
    God, King of the universe, who teaches us to be holy through
    your commandments, and commands us to eat unleavened
    bread. (Amen.)

    The unleavened bread is passed around, and everyone breaks
    off a piece and eats it.

12. Each person breaks off a small piece of *matzah*, puts a little bit of
    horseradish on it. The mother says,

    Blessed are you, Lord our God, King of the universe, who
    teaches us to be holy through his commandments, and com-
    mands us to eat bitter herbs. (Amen.)

    All eat their *matzah* and horseradish, and think about the bit-
    terness of slavery.

13. On another piece of *matzah*, each person puts a little horseradish,
    and this time puts a spoonful of *haroset* on top. One more *matzah*
    piece on top makes a little "sandwich." The *haroset* represents the
    mortar used in making the bricks when they were enslaved. But
    it's sweet, because God was present even in the midst of their suf-
    fering. Everyone eats their sandwich.

14. A festive meal is served. Don't just have the typical discussions
    that you have over dinner. Use this time to reflect on what you
    have learned about Passover and the Last Supper. Children can
    continue to ask their parents what these celebrations are all about.

If the parents don't know, make it a family project to research the answers. Or, discuss how God has redeemed your own lives through Christ, and reflect on the things he has done that have brought you to the point where you are today.

15. The plates are removed and children search for the *afikomen*, which the father hid earlier. Tradition has it that the child who finds it can ask for a gift. This is likely the bread that Jesus held up after supper and said, "This is my body." Feel free to discuss what it means that this "bread of affliction" represents Jesus, and that his sinless, unleavened body was broken for us. The father takes the *afikomen* and holds it up and says,

> Blessed are you, Lord our God, King of the universe, who brings forth bread from the earth. (Amen.)

He breaks it and gives a piece to everyone to eat. This is the last thing that can be eaten, so that the taste lingers in each person's mouth.

16. The father then raises his glass for the third cup of wine, which is called the "Cup of Redemption." This is the cup that Jesus raised after supper and said, "This is my blood." Think about what it means that Jesus shed his blood to redeem us from our sins. Everyone leans back, raises their glass, and the father prays,

> Therefore, we are bound to thank, praise, laud, glorify, extol, honor, bless, exalt, and revere him, who did all these miracles for our ancestors and for us; for he brought us forth from bondage to freedom, from sorrow to joy, from mourning to festivity, from darkness to great light, and from slavery to redemption, and therefore let us sing unto him a new song. Hallelujah!
>
> Blessed are you, Lord our God, King of the universe, Creator of the fruit of the vine. (Amen.)

17. One of the children goes to the front door, opens it and looks out, and looks to see if he sees Elijah outside. According to Malachi 4, Elijah will appear to announce the coming of the Messiah. Have the child return to the table and read Matthew 17:10–13. What does Jesus say about the coming of Elijah?

18. For the fourth and last time, the father leans back, lifts his cup, and prays,

> The breath of all living shall praise your name, O Lord, our God. You redeem, deliver, maintain, and have compassion on us, in all times of trouble and distress, we have no king but you. You are God of the first, and God of the last, and God of all creatures. You are adored with all manner of praise; who governs the universe with tenderness, and his creatures with mercy. Every mouth shall adore you, every knee shall bend, every being shall bow down before you. O Lord, who is like unto you? Great and mighty, tremendous God, most high God, possessor of heaven and earth. Blessed are you, Lord our God, King of the universe, Creator of the fruit of the vine. (Amen.)

> Everyone drinks the last of their wine.

19. It is traditional to sing songs of praise after supper, especially the Psalms of Ascent (Psalm 113–118). Read one or more of these, or sing some songs you find meaningful.

20. Last, everyone exclaims together, "Next Year, In Jerusalem!"

Further Resources

DATES FOR PASSOVER

The dates below are the evenings before the calendar date of Passover, which is the time when the Passover meal is traditionally eaten. Some Jews eat another Passover meal the next evening too. For the seven additional days of the Feast of Unleavened Bread, no leavened food can be eaten.

Friday, March 30, 2018
Friday, April 19, 2019
Friday, April 8, 2020

Recommended Resources

Books and Videos

Bailey, Kenneth E. *Poet & Peasant and Through Peasant Eyes* (combined edition). Grand Rapids: Eerdmans, 1983. From his experience among traditional Middle Eastern peoples, Bailey shares a wealth of cultural insights on Jesus's parables.

Bivin, David. *New Light on the Difficult Words of Jesus: Insights from His Jewish Context*. Holland, MI: En-Gedi Resource Center, 2005. Excellent overview of Jesus's first-century life and teachings in their Jewish context.

Dickson, Athol. *The Gospel according to Moses: What My Jewish Friends Taught Me about Jesus*. Grand Rapids: Baker, 2003. A conservative Christian attends a Reform Jewish Torah study and uncovers rich wisdom for his own faith.

Dosick, Wayne. *Living Judaism: The Complete Guide to Jewish Belief, Tradition, and Practice*. San Francisco: HarperCollins, 1995. Encyclopedic guide to contemporary Jewish tradition and practice.

Evans, Craig. *Fabricating Jesus: How Modern Scholars Distort the Gospels*. Downers Grove, IL: InterVarsity Press, 2006. Excellent popular-level book by a respected scholar on recent theories about the historical Jesus.

Flusser, David, with R. Steven Notley. *The Sage from Galilee: Rediscovering Jesus' Genius*. Grand Rapids: Eerdmans, 2007. An academic study of the Jewish historical reality of Jesus by a renowned Jewish scholar, David Flusser.

Hagner, Donald. *The Jewish Reclamation of Jesus: An Analysis and Critique of the Modern Jewish Study of Jesus*. Grand Rapids: Zondervan, 1984. Reprinted by Wipf and Stock of Eugene, OR, 1997. Hagner surveys several influential Jewish scholarly works on Jesus and comments on their findings from a Christian perspective.

Heschel, Abraham. *The Sabbath*. New York: Farrar, Straus, and Giroux, 2005. A classic work on how time itself is sanctified in Jewish worship.

———. *God in Search of Man: A Philosophy of Judaism*. New York: Farrar, Straus, and Giroux, 1976. A comprehensive study of Judaism. Not light reading, but full of profound insights.

———. *Man's Quest For God*. New York: Scribner, 1954. Another masterful book by Heschel that probes the essence of prayer.

Howard, Kevin, and Marvin Rosenthal. *The Feasts of the Lord*. Nashville, TN: Nelson, 1997. Beautifully illustrated guide to the biblical feasts and their fulfillment by Christ.

Instone-Brewer, David. *Traditions of the Rabbis from the Era of the New Testament*. Vol. 1 of 6-vol. series. Grand Rapids: Eerdmans, 2004. A scholarly study of rabbinic sayings that describe the Judaism of Jesus's day.

Kaiser, Walter C., Jr., and Duane Garrett. *Archaeological Study Bible: An Illustrated Walk Through Biblical History and Culture*. Grand Rapids: Zondervan, 2006. Colorfully illustrated NIV study Bible, full of articles on culture and archaeology that shed light on the biblical text.

Kasdan, Barney. *God's Appointed Times*. Baltimore: Messianic Jewish Publishers, 2007. Nice overview of the feasts in Jewish tradition and the New Testament, with ideas for Christian observance today.

Moffic, Evan. *What Every Christian Needs to Know about Passover*. Nashville: Abingdon Press, 2014. Very good discussion of the significance of Passover from a Jewish point of view.

Pearl, Chaim. *Theology in Rabbinic Stories*. Peabody, MA: Hendrickson, 1997. A delightful collection of rabbinic stories and discussion of the ideas within them.

Pryor, Dwight A. *Behold the Man!* (DVD series & study guide). Dayton, OH: Center for Judaic Christian Studies, 2008. Twelve sessions on the significance of Jesus's Jewishness for Christians today. Excellent for a group study.

———. *Unveiling the Kingdom of Heaven* (DVD series & study guide).

Dayton, OH: Center for Judaic Christian Studies, 2008. Excellent introduction to Jesus's teachings on the kingdom and its implications for our lives.

Safrai, Shmuel, and Menahem Stern, eds. *The Jewish People in the First Century.* 2 vols. Philadelphia: Fortress, 1976. Scholarly and difficult to find, but an outstanding resource on first-century Jewish life and times.

Sampson, Robin, and Linda Pierce. *A Family Guide to the Biblical Holidays.* Woodbridge, VA: Heart of Wisdom, 2001. Comprehensive guide for Christian celebrations of the biblical holidays. A good resource for families.

Schechter, Solomon. *Aspects of Rabbinic Theology.* Peabody, MA: Hendrickson, reprint, 1998 (orig. 1909). An overview of the theology of Judaism by a Conservative Jewish rabbi; older but very readable.

Smith, Michael, and Rami Shapiro. *Let Us Break Bread Together: A Passover Haggadah for Christians.* Brewster, MA: Paraclete, 2005. Coauthored by a rabbi and a pastor, this pamphlet guides Christian groups and families through a Passover Seder.

Stern, David H. *Jewish New Testament Commentary.* Baltimore: Messianic Jewish Resources International, 1992. In-depth, verse-by-verse commentary on the New Testament by a Messianic Jewish scholar. Very good reference.

Telushkin, Joseph. *Jewish Literacy*, rev. ed. New York: William Morrow, 2008. Encyclopedia-like guide to all aspects of Jewish belief, culture, and history. Readable and insightful.

Tverberg, Lois, with Bruce Okkema. *Listening to the Language of the Bible: Hearing It Through Jesus' Ears.* Holland, MI: En-Gedi Resource Center, 2004. Dozens of brief reflections on Hebrew words and Jewish concepts that enrich Bible reading.

Tverberg, Lois. *Listening to the Language of the Bible: Companion Bible Study.* Holland, MI: En-Gedi Resource Center, 2005. A study guide for the book above, for those who want to learn to read the Bible in light of its Hebraic context.

———. *Walking in the Dust of Rabbi Jesus: How the Jewish Words of Jesus Can Change Your Life.* Grand Rapids: Zondervan, 2012. Examines some of Jesus's words in their Jewish context and what this means for living them out today.

————. *Reading the Bible with Rabbi Jesus: How a Jewish Perspective Can Transform Your Understanding*. Grand Rapids: Baker, 2018. A guide to understanding the Scriptures as a first-century disciple, with tools for unlocking language and cultural nuances.

————. *5 Hebrew Words that Every Christian Should Know* (ebook). Holland, MI: OurRabbiJesus.com, 2014.

Vander Laan, Ray. *Faith Lessons* (DVDs and study guides). Grand Rapids: Zondervan, 1998–2018. Outstanding video series that shares insights on the land and culture of the Bible, exploring its implications for Christians today.

Van Loon, Michelle. *Moments & Days: How Our Holy Celebrations Shape Our Faith*. Colorado Springs: Navpress, 2016. Balanced, well-researched guide to the origins of Jewish and Christian festivals and how they relate to each other.

Walton, John, and Craig Keener. *Cultural Backgrounds NIV Study Bible*. Grand Rapids: Zondervan, 2016. Very helpful study Bible for cultural details, particularly the New Testament commentary.

Wilson, Marvin. *Our Father Abraham: Jewish Roots of the Christian Faith*. Grand Rapids: Eerdmans, 1989. A must-read introductory text for anyone wanting to learn more on this topic.

Winner, Lauren. *Mudhouse Sabbath*. Orleans, MA: Paraclete, 2007. As a Christian who has a Jewish past, Winner reflects on how her earlier life enriches her faith and practice.

Young, Brad. *Jesus the Jewish Theologian*. Peabody, MA: Hendrickson, 1995. Excellent study of Jesus's life and teachings in their Jewish context.

Websites

EnGediResourceCenter.com—En-Gedi Resource Center. Educational ministry that teaches about the Jewish context of Christianity. Books and articles by Lois Tverberg and other authors. See *EGRC.net* also.

Hebrew4Christians.com—Hebrew for Christians. Very nice site for learning Hebrew and about Christianity's Jewish heritage.

JCStudies.com—JC Studies. Material by Dwight Pryor and others. Excellent audio/video materials about applying Hebraic study to life today.

JerusalemPerspective.com—Jerusalem Perspective. A large number of excellent articles on Jesus's first-century Jewish context.

OurRabbiJesus.com—Articles by author Lois Tverberg on the Bible and Jesus in their original Hebraic, Jewish context that meditate on the implications for Christians today.

ThatTheWorldMayKnow.com—That the World May Know. Website of Ray Vander Laan, source of *Faith Lessons* video series, leads trips to Israel and Asia Minor. Many articles and resources available.

Glossary

Note: Many of these words have more than one accepted spelling because the English word is a transliteration, which is an approximation because of language differences.

Afikomen (ah-fih-KOH-mun). A piece of *matzah* broken and hidden away early during the Passover meal, which is brought out later and eaten at the end.

Amidah (ah-mee-DAH or ah-MEE-dah; lit., "standing"). The central prayer in Jewish liturgy, repeated three times a day and said while standing. Also called the *Shemoneh Esreh*, (SHMO-neh ES-reh), meaning "eighteen," because originally it was composed of eighteen benedictions, but now a nineteenth has been added.

Berakhah (bear-a-KHAH, or BRA-khah; lit., "blessing"; pl., *berakhot*, bear-a-KHOT). A brief prayer of praise or thanksgiving, acknowledging God as the source of all blessing.

Bet Midrash (bet mid-RASH; lit., "house of interpretation"). Center for study and teaching of the Torah and its rabbinic interpretation. In the first century, it was usually located within a synagogue. It was a "high school" where boys between the ages of thirteen and seventeen studied religious texts, although adults continued to study there in their free time.

Challah (HAL-lah). Braided, sweet bread served on the Sabbath and some festival days.

Daven (DAH-ven). Yiddish word which means "to pray," often used to describe the practice of swaying while reciting prayers. This custom arose among Jews in the Middle Ages.

Essenes. Reform group active in the first century BC and first century

AD. Along with the Pharisees, Sadducees, and Zealots, it was one of the four most influential groups during the time of Christ. The Essenes deplored the corruption of Judaism by pagan elements, but they were not political activists. Some withdrew into the Judean wilderness, where they lived quietly but with great ceremonial purity, preparing themselves for the final battle between the "Sons of Light" (themselves) and the "Sons of Darkness" (most everyone else). The Dead Sea Scrolls contain many of their writings, along with dozens of copies of biblical texts.

Gezerah Shavah (Geh-zer-AH Sha-VAH, lit., "a comparison of equals"). One of Hillel's "Seven Principles of Interpretation," which says that two biblical texts sharing the same word or phrase can be used to interpret each other.

Haggadah (Ha-GAHD-dah, lit., "telling"; also spelled *Aggadah.*). Rabbinic parables and stories, as opposed to law decisions; see *halakhah*. (Also, a *haggadah* is a book of prayers and liturgy traditionally read at a Passover Seder.)

Halakhah (Hal-a-KHAH, lit., "walk"). Hebrew word that is used for legal ordinances in Judaism. (Note that "Torah" is not understood this way, but as "instruction," or "teaching.") *Halakhah* defines how the Torah is applied to your "walk" in life (laws and ethics). Rabbis, including Jesus, taught both *halakhah* (ethics and law) and *haggadah* (stories to explain the Scriptures).

HaShem (hah-SHEM). Hebrew for "the name." Commonly used by modern Jews as a substitute for God's name, out of reverence for God. *Adonai* (meaning "my Lord") is another substitution for God's name. In Jesus's time, "heaven" and "the Holy One" were other substitutions.

Hasidic (hah-SIH-dic). Adjective describing ultra-Orthodox Jews, often in reference to a Jewish movement that began in the 1700s emphasizing mysticism and piety.

Hasidut (hah-see-DOOT). Hebrew word for "piety" that comes from the word *hesed*, which means "loving-kindness." In Hebrew, a person who is pious is a *hasid* (hah-SEED; pl. *hasidim*, ha-see-DEEM).

Haver (ha-VAIR; lit., "friend"; masc. pl., *haverim*, ha-ver-EEM). A student who partners with another in study to discuss a religious text and aid each other in learning. A female study partner is a *haverah* (ha-ver-AH; pl, *haverot*, ha-ver-OTE).

Havruta (hav-ROO-tah). The traditional method of studying Jewish texts together by debating in pairs.

Hillel (hill-LELL). A famous Jewish teacher who was active between 30 BC and AD 10. He was known for his gentleness and moderation in the interpretation of the law. His school of disciples often debated the disciples of Shammai over their stricter interpretations of Jewish law.

Kaparot (kah-pah-ROTE; lit., "covering"). Ritual of sacrificing a chicken to atone for one's sins on the day preceding *Yom Kippur*, the Day of Atonement. The practice arose centuries after the destruction of the temple, and is still done by a few ultra-Orthodox Jews today.

Kavanah (ka-vah-NAH or ka-VAHN-ah; lit., "intention"). To focus one's attention and concentration on being in the presence of God; to direct one's thoughts toward God.

Lechem (LEKH-hem). Hebrew word for "bread," which also refers to food or nourishment in general.

Malkhut shamayim (mahl-KUT shuh-my-EEM; lit., "kingdom of heaven"). Rabbinic term used since before the first century to describe God's activity and reign over those who worship him as king. *Malkhut* means "kingship" or "reign"; *shamayim* means "heavens," a respectful euphemism for God. Exactly the same as "kingdom of God."

Mashiach (mah-SHEE-akh; lit., "anointed"). Hebrew word for Messiah; Greek is *Christos*. It means literally "Anointed One" and refers to the fact that God promised that someone would come who would be specially chosen and anointed as a great king and priest for his people.

Matzah (MAHT-zah). Unleavened bread eaten at Passover.

Messianic Jew. A person who believes that Jesus is the Messiah, but retains his or her Jewish identity. Some Jews avoid using the term "Christian" because of the assumption that Christians are Gentiles.

Midrash (mi-DRASH or MIH-drash; pl. *midrashim*, mi-dra-SHEEM). A rabbinic explanation or commentary on the biblical text. In later centuries, it often expanded biblical stories with legends about the characters in order to explain the text. *Midrash* can also refer to a compilation of commentaries on the text. *Midrashim* date from as early as 400 BC up to the Middle Ages. These commentaries were handed down orally and later compiled in written form. The *midrashim* are extensively quoted in the Talmud.

Minyan (min-YAHN). A gathering of a minimum of ten adult male Jews required for some public prayers. In the first century, women could be included in this number too.

Mishnah (mish-NAH or MISH-nah). The collection of rabbinic rulings and sayings compiled and committed to writing around AD 200. The Mishnah records the sayings of teachers who lived and taught during the previous four hundred years, both before and after the time of Jesus.

Mitzvah (MITS-vah; lit., "command"; pl., *mitzvot*, mits-VOTE). Hebrew word meaning "commandment," referring to a religious obligation, often to a "good deed."

Moed (moe-ED; lit., "meeting"; pl., *moedim*, mo-eh-DEEM). Hebrew word meaning "meeting" or "appointment." The biblical feast days were referred to as *moedim*, God's "appointed times."

Oral Torah. The explanation and interpretations of the laws given by Moses (the "Written Torah") that were passed down in oral form by rabbinic teachers in Jesus's day, and later written down in the Mishnah (see above definition).

Pesach (PAY-sakh; lit., "protect" or "pass over"—*meaning is disputed*). Passover, the first of the seven biblical feasts, held in March or April to remember the exodus from Egypt. Today Passover is still observed by Jews with a ceremonial meal in their homes.

Peyot (PAY-ote or pay-OTE). Side curls worn by some ultra-Orthodox Jews in order to observe the command in Leviticus 19:27 not to shave the edges of one's beard.

Pharisees (lit., "the separated ones" or "separatists"). The roots of this sect can be traced to the second century BC. Unlike the aristocratic

Sadducees, most were common laborers who devoted their spare time to study and teaching. Pondering the lessons of exile and persecution, they concluded that the best hope for the future lay in devotion to God. They carefully studied the Torah to discover how best to live according to the law. As one of the most influential groups in the New Testament period, they determined the character of rabbinic Judaism after the fall of the temple in AD 70.

Pirke Avot (*peer*-KAY *ah*-VOTE; lit. "Chapters of the Fathers"). A section of the Mishnah that contains rabbinic ethical and wisdom sayings from between 200 BC and AD 200. Many comment on the same topics that Jesus did, shedding light on how his words were understood in his time.

Rabbi (lit., "my master"). A term of respect that was used when speaking to teachers of the Scriptures in Jesus's day. After AD 70, "rabbi" became a formal title.

Rosh Hashanah (rosh ha-SHAH-nah; lit., "head of the year"). Jewish New Year, also called *Yom Teruah*, the "day of trumpeting."

Sadducees. Members of the Sadducees came primarily from the ruling priestly and aristocratic classes. They controlled the temple worship. Many people resented them for fattening their purses and securing their position by collaborating with the Romans. Unlike the Pharisees, they did not believe in the resurrection of the dead, and they considered only the Written Torah as binding. Their influence ceased with the destruction of the temple in AD 70.

Seder (SAY-der; lit., "order"). Ritual meal eaten on Passover. The name comes from the fact that the meal follows a traditional order of liturgy and ceremonial foods.

Shabbat (shah-BAHT). Hebrew for "Sabbath," meaning "to cease." A time of ceasing from labor, according to the Bible. Jews observe Shabbat from Friday sunset until Saturday sunset.

Shammai (SHAM-mai or sham-MAI). Famous Jewish scholar of the first century BC who was known for his strict approach to interpreting the laws of the Torah. His school of disciples often debated the more moderate disciples of Hillel during the first century, and these debates shed light on the context of Jesus's sayings.

Shavuot (shav-u-OTE; lit., "weeks"). Hebrew word for the feast that in Greek is called *Pentecost*, meaning "fiftieth day." Seven weeks are counted off after the Feast of Firstfruits to arrive at the day. Commemorates God's giving of his law and covenant on Mount Sinai. The Holy Spirit was poured out on the new believers on this day, as a sign of the new covenant, in which God would put his law in our hearts (Jeremiah 31:33).

Shema (shmah; lit., "hear"). Three Bible passages recited morning and evening by Jews over the millennia, since before Jesus's time. They are Deuteronomy 6:4–9; 11:13–21; and Numbers 15:37–41. The first word of Deuteronomy 6:4, "Hear, O Israel: The Lord our God, the Lord is one." *Shema* means "hear," but it implies action, also meaning "take heed" and "obey." To pray the *Shema* is to commit one's self to loving God and obeying his laws.

Shofar (SHOW-far). A ram's horn that is blown as a trumpet. In biblical times it was sounded for a variety of purposes, but now it is blown on the day of *Rosh Hashanah*, the Jewish new year, and at the end of *Yom Kippur*, the Day of Atonement.

Sukkah (SOO-kah). A booth or tabernacle, a temporary shelter constructed for the Feast of *Sukkot*.

Sukkot (soo-KOTE; lit., "booths"). The Feast of Tabernacles, a harvest festival held in the fall, the last of the seven biblical feasts. For seven days, Jews are commanded to live in booths in order to remember dwelling in the wilderness for forty years after they left Egypt.

Sulha (sul-HAH). A covenantal meal of reconciliation used in Arab cultures. The word *sulha* is the Arabic equivalent of the Hebrew word *shulhan*, which means "table." It derives from the ancient belief that eating at the same table with others is the essence of a peaceful, harmonious relationship.

Synagogue (lit., "assembly"). A local community center that is the place of prayer and study of Scripture. It likely arose during the exile in Babylon when Jews were unable to worship at the temple. In the first century, all kinds of meetings were held there—school during the week, and prayer and study of the Torah on the Sabbath.

Tallit (tah-LEET). In modern Jewish usage, a *tallit* is the prayer shawl, a ceremonial shawl to which tassels are attached. In Jesus's day, the *tallit* was the outer woolen mantle, a rectangle of heavy cloth that bore tassels on its four corners. It was worn in public at all times and could be used as a blanket for sleeping. Underneath was the *haluk* (hah-LOOK), a linen undergarment. Nowadays, Hasidic Jews and some Orthodox Jews wear a small *tallit* (a *tallit katan*, a rectangular cloth carrying the tassels, with a hole for the head) underneath their shirts in order to wear tassels all the time.

Talmid (tahl-MEED; lit., "student"; pl., *talmidim*, tahl-me-DEEM). A disciple or student of a rabbi, one who dedicated himself to life together with a rabbi, humbly serving him and learning the rabbi's understanding of Scripture and his way of living it out.

Talmud (TAHL-mood). Large volume of commentary on the Mishnah. The commentary is printed section by section following each verse of the Mishnah. There are two Talmuds: the Jerusalem (or Palestinian) Talmud, completed about AD 400; and the Babylonian Talmud, completed about a century later. The latter became more widely used.

Tanakh (TAH-nakh or tah-NAHK). The Jewish term for the Bible. It includes the same books as in the Protestant "Old Testament." *Tanakh* is actually an acronym of the first letters that start each of the three main sections. These are the:

- **Torah** (Pentateuch): Five books of Moses (the covenant and laws)
- **Neviim** (neh-vee-YEEM, lit., "prophets"): Joshua, Judges, 1–2 Samuel, other historical books; Isaiah, Jeremiah, and other prophets
- **Ketuvim** (ket-u-VEEM, lit., "writings"): Psalms, Proverbs, Job, Ruth, and others

Tefillah (teh-fee-LAH or teh-FEE-lah; lit., "prayer"). Sometimes used to refer to the *Amidah*, the central prayer in Jewish liturgy.

Tefillin (teh-FEE-lin). Phylacteries, leather boxes containing Scriptures that were worn on the forehead and left arm to fulfill the command in Deuteronomy 6:8: "Tie them as symbols on your hands and bind them on your foreheads." In Jesus's time, these were worn most of the day, but now they are worn only during prayer on weekdays.

Torah (TOR-ah; "teaching, instruction"). Refers to the first five books of the Bible, also called the Pentateuch. Christians often translate Torah as "law," while Jewish translations usually render it "teaching."

Tzitzit (TSEE-tseet; pl., *tzitziyot*—tsee-tsee-YOTE). Tassels attached to the hem of a garment, called a *tallit*, in accordance with the command to wear tassels in Numbers 15:37–41. (See *tallit* for more.)

Yarmulke (YAR-muhl-kuh). A fabric skullcap worn traditionally by Jewish men. Some men wear one at all times, while others wear it only for religious occasions.

Yeshiva (yeh-SHEEV-ah). Orthodox Jewish school for religious learning in modern times. Some schools teach younger students, and some prepare adults to become ordained as rabbis.

Yeshua (yeh-SHU-ah). Jesus's name as it would have been said in Hebrew. It is a shortened form of *Yehoshua*, which in English is "Joshua." Both mean "God's salvation," which is why the angel said, "You are to give him the name Jesus, because he will save his people from their sins" (Matthew 1:21).

Yom Kippur (yome kih-PUHR; or yome KIP-pur, lit., "day of covering"). Day of Atonement. The most holy day of the year for Jewish people, when they fast and pray for forgiveness of sins. In biblical times the sins of the nation were laid on the head of a scapegoat, which was then driven into the wilderness, and the high priest entered the Most Holy Place of the temple to make atonement for the sins of the nation.

Zealots. The Zealots originated during the reign of Herod the Great. A political party with religious underpinnings, this group advocated the violent rebellion of Israel against Rome. The Galilee region where Jesus lived and taught was a Zealot stronghold. This movement came to the fore in the Jewish revolt against Rome in AD 66–70 and disappeared afterward.

Notes

Chapter 1: Joining Mary at the Feet of Jesus

1. See Shmuel Safrai, "The Place of Women in First-Century Synagogues," *Jerusalem Perspective* 40 (1993): 3–6, 14. Wealthy women, who often took charge of the family's charitable contributions, sometimes supported rabbis, just as Joanna and other women supported Jesus in Luke 8. See Tal Ilan, *Integrating Women into Second Temple History* (Peabody, MA: Hendrickson, 1999), 15–31.
2. Mishnah, *Pirke Avot* ("Sayings of the Fathers") 1:4. This saying is attributed to Yose ben Yoezer, one of the earliest rabbinic teachers, who lived in the second century BC.
3. In Greek the literal words of Paul were that he had trained "at the feet" of Gamaliel. The NIV obscures this metaphor by translating the line as, "I studied under Gamaliel and was thoroughly trained."
4. David Bivin, *New Light on the Difficult Words of Jesus* (Holland, MI: En-Gedi Resource Center, 2005), 14.
5. For instance, it's only been in the past dozen years that it has been established how strongly Jewish the Galilee area was where Jesus grew up. For decades, scholars assumed that the Galilee area was a land of peasants cut off from the religious fervor of Jerusalem. So it's hardly surprising, for instance, that more than twenty years ago, Philip Yancey portrayed the Galilee area as "lax in spiritual matters," in *The Jesus I Never Knew* (Grand Rapids: Zondervan, 1995), 59–60. But more recently, archaeology has revealed that Jesus lived among very observant Jews, known for their national and religious zealotry. This makes an enormous difference in how we repaint the cultural backdrop of Jesus's ministry. See Mark Chancey, *The Myth of a Gentile Galilee* (Cambridge, UK: Cambridge University Press, 2002). Noted scholar Craig Evans points out that seeing the Jewishness of Jesus's upbringing can counter some of the more questionable theories about Jesus's teachings, for instance that they arose out of his youthful encounters with pagan Greek philosophers. See Craig Evans, *Fabricating Jesus: How Modern Scholars Distort the Gospels* (Downers Grove, IL: InterVarsity Press, 2006), 100–122.
6. This explains why, in Matthew 2, the wise men came to honor Jesus as the newborn king of Israel with gold, frankincense, and myrrh. In that

world, these were gifts fit for a king. This also parallels the life of Solomon, when the queen of Sheba brought him extremely expensive gifts, including enormous amounts of spices. See 1 Kings 10.

7. It should be noted that while John's gospel describes Mary's anointing of Jesus as occurring the evening before his triumphal entry, Matthew 26:6 and Mark 14:3 place it later during Holy Week, a couple of days before his arrest and crucifixion. (Matthew and Mark do not identify the woman, but John says specifically in John 11:2 that it was Mary.)

8. Posted at www.calvin.edu/worship/stories/bailey_bonus.php (accessed July 8, 2008).

9. Philip Yancey, *The Jesus I Never Knew* (Grand Rapids: Zondervan, 1995), 50.

Chapter 2: Why a Jewish Rabbi?

1. Mishnah, *Pirke Avot* 5:27.
2. The recommended ages of study are found in the Mishnah, *Pirke Avot* 5:21.
3. Shmuel Safrai and Menahem Stern, eds., *The Jewish People in the First Century* (Amsterdam: Van Gorcum, 1976), 968.
4. Babylonian Talmud, *Shabbat* 31b.
5. Often Jesus was addressed as "rabbi" in the earlier sense of the word. Many modern scholars prefer to call Jesus a "sage" instead of a "rabbi" because he lived just a few years before the rabbinic period, which began in AD 70. Because Jesus was a greatly esteemed Jewish scholar of the Scriptures, we've used "rabbi" to speak of him here.
6. The professions of rabbis are described in Isadore Singer et al., "Rabbi," *Jewish Encyclopedia* (New York: Funk and Wagnalls, 1905–1906), in public domain at www.jewishencyclopedia.com; Safrai and Stern, *The Jewish People in the First Century*, 953. The term for carpenter is *tekton* and more likely refers to a builder, because they more typically worked with stone than wood.
7. Safrai and Stern, *The Jewish People in the First Century*, 965.
8. Dan Brown, *The DaVinci Code* (New York: Anchor, 2006), 245.
9. Mishnah, *Pirke Avot* 5:21.
10. David Bivin, *New Light on the Difficult Words of Jesus*, 67.
11. Brad Young, *Jesus the Jewish Theologian* (Peabody, MA: Hendrickson, 1995), xiii.
12. Joseph Frankovic, "Is the Sage Worth His Salt?" *Jerusalem Perspective* 45 (July–August 1994): 12–13.
13. Athol Dickson, *The Gospel according to Moses* (Grand Rapids: Baker, 2003), 63.
14. Craig A. Evans and W. H. Brackney, eds., *From Biblical Criticism to Biblical Faith* (Macon, GA: Mercer University Press, 2007), 41–54.

15. The discussion on divorce is in Matthew 19:3–11. See David Instone-Brewer, *Divorce and Remarriage in the Bible: The Social and Literary Context* (Grand Rapids: Eerdmans, 2002).

16. In the 1970s and 1980s, many scholars felt that early Jewish sources like the Mishnah were not useful for describing Jesus's setting because they were written down later, although they appear to quote sayings and describe traditions from the first century. The influential Jewish scholar Jacob Neusner is well known for raising these concerns. In the past decade, however, confidence has grown that these sources are reliable when used with care. See David Instone-Brewer, *Traditions of the Rabbis from the Era of the New Testament* (Grand Rapids: Eerdmans, 2004), 28–40, and the review article by Instone-Brewer, "The Use of Rabbinic Sources in Gospel Studies," *Tyndale Bulletin* 50 (1999): 281–98.

    Some of the works that were criticized for using rabbinic sources to interpret the New Testament are now being reprinted. For instance, the book *Memory and Manuscript* by Birger Gerhardsson (Grand Rapids: Eerdmans, 1998, first published in 1961) was discounted for decades because it compared Jesus's teaching methods to those of the early rabbis. Neusner, who had strongly criticized the book, advocated its republication and even wrote an apologetic foreword in the 1998 version.

    In *Sitting at the Feet of Rabbi Jesus, we have made every effort to use early sources rather than later rabbinic material to describe the setting of Jesus. We do occasionally quote Jewish wisdom from the Babylonian Talmud and later works, without assuming that they describe the reality of Jesus's time.*

17. The idea of God as king can be found in 1 Samuel 8:7; Psalm 24; 47; as shepherd in Isaiah 40:11; Jeremiah 23; 31; Ezekiel 34; and as a farmer or vineyard owner in Psalm 80 and Isaiah 5. These images are found many other places too.

18. From Rabbi Haggai bar Eleazar, *Midrash Psalms*, 119:3. Quoted by Brad Young in *The Parables: Jewish Tradition and Christian Interpretation* (Peabody, MA: Hendrickson, 1998), 192. Rabbi Eleazar lived between one and two hundred years after Jesus. Since we can't know either way, scholars generally assume that he and other later rabbis didn't know of Jesus's teaching, and that the similarities between them come from a common cultural context. Scholars do assume that Jesus knew the influential teachings of Hillel and Shammai, however.

19. Mishnah, *Pirke Avot* 5:15.

20. Rabbi Meir Zlotowitz, *Ruth: A New Translation with a Commentary Anthologized from Talmudic, Midrashic and Rabbinic Sources* (Brooklyn, NY: Mesorah Publications), xxxi–xxxiii.

21. Babylonian Talmud, *Hagigah* 15b.

Chapter 3: Stringing Pearls

1. Martin Abegg, Michael Phelps, and Hershel Shanks, "Will Marty Abegg Ever Find a Job? Scholar Thrives Despite Unauthorized Publication," *Biblical Archaeology Review* 29 (January–February 2003): 36–39. Abegg wrote a simple computer program to reconstruct the text from an unpublished concordance, and then checked it against photographs of the scrolls.

2. The Hebrew of Psalm 8:2 is obscure and the 2011 NIV has reworded both OT and NT quotations so that they sound better in English. In the 1984 NIV, the translation is word-for-word, which makes Jesus' quotation of Psalm 8:2 more obvious.

3. From the foreword by Rabbi David Wolpe in *Jesus the Jewish Theologian*, by Brad Young, xiv.

4. Other Jewish texts from Jesus's time also associated Lamech with the phrase "seventy-seven times" and with an attitude of vengeance. See the *Testament of Benjamin* 7.

5. Craig Keener, *Commentary on the Gospel of Matthew* (Grand Rapids: Eerdmans, 1999), 388. A *seah* is actually a measure of volume. Scholars differ as to the size of a *seah*, estimating it between six and thirteen liters. With these estimates, one *seah* of flour would have weighed between eight and sixteen pounds.

6. Other rabbis sometimes used leavening in a positive way too, as an invisible but potent permeating force. See Young, *Jesus the Jewish Theologian*, 79–80. The story of Abraham's feast was also noted by early rabbis as a lesson for living, because Abraham had only offered to get a little water and something to eat, and instead he laid out a sumptuous feast. Shammai pointed out that we should "Say little and do much"—do everything we promise, and then some (*Avot d'Rabbi Natan* 13:3).

7. Many prefer to refer to the Old Testament as the "Hebrew Bible" or "Hebrew Scriptures," because "Old Testament" is a Christian term that contrasts that text with the New Testament, making the texts that Jews still read sound obsolete. We use the expression "Old Testament" here because of its familiarity. Also, in Eastern cultures, old age is associated with great wisdom, not with obsolescence.

8. There were thirty-seven copies of the Psalms, thirty copies of Deuteronomy, and twenty-one copies of Isaiah found at Qumran. Other books of the Torah were well represented too. See Jonathan Campbell, *Deciphering the Dead Sea Scrolls* (Oxford, UK: Blackwell, 2002), 34.

9. See Edward Ellis, *History and Interpretation in New Testament Perspective* (Leiden: Brill, 2001), 126–29. For more on Hillel's Rules, see Brad Young, *Meet the Rabbis* (Peabody, MA: Hendrickson, 2007), 165–71.

10. Joseph Frankovic, "Remember Shiloh!," *Jerusalem Perspective* 46 &

47 (September–December 1994), 24–31. Available online at www.
jerusalemperspective.com/2714/. It should be said that the link between
the two love commands may have been made before Jesus's time. See
David Daube, *The New Testament and Rabbinic Judaism* (Peabody, MA:
Hendrickson, 1998), 247.

11. See David Instone-Brewer, *Techniques and Assumptions in Jewish Exegesis
Before 70 CE* (Tübingen: Mohr Siebeck, 1992). An often-quoted theory is
that Jesus used a method called "*PaRDeS*," an acronym for four different
ways Scripture can be interpreted (*Pashat*—in a plain sense; *Remez*—as
a hint; *Drash*—in an allegorical or homiletical way; *Sod*—in a secret
way). Although Jesus did use early forms of what later was called *Pashat*,
Remez, and even *Drash*, this terminology is from after his time. And, the
PaRDeS method, especially *Sod*, includes mysticism that Jesus didn't use.
See David Bivin, "Medieval Jargon on First-century Lips," July 1, 1999 at
www.jerusalemperspective.com/1898/. Also, see David Stern, *The Jewish
New Testament Commentary* (Clarksville, MD: Messianic Jewish Resources
International, 1992), 11–14.

12. From *Song of Songs Rabbah* 1:10, as quoted by Philip Culbertson, *A Word
Fitly Spoken: Context and Transmission and Adoption of the Parables of Jesus*
(New York: State University of New York Press, 1995), 101.

13. The allusions from Psalm 2 and Isaiah 42 are widely recognized by scholars.
Genesis 22 is less so, but not unlikely. See Craig Keener, *A Commentary
on the Gospel of Matthew*, 135. Also, see James Dunn and John Rogerson,
Eerdmans Commentary on the Bible (Grand Rapids: Eerdmans, 2003), 1010.

14. God also makes a statement like this at the transfiguration, when Jesus's
disciples see him in glory on a mountaintop. At that time a different text
is spoken, "Listen to him," from Deuteronomy 18:15. In this passage God
promises to send another prophetic leader like Moses. This text was widely
understood to refer to the Messiah. See Young, *Jesus the Jewish Theologian*,
209–11; David Flusser, *The Sage from Galilee: Rediscovering Jesus' Genius*
(Grand Rapids: Eerdmans, 2007), 103.

15. Part of why Jesus did this was because it would be crass, even blasphemous,
to openly make this claim. A century later, Bar Kokhba, used indirect self-
references to hint that he was the Messiah, calling himself "Nasi," meaning
the "Prince." The name Bar Kokhba means "Son of the Star," and "star"
was another messianic reference.

16. See Philip Payne, "Jesus' Implicit Claims to Deity in His Parables," *Trinity
Journal* 2 (1981): 3–23.

17. See Young, *Jesus the Jewish Theologian*, 243–52; also Flusser, *The Sage from
Galilee*, 107–16.

18. In the visions of Jesus's second coming in Revelation, John sees a scene of
someone "like a son of man" coming in glory (see Revelation 1:13; 14:14).

19. Robert Funk, Roy Hoover, and the Jesus Seminar, *The Five Gospels: The Search for the Authentic Words of Jesus* (San Francisco, HarperCollins, 1997), 4–5.
20. See Randall Buth, "'Son of Man': Jesus' Most Important Title," *Jerusalem Perspective* 25 (March–April 1990): 11–15. Available online at www.jerusalemperspective.com/2471/.
21. Sally Lloyd-Jones, *The Jesus Storybook Bible: Every Story Whispers His Name* (Grand Rapids: Zondervan, 2007).

Chapter 4: Following the Rabbi

1. Ange Sabin Peter, "A Japan Story," *Ceramics Technical* 23 (2006): 95–97.
2. John Singleton, ed., *Learning in Likely Places: Varieties of Apprenticeship in Japan* (New York: Cambridge University Press, 1989), 16–17.
3. Safrai and Stern, *The Jewish People in the First Century*, 958. The practice of an apprentice as a young boy (or occasionally a girl) going to live with a craftsman has been traditional in Europe over the centuries too. See Barbara Hanawalt, *Growing Up in Medieval London: The Experience of Childhood in History* (New York: Oxford University Press, 1993), 129–33.
4. Mishnah, *Pirke Avot* 1:1.
5. Elisha is often held up as a model disciple, especially for his humble service and commitment to Elijah. See Babylonian Talmud, *Berakhot* 7a, and Rabbi Menashe Bleiweiss, "Elisha ben Shaphat: The Wonder Years," at http://nebula.wsimg.com/0a1ab8e2288e9b6dacaf2e56081e2b2c ?AccessKeyId=DFFED978B208E263454C&disposition=0&alloworigin=1 (accessed June 30, 2017).
6. Safrai and Stern, *The Jewish People in the First Century*, 964.
7. Mishnah, *Pirke Avot* 6:4.
8. Mishnah, *Bava Metzia* 2:11.
9. Ibid. Also, see Shmuel Safrai, "Master and Disciple," *Jerusalem Perspective* 29 (1990): 3–5, 19. Other articles on first-century discipleship are available at jerusalemperspective.com. An excellent discussion can also be found in David Bivin's *New Light on the Difficult Words of Jesus*, 17–21.
10. Babylonian Talmud, *Makkot* 10a.
11. Babylonian Talmud, *Ketubot* 96a.
12. Safrai and Stern, *The Jewish People in the First Century*, 964.
13. Babylonian Talmud, *Taanit* 7a.
14. David Brooks, "The Obama-Clinton Issue," *The New York Times* (December 18, 2007).
15. From an unpublished sermon by Joseph Stowell, August 14, 2008. The Jerusalem visitor mentioned in this story is Dr. Ed Dobson.

Chapter 5: Get Yourself Some Haverim

1. Mishnah, *Pirke Avot* 1:6.
2. Mishnah, *Pirke Avot* 3:32. Attributed to Hananya ben Teradion, from the early second century. Another rabbi, Halafta ben Dosa, said a similar thing a few decades later (*Pirke Avot* 3:7). The similarity of these sayings to the words of Jesus may either be evidence that the rabbis knew of his teachings or that they were simply speaking from a common cultural background, one that emphasized the spiritual richness of studying with others.
3. Nahum Goldmann, *Memories* (London: Weidenfeld & Nicolson, 1970), 6.
4. In 1 Corinthians 10:1, Paul says, "For I do not want you to be ignorant of the fact, brothers and sisters, that *our* ancestors were all under the cloud and that they all passed through the sea" (italics added). He is preaching primarily to Gentiles, but speaks as if these non-Jews are part of the extended family and can learn from their ancestors' experience.
5. Eugene Peterson, *A Long Obedience in the Same Direction* (Downers Grove, IL: InterVarsity Press, 2000), 166–67.
6. Pastor Robert C. Stone, "Spiritual Friendships Pt. 1: Qualities That Build Friendships"; online at www.eagleflight.org/ministrycentral/friendship.html (accessed June 30, 2017).
7. See David Smith, *The Friendless American Male* (Ventura, CA: Regal, 1983), 21.
8. Mishnah, *Pirke Avot* 2:5.

Chapter 6: Rabbi, Teach Us to Pray

1. Abraham Heschel, *Man's Quest for God* (New York: Scribner, 1954), 15.
2. Yigael Yadin, "Tefillin from Qumran," *Eretz-Israel* 9 (1969): 60–83.
3. Safrai and Stern, *The Jewish People in the First Century*, 799; Bivin, *New Light on the Difficult Words of Jesus*, 51–53.
4. Shmuel Safrai, "Did Jesus Wear a Kippah?" *Jerusalem Perspective* 36 (January–February 1992): 11. Safrai points out that in third-century frescoes found in ancient synagogues, men were bareheaded. But the Babylonian Talmud (written around AD 500) said that some men covered their heads. Only in the Middle Ages did the practice become common.
5. See Safrai and Stern, *The Jewish People in the First Century*, 798.
6. Rabbi Wayne Dosick, *Living Judaism* (San Francisco: HarperSanFrancisco, 1995), 250–51.
7. With the exception of a few prayers in Aramaic, Orthodox Jewish prayer is entirely in Hebrew. It is permissible to pray in any language, but Hebrew is traditional for communal prayer. Reform Jews, however, often pray in their

native language. According to Shmuel Safrai, all of the prayers found in rabbinic literature, without exception, are in Hebrew. These include both personal and communal prayers. See "Literary Languages in the Time of Jesus," *Jerusalem Perspective* 31 (March–April 1991): 3–8.

8. This translation is from the JPS *Tanakh* (New York: Jewish Publication Society, 1985). The *Shema* is composed of three passages from Scripture: Deuteronomy 6:4–9; 11:13–21; Numbers 15: 37–41. The Shema is technically not a prayer, but a daily recommitment to loving and serving God.

9. *Amidah*, in fact, means "standing," because the prayer is said while standing.

10. Some ancient sources say that in earlier times the *Amidah* was prayed two times a day, morning and afternoon, but after AD 70, it was prayed three times a day. The Shema was recited each morning and evening.

11. Joseph Heinemann, *Prayer in the Talmud* (New York: De Gruyter, 1977), 46.

12. Dosick, *Living Judaism*, 9–10.

13. Bivin, *New Light on the Difficult Words of Jesus*, 59–66.

14. *Didache* 8:3.

15. Scholars believe that in the time of Christ, women could be counted in the number, unlike today. See Shmuel Safrai, "The Place of Women in First-Century Synagogues," 3–6, 14. Also, in first-century synagogues men and women sat together. Dividing the sexes became customary centuries later.

16. For instance, in God's promise of a descendant to King David, he said, "I will be his father, and he will be my son" (2 Samuel 7:14). See also Psalms 2:7 and 89:26–28. A few other Jewish teachers spoke of God as "Abba," but this was unusual. See Brad Young, "The Lord's Prayer (2): 'Our Father Who Art in Heaven,'" *Jerusalem Perspective* 10 (July 1988): 1–2.

17. Josa Bivin, "Don't Throw Away That Piece of Bread!," *Jerusalem Perspective* 29 (October 1999), available at blog.jerusalemperspective.com/ 6174/ (accessed June 30, 2017).

18. For instance, see Psalm 121:7 or Job 5:19. In these passages the word *ra* is translated as "harm." Psalm 121:7 says, "The LORD will keep you from all harm," speaking of physical danger rather than moral evil.

19. See Randall Buth, "Deliver Us from Evil," *Jerusalem Perspective* 55 (April–June 1999): 29–31.

20. Mishnah, *Pirke Avot* 2:13.

21. Mishnah, *Berakhot* 9:3.

22. Babylonian Talmud, *Shabbat* 165b.

23. Annie Dillard, *Teaching a Stone to Talk: Expeditions and Encounters* (New York: Harper & Row, 1982), 40.

24. Heschel, *Man's Quest for God*, 84.

25. Babylonian Talmud, *Berakhot* 32b.

Chapter 7: For Everything a Blessing

1. As quoted in Joseph Hertz, *A Book of Jewish Thoughts* (Oxford: Oxford University Press, 1922), 283.

2. *Fiddler on the Roof* (Santa Monica, CA: MGM Home Entertainment, 1998). Originally released in 1971.

3. Most translators believe that the two meanings of *barakh* ("to kneel" and "to bless") are coincidental. Others suggest that in ancient times, the word for kneeling later took on the meaning of blessing, because one kneels to receive a blessing and also to worship God. See the discussion of *barak* (I) and (II) in *The New International Dictionary of Old Testament Theology and Exegesis*, ed. Willem VanGemeren (Grand Rapids: Zondervan, 1997), 1:755–67.

4. The Mishnah, which was written down about AD 200 and preserved traditions from Jesus's time, includes the shorter prayers. By the time of the writing of the Jerusalem Talmud, between 300–400, the rabbis decreed that one should remind oneself that God is "king of the universe" in every prayer so that one acknowledged his kingship over oneself. This is similar to how the rabbis said that people "received the kingdom of heaven" when they said the *Shema*. See chapter 13 for more.

5. The texts of the blessings (with minor updates) are from the article "Benedictions" by Cyrus Adler and Kaufmann Kohler, *Jewish Encyclopedia* (New York: Funk and Wagnalls, 1901–1906) in public domain at www.jewishencyclopedia.com/articles/2931-benedictions (accessed June 30, 2017).

6. The prayer after using the bathroom is, "Blessed is he who has formed man in wisdom and created in him many orifices and many cavities. It is obvious and known before your throne of glory that if one of them were to be ruptured or one of them blocked, it would be impossible for a man to survive and stand before you. Blessed are you that heals all flesh and does wonders" (Babylonian Talmud, *Berakhot* 60b). A wonderful article about this prayer by Kenneth Prager, MD, entitled "For Everything a Blessing," appeared in the *Journal of the American Medical Association* 277 (20) (May 28, 1997): 1589.

7. *Reb Dovid Din*, an oral tradition cited in *Hasidic Tales*, 149, quoted in Philip Yancey, *Prayer: Does It Make Any Difference?* (Grand Rapids: Zondervan, 2006), 68–69.

8. The NIV renders the word "blessed" as "gave thanks."

9. Mishnah, *Berakhot* 6:1.

10. See, for instance, the NASB. Others, like the NIV, say "gave thanks," which explains more clearly what he was doing. See Young, *Jesus, the Jewish Theologian*, 122–23.

11. David Flusser, "A Lost Jewish Benediction in Matthew 9:8," *Judaism and the Origins of Christianity* (Jerusalem: Magnes, 1988), 535–42.

12. This is called the *Birkat ha Gomel* and is now prayed publicly at the synagogue after going through a significant experience of God's deliverance, such as being released from prison, surviving a serious illness, giving birth, or completing a dangerous journey.
13. *Midrash Psalms* 117. See "Rain in Jewish Tradition" at www. jewishnaturecenter.org/html/jewish_rain.html (accessed February 19, 2008).
14. Lauren Winner, *Mudhouse Sabbath* (Brewster, MA: Paraclete, 2003), 55.
15. Ibid., 60.

Chapter 8: A Passover Discovery

1. Mishnah, *Pesahim* 10:5.
2. Some have thought that the Last Supper was not a Passover meal because John's gospel sounds as if the supper was held the evening before the feast, although the other Gospels clearly refer to it as a Passover (e.g., Luke 22:15). For an excellent discussion of the approaches to this debate, as well as strong evidence for the meal actually as a Passover, see Joachim Jeremias, *The Eucharistic Words of Jesus* (London: SCM, 1966), 15–88.
3. Mishnah, *Pesahim* 10:8. See David Daube, *The New Testament and Rabbinic Judaism* (Peabody, MA: Hendrickson, 1998), 332–35.
4. Scholars now believe that the idea that Jesus was entirely rejected by the Jewish people is mistaken, because in Acts, numerous accounts describe large numbers of Jewish believers (e.g., Acts 21:20), and of course, the disciples and all of the early church was Jewish. The Jewish people were *divided* over Jesus, although the religious leadership rejected him. See Jacob Jervell, *Luke and the People of God* (Minneapolis: Augsburg, 1972), 41–74; Oskar Skarsaune and Reidar Hvalvik, *The Jewish Believers in Jesus* (Peabody, MA: Hendrickson, 2007). An excellent resource on the Passover plot is the audio series "Misconception about Jesus and the Passover," by Dwight A. Pryor. It is available at www.jcstudies.com.
5. Jeremias, *The Eucharistic Words of Jesus*, 206.
6. See Geza Vermes, *Scripture and Tradition in Judaism: Haggadic Studies*, 2nd ed. (Leiden: Brill, 1983), 214–19. The Jewish scholar Vermes says that the sacrifice of Isaac was a prominent image in the early Passover celebration, much more in Jesus's time than today. Jewish tradition emphasizes the heroic obedience of Isaac as much as the faith of Abraham. They point out that Isaac had to be an adult in order to carry the wood for the sacrifice, which would have weighed well over a hundred pounds. With this interpretation in mind, the parallels between Isaac and Jesus are even clearer.
7. The Jewish calendar is based on a lunar cycle with an occasional "leap month" added, so its dates change each year relative to our own calendar, which is based on a solar calendar.

8. See Bruce Okkema, "Has DaVinci Painted Our Picture of Jesus?" at www. egrc.net/articles/director/articles_director_0404.html (accessed June 30, 2017).

9. See David Daube, "He That Cometh" (lecture given at St. Paul's Cathedral, London, October 1966). Also see Deborah Carmichael, "David Daube on the Eucharist and the Passover Seder," *Journal for the Study of the New Testament* 42 (1991): 45–67.

10. Nowadays, three pieces are used in the *afikomen* ritual, and the middle one is broken. Some see this as a picture of the Trinity and say that the middle piece, the Son, was broken and taken away. The tradition of using three pieces, however, arose after Jesus's time.

11. Firstfruits always occurred on the first day of the week after the Sabbath following Passover. Because Passover could be on different days of the week, depending on the year, the Feast of Firstfruits sometimes fell several days after Passover. It was celebrated on Sunday in Jesus's time, and Karaite Jews still celebrate it on Sunday. Later, the rabbis moved it to the day after the Feast of Unleavened Bread.

12. Modern theologians read Ezekiel 37 as a prophecy given during the Babylonian exile that God would "resurrect" his people by regathering them into their land. But in the first century, the text was understood by both Jews and Christians as pointing to the future resurrection of the dead. In the early church it was read every week. See Gary T. Manning, *Echoes of a Prophet: The Use of Ezekiel in the Gospel of John and the Literature of the Second Temple Period* (New York: T&T Clark, 2004), 70, 96–97.

13. The earliest reference to the *Dayeinu* in Jewish writings is from around 1000. But a Christian sermon from the second century AD includes a Passover liturgy based on this song. This earlier evidence suggests that the *Dayeinu* might have even been known in Jesus's time. See Eric Werner, "Two Hymns for Passover and Good Friday," in *The Sacred Bridge: The Interdependence of Liturgy and Music in the Synagogue and Church in the First Millennium* (New York: KTAV, 1959), 127–48.

Chapter 9: Discovering Jesus in the Jewish Feasts

1. Abraham Joshua Heschel, *The Earth Is the Lord's / The Sabbath* (New York: Harper Torchbooks, 1966), 8.

2. Mauna Kea, a summit on the same island, is actually slightly higher than Mauna Loa. But Mauna Loa is far more massive underwater. It may not be the tallest mountain above the surface, but it is the world's largest mountain.

3. In this chapter we are speaking of the "feasts" as the seven observances that were commanded in Leviticus 23. Later two more celebrations, Hanukkah and Purim, were added. The Sabbath is also understood to be a feast day.

4. Part of the reason that Pentecost was thought of as occurring in the upper room was because Acts 2:2 speaks of wind filling the "house," but this likely refers to the temple. The temple is often referred to as "the house of God" or simply "the house" in Scripture. Even today in Hebrew, the Temple Mount is called *har habayit*, which means "the mountain of the house."

5. Several pieces of evidence suggest that these Shavuot traditions were at least two or three hundred years older than in Jesus's time. In the past, scholars have believed that they arose after Jesus. See Moshe Weinberg, *Normative and Sectarian Judaism in the Second Temple Period* (New York: Continuum, 2005), 268–78.

6. Walter C. Kaiser Jr., Peter H. Davids, F. F. Bruce, and Manfred T. Brauch, eds., *Hard Sayings of the Bible* (Downers Grove, IL: InterVarsity Press, 1996), 519.

7. Even though Nisan, the month of Passover, is the first month of the festal year according to Exodus 12:1, the Jewish calendar year begins six months later, with Tishri. This is when Sabbatical and Jubilee years always began.

8. Ancient historians like Josephus declared that up to 2.5 million pilgrims attended the feast. Modern scholars are skeptical of such high numbers, making estimates between 200,000 and 1,000,000. See Bruce W. Winter and Andrew D. Clarke, *The Book of Acts in Its Ancient Literary Setting* (Grand Rapids: Eerdmans, 1993), 259–65.

9. Mishnah, *Sukkah* 5:1.

10. Orthodox Jews traditionally do not drive on Shabbat, and in some ultra-Orthodox areas they turn off the traffic lights to discourage others from driving through and disturbing the *shalom* of the day.

11. Nan Fink, *Stranger in the Midst: A Memoir of Spiritual Discovery* (New York: Basic Books, 1997), 96, quoted in Winner, *Mudhouse Sabbath*, 2.

12. Lis Harris, *Holy Days: The World of a Hasidic Family* (New York: Touchstone, 1995), 68–69, quoted in Winner, *Mudhouse Sabbath*, 6–7.

13. Heschel, *The Earth is the Lord's / The Sabbath*, 8.

Chapter 10: At Table with the Rabbi

1. See Marc Angel, *A Sephardic Passover* (Jerusalem: KTAV, 1988), 65.

2. J. R. R. Tolkien, *The Hobbit* (Boston: Houghton Mifflin, 1937), 30–31.

3. Of the twenty times in the NASB in which it says that Jesus and others reclined "at the table," only one instance of this phrase actually appears in the original Greek text. The others were added by translators. The original texts simply say they "reclined."

4. The tabernacle had a table for the showbread. A common, but mistaken notion is that people sat or reclined around a U-shaped table called a *triclinium* in New Testament times. A *triclinium* is actually a room found in

wealthy homes that had a U-shaped platform where cushions were placed. Diners would recline on cushions in a semicircle, and food would be placed on a small table in the middle.

5. To "eat at a ruler's table" meant that you were under the ruler's protection and provision. For instance, 1 Kings 18:19 says that 450 prophets of Baal and 400 prophets of Asherah ate "at Jezebel's table." The expression is not so much about literal eating as a strong bond of relationship.

6. This is why Lot offered his daughters to the men of Sodom when they wanted him to bring out his angelic visitors (Genesis 19:8). As horrible as his action was, Lot felt obligated to protect his visitors at any cost.

7. For more, see the *Dictionary of Biblical Imagery*, ed. Leland Ryken et al. (Downers Grove, IL: InterVarsity Press, 1998), 402–6.

8. In Exodus 33:20, God told Moses, "You cannot see my face, for no one may see me and live." In Leviticus 10:1–2, Nadab and Abihu are killed when they enter God's presence in an unauthorized manner. Mentioning them here appears to be a hint at the utter uniqueness of this situation, where human beings could safely enter God's presence.

9. *Didache* 14:2.

10. Most of these traditions postdate Jesus, but are lovely and wise nonetheless.

11. This special bread is made in honor of God's provision of bread. Two loaves are served because God instructed the Israelites in the wilderness to gather twice as much manna before the Sabbath.

12. Ephraim and Manasseh were the two sons of Joseph who became fathers of two of the largest tribes of Israel. Sarah, Rebecca, Rachel, and Leah are the four great matriarchs, the mothers of all Israel. The last prayer is called the Priestly (Aaronic) Benediction and is found in Numbers 6:24–26.

13. Mishnah, *Pirke Avot* 3:2–3.

14. The delightful implication is that if you're on a diet, you should take a day off on Shabbat! In contrast, some Christians often have fasted on their holy days, associating holiness with denial rather than joy and celebration.

15. The exception is Yom Kippur, which is still observed even on the Sabbath, because it is a "Sabbath of Sabbaths" (Leviticus 16:31).

16. An outstanding book on Christian observance of a Sabbath is Marva Dawn's *Keeping the Sabbath Wholly* (Grand Rapids: Eerdmans, 1989).

17. Ilan Zamir, *The Sulha: Reconciliation in the Middle East* (San Francisco: Purple Pomegranate Productions, 1989).

18. Kenneth Bailey, *Poet & Peasant and Through Peasant Eyes* (Grand Rapids: Eerdmans, 1983), 161–62.

19. Young, *Jesus the Jewish Theologian*, 143–54.

20. Joachim Jeremias, *New Testament Theology* (London: SCM, 1971), 115–16.

Chapter 11: Touching the Rabbi's Fringe

1. *TANAKH: A New Translation of the Holy Scriptures according to the Traditional Hebrew Text* (New York: Jewish Publication Society, 1985).

2. Solomon Schechter, *Aspects of Rabbinic Theology* (Peabody, MA: Hendrickson, reprint, 1998 [orig. 1909]), 121.

3. See Abraham Heschel, *Moral Grandeur and Spiritual Audacity: Essays* (New York: Farrar, Straus, and Giroux, 1997), 65.

4. Jacob Milgrom, *JPS Torah Commentary: Numbers* (New York: Jewish Publication Society, 1990), 410–14.

5. Made from a rare type of snail, this dye eventually became so costly that it was no longer required, and the formula for making it was lost. In just the past few years, the process for this dye has been rediscovered. See Ari Greenspan, "The Search for Biblical Blue," *Bible Review* 19 (February 2003): 32–39. Also see www.tekhelet.com (accessed June 30, 2017).

6. Jacob Milgrom, "The Tassel and the Tallit," The Fourth Annual Rabbi Louis Fineberg Memorial Lecture (University of Cincinnati, 1981). (Quoted in the article "The Meaning of Tekhelet" by Baruch Sterman at www.baruchsterman.com/Essays/MeaningOfTekhelet.pdf (accessed June 30, 2017).

7. Ann Spangler and Jean E. Syswerda, *Women of the Bible* (Grand Rapids: Zondervan, 2007), 324–25.

8. The tassels were to be attached to the corners (*kanafim*) of the garment. Because *kanafim* also means "wings," some suggest that she grasped his *tzitzit* because she believed that as the Messiah, he would fulfill Malachi 4:2, "But for you who revere my name, the sun of righteousness will rise with healing in its wings [*kanafim*]." (1984 NIV).

9. Thomas Cahill, *The Gifts of the Jews: How a Tribe of Desert Nomads Changed the Way Everyone Thinks and Feels* (New York: Doubleday, 1998), 154.

10. The Israelites felt the same way. God had to give them special permission so that they could eat meat without sacrificing the animal (see Deuteronomy 12:15).

11. When God chose people for a special purpose, he commonly gave them dietary restrictions to observe. Priests and those who took a Nazirite vow (Numbers 6:1–21) were separated from others, in part, by extra dietary rules. See Gordon J. Wenham, "The Theology of Unclean Food," *Evangelical Quarterly* 53.1 (January–March 1981): 6–15; also Jacob Milgrom, *Leviticus 1–16* (Anchor Bible Commentary; New York: Doubleday, 1991), 726.

12. For more on how "an eye for an eye" was understood, see Nahum Sarna, *Exploring Exodus* (New York: Shocken, 1996), 185–89. This is part of a longer essay (pp. 158–89) that explains the distinctive features of the Sinai

laws in comparison to other ancient codes that shows their surprisingly humane spirit in their time.

13. See William J. Webb, *Slaves, Women & Homosexuals: Exploring the Hermeneutics of Cultural Analysis* (Downers Grove, IL: InterVarsity Press, 2001), 31–33.

14. A. J. Jacobs, *The Year of Living Biblically: One Man's Humble Quest to Follow the Bible as Literally as Possible* (New York: Simon & Schuster, 2007), 4–8, 165–67.

15. Quoted in Mark I. Pinsky, *The Gospel according to the Simpsons* (Louisville: Westminster John Knox, 2001), 32.

16. For a discussion of Peter's vision and the impurity laws regarding Gentiles, see Hilary Le Cornu, *A Commentary on the Jewish Roots of Acts* (Jerusalem: Netivya Bible Instruction Ministry, 2003), 562–88.

17. Douglas Moo, *The Epistle to the Romans* (Grand Rapids: Eerdmans, 1996), 641.

18. Joseph Telushkin, *The Book of Jewish Values* (New York: Bell Tower, 2000), 70–71.

Chapter 12: Jesus and the Torah

1. B. Cobbey Crisler, "The Acoustics and Crowd Capacity of Natural Theaters in Palestine," *The Biblical Archaeologist* 39 (1976): 128–41. At the time of this writing, a grove of fruit trees is planted on the land near the Cove of the Sower, which absorbs the sound. But you can still see the curve of the shoreline as you drive along the modern road on the western shore of the Sea of Galilee.

2. Philologos, "A Thorn in One's Side," *Jewish Daily Forward* (Friday, May 23, 2003). Online at www.forward.com/articles/a-thorn-in-one-s-side/ (accessed June 30, 2017). Other rabbis said similar things; for instance, "Should all the nations of the world unite to uproot one word of the Torah, they would be unable to do it" (*Leviticus Rabbah* 19:2). See Bivin, *New Light on the Difficult Words of Jesus*, 94–96.

3. For instance, "Go away to a place of study of the Torah, and do not suppose that it will come to you. For your fellow disciples will *fulfill* it in your hand. And on your own understanding do not rely" (Mishnah, *Pirke Avot* 4:14). In this line, "fulfill" means to clarify the meaning of the Scriptures. See also Mishnah, *Horayot* 1:3, which talks about "abolishing" and "fulfilling" laws. In a rabbinic debate from around AD 100, Rabbi Eliezer said to Rabbi Akiva, "Would you uproot [abolish] what is written in the Torah?" (Mishnah, *Pesahim* 6:2). For more on "abolish" versus "fulfill," see Bivin, *New Light on the Difficult Words of Jesus*, 93–102; Daube, *The New Testament and Rabbinic Judaism*, 60–61.

4. Mishnah, *Pirke Avot* 1:1.

5. Donald Hagner remarks, "Jesus came denouncing legalism, a perversion of the Law even as most of the Pharisees themselves would have denounced it; he did not come to overthrow Judaism, to bring a new religion, or to set up a new law code." See Donald A. Hagner, *The Jewish Reclamation of Jesus: An Analysis and Critique of Modern Jewish Study of Jesus* (Grand Rapids: Zondervan, 1984), 118.

6. Mishnah, *Sanhedrin* 10:1. Paul quotes this sentiment in Romans 11:26, when he says, "All Israel will be saved."

7. David Stern, *Jewish New Testament Commentary* (Clarksville, MD: Jewish New Testament Publications, 1992), 69–70.

8. Abraham Heschel notes that rabbinic sources also commented that the rulings of Shammai's disciples were sometimes greatly excessive, to the point of being unlivable. See *Heavenly Torah: As Refracted through the Generations* (New York: Continuum: 2005), 722–24. The disciples of Shammai were in the majority until AD 70, after which the Hillelites came into power.

9. Stern, *Jewish New Testament Commentary*, 69.

10. *Sifre Deuteronomy* 187:11 (from between AD 200 and 300).

11. Babylonian Talmud, *Sukkah* 52a.

12. Babylonian Talmud, *Bava Metzia* 59a. Jews are particularly sensitive to the sin of humiliation, having been ridiculed for their piety over the centuries. They have a long list of ethical rules to prevent shaming of others, and much wisdom on the damage gossip can do. An excellent resource is Rabbi Joseph Telushkin, *Words That Hurt, Words That Heal* (New York: Harper, 1998).

13. Donald Hagner writes, "Jesus is the finally authoritative interpreter of Torah: he penetrates in every instance beyond the letter of the Law to the will of God. The solution to the problem of Jesus and the Law is not simply to be found in elevating of written Torah over the oral tradition of the Pharisees nor in the giving of primacy to the ethical over the ritual and ceremonial legislation, true though both of these observations are. It is to be found rather in the definitive (because eschatological) interpretation of the Law given by the bringer of the kingdom" (see *The Jewish Reclamation of Jesus*, 128). Hagner also points out that in several places in rabbinic literature, the rabbis predict that the Messiah will bring a new and greater understanding of the Torah.

14. Babylonian Talmud, *Shabbat* 31a.

15. Hagner, *The Jewish Reclamation of Jesus*, 152, 159–70.

16. Rabbi Dovid Rosenfeld, "Chapter 2: Mishna 10–11c: G-d's Immanent Presence," www.torah.org/learning/pirkei-avos-chapter2–10and11c (accessed June 30, 2017).

17. Margie Mason, "Vietnamese Man, on Anti-Abortion Mission, Opens Home to Moms and Babies," *Arizona Daily Star*, March 25, 2008, http://tucson.com/news/vietnamese-man-on-anti-abortion-mission-opens-home-to-moms/article_a553de02-d6e6-56b1-ad97-1e232c5e2dbf.html (accessed June 30, 2017).

18. Babylonian Talmud, *Shabbat* 31a.

19. Babylonian Talmud, *Makkot* 24a. (Just a note, the New Testament contains over a thousand commands.)

20. Athol Dickson, *The Gospel according to Moses: What My Jewish Friends Taught Me about Jesus* (Grand Rapids: Baker, 2003), 72.

21. Rabbi Joseph Telushkin, *The Book of Jewish Values* (New York: Bell Tower, 2000), 222–23.

Chapter 13: The Mysterious Kingdom of God

1. This is the opening line of the *Kaddish* (meaning "Sanctified"), an ancient prayer liturgy that was recited by rabbis after a sermon or study of the Scripture. It is now said during the synagogue service and by mourners as an affirmation of faith in God despite their loss.

2. Philip Yancey, *The Jesus I Never Knew* (Grand Rapids: Zondervan), 239.

3. Ibid., 241.

4. David Bivin, *New Light on the Difficult Words of Jesus*, 55–58. Even now, most Orthodox Jews do not refer to God directly but speak of him as "HaShem," which actually means "the name." Also, "Adonai" ("my Lord") is pronounced rather than uttering God's name, Y H W H, out loud when reading Scripture.

5. This might seem obvious if you compare sayings where "kingdom of God" and "kingdom of heaven" are clearly interchangeable; see, for instance, Matthew 13:31 and Mark 4:30–31, where the kingdom is compared to a mustard seed. But this question alone has confounded some Christians because of our general lack of knowledge of Jewish idioms and euphemistic ways of speaking of God.

6. Although Aramaic was widely spoken in first-century Israel, rabbis of that era often taught in Hebrew. The Mishnah and other early collections of rabbinic sayings are all in Hebrew, but later texts like the Talmud are in Aramaic. It is likely Jesus was trilingual, knowing Hebrew, Aramaic, and some Greek, since he lived in an occupied land with much foreign commerce. See Randall Buth, "The Language of Jesus' Teaching," *Dictionary of New Testament Background*, ed. Craig Evans and Stanley Porter (Downers Grove, IL: InterVarsity Press, 2000), 86–91.

7. The multifaceted Jewish understanding of the kingdom of God is described

by Solomon Schechter in *Aspects of Rabbinic Theology*, 65–115.

8. Ironically, at various periods in history, Christians persecuted Jews for this very prayer, mistakenly perceiving it as being said against them as the worshippers of idols. However, it likely predates Christianity and it is possible that Jesus himself prayed this prayer. See "Alenu," Kaufmann Kohler, www.jewishencyclopedia.com/articles/1112-alenu (accessed June 30, 2017). The text of the prayer is in the public domain in that article and rendered with minor updates in language here.

9. Two scholarly sources on Jesus's Jewish understanding of the kingdom of God are in Flusser, *The Sage from Galilee*, 76–96, and Young, *Jesus the Jewish Theologian*, 49–84. Lay readers will find an excellent introduction in the DVD series *Unveiling the Kingdom of Heaven* by Dwight A. Pryor (Dayton, OH: Center for Judaic-Christian Studies, 2008); see www.jcstudies.org.

10. For more on God's kingdom being "seen" at the Red Sea, see Bivin, *New Light on the Difficult Words of Jesus*, 128. The Sabbath prayer can be found in Joseph Hertz, *Authorized Daily Prayerbook*, rev. ed. (New York: Bloch, 1961), 371.

11. For thousands of years, the phrase "finger of God" has been used in the Passover ceremony to refer to the way God had revealed his kingly reign by defeating the Egyptians and their gods and by liberating his people at the parting of the Red Sea. See R. Steven Notley, "By the Finger of God," *Jerusalem Perspective* 21 (July/August 1989): 6–7.

12. See Craig Evans, "Messianic Hopes and Messianic Figures in Late Antiquity," *Journal of Greco-Roman Christianity and Judaism* 3 (2006): 9–40.

13. Charles Colson, *God and Government: An Insider's View on the Boundaries between Faith and Politics* (Grand Rapids: Zondervan, 2007), 94–95.

14. Passages about "the day of the Lord" include Isaiah 13 and Zechariah 14.

15. James Carroll, *Constantine's Sword: The Church and the Jews* (New York: Mariner, 2002), 78, 80.

16. Flusser, *The Sage from Galilee*, 77.

17. Hagner, *The Jewish Reclamation of Jesus*, 137–41.

18. John the Baptist also said, "His winnowing fork is in his hand to clear his threshing floor and to gather the wheat into his barn, but he will burn up the chaff with unquenchable fire" (Luke 3:17). Here, the picture is of the righteous being separated from the wicked, as when a farmer throws grain into the air with a fork, allowing the chaff to be carried away by the wind. Again, he uses the image of fire to picture the coming judgment.

Jesus tells a similar parable about a farmer who wishes he could separate his crop from noxious weeds, which look much like wheat in the early stages of their growth. But the wise farmer will wait until harvest time to separate the wheat and the weeds. Once again, Jesus puts off the time of winnowing and burning the chaff until the very end. (See the note to

Matthew 13:26 in the *Archaeological Study Bible* [Grand Rapids: Zondervan, 2005], 1583).

19. Babylonian Talmud, *Ta,anit* 7a. The rabbinic emphasis on God's mercy predates Jesus, who appears to expand on the ideas of his time to teach about his merciful kingdom. See Flusser, *Judaism and the Origins of Christianity*, 469–93.

20. Mishnah, *Berakhot* 2:2. Attributed to Joshua ben Korhah, around AD 150. An earlier rabbi, Gamaliel II, also connected the "kingdom of God" with saying the Shema (see *Berakhot* 2:5). Nowadays, the phrase that is commonly used to refer to the first part of the Shema is *kabalat ol malkhut shamayim*, which is literally, "receiving the yoke of the kingdom of heaven." Later manuscripts of the Mishnah insert the word "yoke," but earlier ones do not. It appears, then, that in Jesus's time the idiom was "receiving the kingdom of heaven," which is identical to the phrase that Jesus himself used (David Bivin, personal communication).

21. The phrase "will enter" sounds like it refers to the future here, but in Hebrew, the future (imperfect) tense is also used for the proverbial sense, e.g., "A stitch in time *will* save nine."

Chapter 14: Becoming True Disciples of Our Jewish Lord

1. For an excellent overview of the history of Christian anti-Semitism and the heresy of Marcion, see Marvin Wilson, *Our Father Abraham: The Jewish Roots of the Christian Faith* (Grand Rapids: Eerdmans, 1989), 87–110. There *have* been times in previous centuries in which Christians showed interest in their Jewish "roots." For instance, the early American Puritans stressed Hebrew and Old Testament studies and gave their children names like Abraham and Jacob. But this interest has been not nearly as common as the opposite perspective. See ibid., 127–31.

2. John Sailhamer, *Introduction to Old Testament Theology* (Grand Rapids: Zondervan, 1995), 135. Also, Louis Jacobs, *The Jewish Religion: A Companion* (Cambridge, UK: Oxford University Press, 1995), 79.

3. See pp.248–58 for more details on the Seder.

4. Dr. Notley, professor of biblical studies at Nyack College, is the coauthor of *The Sacred Bridge* (Jerusalem: Carta, 2006), a highly respected historical atlas of the biblical world.

5. Dwight Pryor, "Walk After Me!" *Jerusalem Perspective* 55 (April–June 1999): 10–11, online at www.jerusalemperspective.com/2829/ (accessed June 30, 2017).

6. James Kugel has written several books exploring how the Jewish Scriptures were interpreted in ancient times. See, for instance, *The Bible as It Was* (Cambridge, MA: Belknap, 1999).

7. *Mezuzah* means "doorpost" and came to be the name of the object. The plural is *mezuzot* (meh-zu-ZOTE). For more on customs associated with the *mezuzah*, see Haim Halevy Donin, *To Be a Jew: A Guide to Jewish Observance in Contemporary Life* (New York: Basic Books, 1991), 152–55; also Dosick, *Living Judaism*, 247–49.

Scripture Index

General Index